Inuit and Whalers on Baffin Island
through German Eyes

Ludger Müller-Wille and Bernd Gieseking

# Inuit and Whalers on Baffin Island through German Eyes

Wilhelm Weike's Arctic Journal and Letters (1883-1884)

*Translated by William Barr*

Baraka
Books
Montréal

Canada Council    Conseil des Arts
for the Arts      du Canada

We acknowledge the support of the Canada Council for the Arts which last year invested $20.1 million in writing and publishing throughout Canada.

Authorized English translation of the first edition in German published as *Bei Inuit und Walfängern auf Baffin-Land (1883/1884). Das arktische Tagebuch des Wilhelm Weike.* Edited by and © Ludger Müller-Wille and Bernd Gieseking. (Mindener Beiträge, Vol. 30). Minden: Mindener Geschichtsverein 2008. 321 pp., 17 figures. ISBN 978-3-929894-31-8). English translation published by permission.

Wilhelm Weike's original German texts and photos © American Philosophical Society (Philadelphia, Pennsylvania, USA). Texts in translation and photos reproduced and published by permission.

English translation © William Barr 2011.

Translation consulting, editing and revisions of English version by Linna Weber Müller-Wille and Ludger Müller-Wille.
Cartography and image digitization by Ragnar Müller-Wille.
Cover: front – Wilhelm Weike and Inuit companions (American Philosophical Society, Philadelphia), back – Pangnirtung. Painting by Maurice Haycock, 1900-1988 (Department of Geological Sciences, University of Saskatchewan, Saskatoon)

Copyright © Baraka Books

Published by Baraka Books of Montreal.
6977, rue Lacroix
Montréal, Québec H4E 2V4
Telephone: 514-808-8504
info@barakabooks.com
www.barakabooks.com

Book design and cover by Folio infographie

Printed and bound in Quebec
ISBN 978-1-926824-11-6

**Library and Archives Canada Cataloguing in Publication**

Weike, Wilhelm, 1859-1917
   [Bei Inuit und Walfängern auf Baffin-Land (1883/1884). English]
   Inuit and whalers on Baffin Island through German eyes: Wilhelm Weike's arctic journal and letters (1883-1884) / [edited and annotated by] Ludger Müller-Wille and Bernd Gieseking; translated by William Barr.

   Translation of: Bei Inuit und Walfängern auf Baffin-Land (1883/1884).
   Includes bibliographical references and index.

   ISBN 978-1-926824-11-6

   1. Weike, Wilhelm, 1859-1917—Travel—Nunavut—Baffin Island. 2. Boas, Franz, 1858-1942.—Travel—Nunavut—Baffin Island. 3. Inuit—Nunavut—Baffin Island—Social life and customs—19th century. 4. Whaling ships—Nunavut—Baffin Island—History—19th century. 5. Baffin Island (Nunavut)—Social life and customs— 19th century. 6. Baffin Island (Nunavut)—Description and travel. 1. Müller-Wille, Ludger, 1944- II. Gieseking, Bernd III. Barr, William, 1940- IV. Title. V. Title: Bei Inuit und Walfängern auf Baffin-Land (1883/1884). English.

   FC4317.1.W3413 2011      917.19′52042      C2011-905620-8

Legal Deposit, 4th quarter, 2011
Bibliothèque et Archives nationales du Québec
Library and Archives Canada

Trade Distribution & Returns
Canada                              United States
LitDistCo                           Independent Publishers Group
1-800-591-6250; orders@litdisctco.ca   1-800-888-4741; orders@ipgbook.com

# TABLE OF CONTENTS

## PART 2
## WILHELM WEIKE (1859-1917)—
## LIFE IN GERMANY AND ON BAFFIN ISLAND

# LIST OF FIGURES

# PREFACE

# The arctic year of
# an ordinary German

Wilhelm Weike, born on November 28, 1859 in rural Häverstädt near Minden in eastern Westphalia, Germany, is mentioned in historical records variously as a domestic servant, gardener, business attendant, and porter. Almost by accident he would participate in a scientific expedition to the Inuit and whalers of Baffin Island in Canada's Eastern Arctic that would become quite a sensation in German polar research in the 1880s.

The scientist Franz Boas, born on July 9, 1858, came from a Jewish family in Minden. He planned a research trip to the Inuit of the Canadian Arctic for the year 1883-84 to carry out geographical and ethnological investigations. From his youth he had been fascinated by the reports of explorers going to the Arctic. He had studied physics, geography and philosophy, completing his doctorate in physics. For this expedition his declared aims were investigations into the natural history and geodetic surveys. But Boas' real aim was to make contact with the Inuit, the indigenous people of the Arctic, to get to know their culture and to live and travel with them. His research goal was to relate their life-style to their movements on land, sea, and pack ice and to their pattern of settlement as well as to the utilization of available resources.

For this trip Franz Boas was looking for assistance and support from somebody who, above all, would unburden him from the problems and duties of everyday life while travelling, relieve him of domestic chores, and also be available as a "Jack-of-all-trades" with regard to his endeavours. What he was seeking was a reliable, diligent, literate person with

Wilhelm Weike in Berlin, 1886 (Photo: Studio E. Hering, Berlin; *American Philosophical Society*)

Franz Boas as a one-year volunteer in the 15th Infantry Regiment in Minden, 1881-1882 (Photo: Studio J. Hülsenbeck, Minden; *American Philosophical Society*)

wide experience of everyday practical matters, who possessed some organizational talent, understood his work, and above all, could adapt to new, strange living conditions. Plans to engage a lieutenant in the German Army as a member of the expedition fell apart shortly before the departure date. Simultaneously Boas had been looking for somebody who was to accompany him to the Arctic as his servant. Thus his eye fell on an employee in his parents' house.

It was probably the businessman Meyer Boas Sr who offered his servant Wilhelm Weike to accompany and support his son on his trip. Weike had been living in the Boas house in Minden, working as a gardener and domestic servant since 1879. Weike agreed to join the expedition. At that point Franz Boas was 24 years old; at age 23 Wilhelm Weike was even younger. The relationship between Boas and Weike was dictated by the formal constraints of German society at the end of the nineteenth century. That social distance, in terms of boundaries and norms, would persist throughout their shared sojourn in the Arctic as well as later on in their lives.

Weike, a smart young man, was appropriately prepared; he learned to cook, to sole shoes, and to pour bullets and everything that was essential and could be anticipated, by the standards of the time, for such a journey. Moreover, Weike could read and write. Franz Boas made Weike keep a journal, probably in anticipation of his entries being useful to him. Weike's journal represents a unique account of an ordinary man encountering a remote world that is totally alien to him. The journal makes clear that Weike succeeded, with practical sense and dexterity, in tackling the most varied everyday hands-on demands in the Arctic, in adapting to the conditions of a strange country and environment, and in meeting the demands of an expedition. It also describes the social contacts with Inuit and whalers. The journal reflects everyday aspects and chores and throws light on Weike's character and his inner attitudes, which were free of cultural or racial arrogance and were marked by curiosity, frankness, and interest in anything new and strange. He treated people with respect and acceptance and his human warmth permitted him to get close to people and to overcome difficulties in communicating. Thus, through his warm-heartedness he balanced Boas' scientific training and outlook.

Right at the start of the trip Weike, coming from the small town of Minden, was amazed at the "metropolis" of Hamburg, the *Germania*'s departure point as it sailed for the Canadian Arctic. This expedition was almost a world-trip for him. The *Germania* sailed across the North Sea past Scotland and the Greenland coast, and finally to the Arctic waters off Baffin Island. After their year-long sojourn and extended travels on Baffin Island, they returned to Minden via St. John's, Halifax, New York, and Hamburg. After only a little more than a year Weike was married and moved to Berlin early in 1886 where he died on June 11, 1917.

Franz Boas, returning briefly to Germany to extend his academic studies and degree, moved to the United States where he had a long scientific career in cultural anthropology at Columbia University. He died in New York on December 21, 1942.

The year 2008 was the 150th anniversary of Franz Boas' birth and the 125th anniversary of the arrival of the expedition at Baffin Island. Both were extensively commemorated in a number of events and publications in Minden and elsewhere in Germany. Boas' journals of the Arctic expedition had been published already in German and in English (Müller-Wille 1994, 1998). As authors and editors we felt that these anniversaries provided an excellent opportunity to publish Weike's parallel Arctic journal that, as we knew, was preserved and had survived thanks to Franz Boas' personal diligence. Publication of the German-language book was generously funded by the *Mindener Geschichtsverein* (Historical Society of Minden) and it was launched at a public event in Minden on June 4, 2008. The book presents the first-hand description of Weike's daily work, experiences, encounters, and impressions—rich in detail, fascinating, and often wonderfully funny. In terms of literature Weike's writings are an unusual and extraordinary document that, one may assume, was not intended for publication either by Weike or by Boas.

The purpose of the publication of Wilhelm Weike's parallel journal is to make his voice heard beside that of Franz Boas' overpowering scientific presence. As an ordinary man—he remained so throughout his life—Weike was not a historical figure. And so, after more than 125 years a permanent record to his previously hidden literary bequest was made available to the public in Germany.

The English edition of Weike's journal and letters was prepared to provide English-language readers everywhere, but particularly in Nunavut and other circumpolar regions, with access to Weike's writings. This way Weike, through his written words, could travel back to the Canadian Arctic giving Inuit and Qallunaat alike insight into this historical document that conveys the simple, unaltered, and external observation and perception of the life of Inuit and whalers on Qikiqtaaluk (Baffin Island) during the early 1880s. Appropriately, William Barr, who already had translated Franz Boas' Arctic diaries, translated it into English free of charge, as before. Linna Weber Müller-Wille did the final linguistic editing of the English version that we had revised and adapted in a few places in our text without touching the writing by Wilhelm Weike. Both she and Ragnar Müller-Wille were a source of inspiration and support during the preparation of both the German and English editions. William Barr and we are thankful to Robin Philpot, the publisher of Baraka Books, for his encouragement and engagement to include this book in his collection of extraordinary texts.

Since 2008 Wilhelm Weike and also Franz Boas have been given further attention and recognition. On November 28, 2009, on the occasion of the 150th anniversary of Weike's birthday, a group of dedicated Mindeners—curator, actors, a cabaret artist, and a journalist (Ursula Bender-Wittmann, Petra Fröhlich, Bernd Gieseking, Jürgen Langenkämper and Thea Luckfiel)—held a well-received play reading at the old Boas house at the Minden Market featuring texts by Weike, Boas, and Inuit. On October 24, 2010 the world premier of Bernd Gieseking's 20-scene play *"Die Farbe des Wassers"* (The Colour of Water) was staged by the Minden City Theatre, which dramatizes the Boas-Weike-Inuit relationships during their Arctic sojourn (Gieseking 2010). After years of lingering as the master's servant in a very small footnote in Franz Boas' major publication on Inuit society Weike's appearance in the public eye does not seem to end whether in Germany, Canada, The United States, Nunavut or elsewhere.

*Ludger Müller-Wille* and *Bernd Gieseking*
St-Lambert (Québec) Canada / Dortmund,
Germany, September 2011

# INTRODUCTION

# Wilhelm Weike with Franz Boas among Inuit and whalers – duties and chronicling

Wilhelm Weike arrived back in Minden from Baffin Island on October 9, 1884, having returned from an adventurous journey involving at least one life-threatening episode. Next day Weike reported his return to the authorities, and in the Minden register for that year there appears, for October 10, 1884, under the heading "place of last residence" the entry "North Pole." He hadn't travelled quite as far as that, but for a Prussian official in Minden, places, landscapes, and islands such as Anarnitung, Cumberland Sound or Baffin Island were seemingly synonymous with the North Pole or so Wilhelm Weike let him believe.

In various respects Franz Boas was a pioneer in his perceptions and ideas. Thus he was unusual in that as a young scientist he wanted to ensure that he had a second observing voice, by asking Wilhelm Weike, who accompanied him as his servant, to keep a regular journal. And Wilhelm Weike fulfilled this duty faithfully; he thus created and bequeathed a first-hand vision of the everyday affairs of an arctic expedition, of his relationship with Boas, of the social interaction of the whalers of widely differing nations, living in the Arctic and of his encounters with the numerous Inuit.

He experienced contacts, exchanges, friendship, and collaboration with over 150 of the Inuit living there, and names over fifty of them in his journal. From later letters between Franz Boas and James Mutch

(1848-1931), the head of the Scottish whaling station of the Crawford Noble Company (Aberdeen, Scotland) on Kekerten Island, one may gather that there was a "liaison" between Wilhelm Weike and Tookavay, an Inuit woman who at that time was living at the Inuit settlement at this station on Kekerten Island (or Qeqerten, the spelling used by Franz Boas). Kekerten Island served as the base for the two Germans in the winter of 1883-84.

Wilhelm Weike begins the journal with his travel preparations in Minden on June 10, 1883. The actual sea voyage starts on June 22. In the early hours of the morning *Germania* sailed from the mouth of the Elbe off Cuxhaven. The final entry in the journal occurs on September 1, 1884 on board *Wolf*, a whaling ship out of St. John's, Newfoundland. On the homeward voyage Weike travelled along the east coasts of Canada and the United States to New York. From there Weike made the ocean crossing to Germany; he reached Minden in October 1884, and Boas not until March 1885.

There exists only a copy of Wilhelm Weike's journal. Like most of the other documents on Weike's life, the original seems to have disappeared or was destroyed and cannot be traced. The building of his last residence in Berlin was bombed and levelled during World War II and most traces of it are lost. Despite these circumstances some phases of his life could be traced, which the authors present in their commentary following the journal and letters.

Franz Boas came back to Germany for only fifteen months and then moved to the United States in July 1886. He became a trend-setting scientist in the field of cultural anthropology, and an influential curator, professor, and author (Tilg and Pöhl 2007). His complete literary bequest is housed at the American Philosophical Society in Philadelphia. The copy of Weike's journal is also located there. In April 1886, while working on his post-doctoral thesis (*Habilitation*), Franz Boas mentioned to his parents that he was having Weike's journal copied. At that time he entertained the plan of writing a popular description of his arctic experiences. This book did not materialize. But that plan explains Franz Boas' particular interest in Weike's writings, which would have been of particular value for that undertaking. Even while they were travelling together Boas was curious as to what Weike was writing every day, "*as*

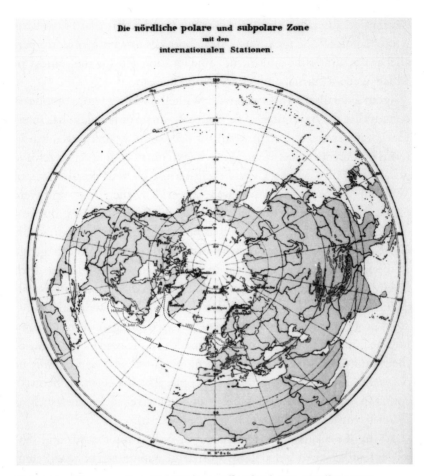

Outward and homeward voyage, Minden - Baffin Island, 1883-1884 (Base map: Neumayer & Börgen 1886, Vol. 1, facing p. 1; additional cartography: Ragnar Müller-Wille)

*if he were enjoying endless experiences.*" (Franz Boas/parents, letter diary, *Germania*, July 2, 1883).

Wilhelm Weike kept his journal conscientiously, steadily and observantly; entries are missing on only a few days. It is an independent document, vivid in its picturesque descriptions, precise in the ethnographic observations, authentic in terms of the immediate rendering of multifarious impressions, and finally, gripping as a representation of the encounter between an ordinary man and an alien world. Weike's writings are directly linked to the journals and letters that Franz Boas wrote (Müller-Wille 1994, 1998), since both documents evolved in parallel at the same time and in the same location. This is the context in which Weike's journal and letters should be read.

From a detailed comparison with Wilhelm Weike's letters it appears certain that the transcriber of the journal—male or female—has intervened extensively, at least in terms of orthography, and partly also in terms of sentence structure in Weike's text, possibly in order to achieve greater legibility. In the German edition the obvious peculiarities of Wilhelm Weike's orthography were retained by the editors and were only adjusted to present-day standards where the meaning was unclear.

Weike wrote sounds and words as he heard them. In his journal the German language is mixed up with words and terms from the language of the Inuit, known as Inuktitut in the Eastern Arctic, and also with English vocabulary, probably just as in his normal daily oral communication with the Inuit and the whalers. Wilhelm Weike writes the numerous proper names in many different ways providing some insight into how he interpreted what he heard phonetically. He renders the name of their Inuit companion, spelled Ssigna by Boas, as *Singna, Sinar* or *Singnark*, among others. To other people, like his constant Scottish counterpart at the station, James Mutch, he gives nicknames such as *Mi=Mö* (Mister Mutch) or *Sim Mo* (Jim Mutch).

All Inuit personal and place names as well as Inuit words and sentences that Weike recorded in his journal are maintained in his different original spellings. For historical reference the names are presented in the footnotes as Franz Boas published them in various places (Boas 1885a: Appendix I, 90-95; 1888: Glossary, 659-675; 1894:97-114; furthermore Boas in Müller-Wille 1994:267-269, 277-280, 287-294; 1998:273-276, 285-298). An exception is made for the letter *k'* for the velar *k* at the beginning of words and the Greek letter *x* (pronounced "kai") within words. Boas used them consistently in his major publication *Baffin-Land* (1885a) but he changed them in almost all cases to the letter Q/q in his later publications (1888, 1894). This use of Q/q is standard today and is therefore applied throughout this book (cf. Dorais 1996:179ff. for the discussion of the evolution of orthographies for Inuit languages). Other Inuit vocabulary is presented in the accepted standardized Inuit orthography for the Eastern Canadian Arctic based on various sources as indicated (e. g., Schneider 1985).

On a later occasion, after the arctic expedition, in a critical assessment of his formal writing abilities, Weike wrote that writing was not his forte. He was not very particular when it came to punctuation and capitalization. His sentence structure and vocabulary are stamped with his east Westphalian dialect, belonging to the Low Saxon variety of Low German. In numerous locations the editors have added punctuation, to make the text more accessible to the reader.

The few surviving letters by Weike must be seen differently from his journal. His letters, added here to the journal, derive from three periods. The first letters belong to the period of their travels and were sent back to Minden with the *Germania* on September 16, 1883; and the last one with the *Catherine* on October 3. These letters are forthright reports of his first impressions of the sea voyage and of his arrival in arctic Baffin Island. The addressees are not always immediately identifiable. His later letters were sent to Boas from Minden and Berlin.

As regards the Arctic letters, and this applies to both Franz Boas' correspondence and Wilhelm Weike's letters, it must be said that Boas' mother and sisters made numerous copies of these letters for the widely scattered, international Boas clan, so that often many copies of the same letter exist in the family correspondence in the American Philosophical Society Archives. Yet several letters in Weike's original handwriting have survived in the Boas bequest. Weike often wrote his journal and letters in ink, i.e., using an inkpot and a quill pen, sometimes at temperatures below -40°. Both he and Boas often had to thaw the frozen ink over an open flame, or with their bodily heat.

Wilhelm Weike's unknown transcriber in Berlin, like Weike himself, used the German Gothic script of their time (called *Spitzschrift* or *Kurrentschrift*). In the copy, almost all personal and place names used by the Inuit and whalers, English and Inuit words, and also, generally, dates (weekdays and months) were rendered in the Roman script. The basic texts used by the editors were the documents present in the Boas bequest at the American Philosophical Society Archives, either the originals or copies on microfilm. To make the text more accessible, the editors have used footnotes to explain the numerous situations, concepts, and words as well as some complex cultural aspects of the Inuit such as shamanism, whose meanings would not always be comprehensible to the reader. Some extracts from Weike's journal have already been published in German (Müller-Wille 1994) and in English (Müller-Wille 1998) and some were also included by Bernd Gieseking in a collation of text pieces in his dramatic reading *Im Eis* (In the Ice; 1998) accompanied by original music and audiovisual effects.

Some symbols and abbreviations used in the journal's text and in footnotes are explained as follows:

I. = Inuktitut with English translation in the footnotes is rendered in Roman orthography that is used along with the Standard Syllabic Orthography in the Eastern Canadian Arctic. Translations are based on Boas (1885a, 1894), Schneider (1985), Boas in Müller-Wille (1994, 1998), and others as indicated. The spelling of Inuit personal names and place names is taken from Boas (1885a, 1888, 1894) with the alterations mentioned above.

... Illegible or inexplicable words.

(...) Words left out of the original text; probably the transcriber could not always decipher Weike's handwriting and in some places inserted a question mark where the material could not be read.

( ) A spelling mistake in the original copy: only corrected if the sense of the word could not be understood; if given in italics it represents Weike's original renderings.

[ ] Insertions (e.g., letters left out), corrections and additional text material added by the journal's editors.

Text pieces in brackets are not part of Wilhelm Weike's journal or letters. These sections include quotations rendered in italics from Franz Boas' published journals and letters (Müller-Wille 1998). The footnotes contain translations and supplementary information about situations, individuals and facts and explanations of the text. All original texts and quotations, except where indicated otherwise, derive from the Franz Boas Professional Papers kept at the American Philosophical Society in Philadelphia, Pennsylvania (U.S.A.).

PART I

WILHELM WEIKE
Arctic Journal and Letters
(1883-1884)

Edited and annotated by
Ludger Müller-Wille and Bernd Gieseking

# Preparations and voyage on board the *Germania* (June 10 to August 27, 1883)

*Sunday, 10 June.*
Now our voyage is getting ever closer. This morning I left here at 3:30 a.m. to say goodbye to my relatives, my father, and brother;[1] I got back at 10 p.m. very tired and soaked through. Tonight Dr Boas travels to Hamburg to make further preparations there.

*Monday, 11 June.*
Today I fetched the halyards for our flags as well as the little medical kit. E. Limberg had sprained his leg, I twisted it straight again and twice massaged it. And when I went to the train station, I was together with F. Hirsch.[2]

*Tuesday, 12 June.*
I've also been making progress at my shoemaking; I've soled a pair of shoes and straightened some hooks. We've also received our alpenstocks that are equipped with 7-cm-long steel points, along with two spare points for each alpenstock.

*Wednesday, 13 June.*
Dreary weather and a lot of work.

---

1. At his brother's and stepfather's house in Häverstädt near Minden. Weike's father had died early in 1861.
2. Individuals and circumstances unknown.

*Thursday, 14 June.*
Dealing with H. Ca. and B. St.³ has not been easy, but still the situation has been resolved.

*Friday, 15 June.*
The temperature has changed rapidly. It was a warm day; hence it was inevitable that there was a thunderstorm. Dr Boas returned from Hamburg this morning, to take his final farewells from home; this will not be very easy. Now we'll soon be up-to-date with all our things, including the most minute; and high time too!

*Saturday, 16 June.*
It was a very warm day; our beds, and the other things that were still here, have been sent off. Dr Boas travels back to Hamburg tonight and I'll be travelling later, since I still have a lot to do there.

*Sunday, 17 June.*
My farewell from Minden was very hurried; it was already 12 o'clock when the message arrived that I should come. Then I first had to pack my things, and then I still had to take care of something in town, and I hurried to do so. It was not long before I had to leave; there were several friends at the station to see me off. How beautiful the countryside looks with the splendour of the grain fields.

*Monday, 18 June.*
In small towns one has no concept at all of life in the large city; the hustle and bustle on the streets with horse-drawn trams and other vehicles, and when one sees the business activity, with the toing and froing from one house to the next.

*Tuesday, 19 June.*
There was still much to do and things to get, since I was already sleeping on board.⁴ There was a great deal to be done before I went to bed.

---

3. Ditto.
4. On board *Germania*, the two-masted schooner (221 grt, 26 m long) of the German Polar Commission. In September 1882 it left 11 men (seven scientists and four workers) at Kingua, the site of the German station on Baffin Island, and picked them up

At 8 o'clock I went with the cook[5] to Altona; we came back in the early hours of the morning; it was already [daylight].

*Wednesday, 20 June.*
Things got under way very early this morning. Since we were leaving harbour at noon today, there was a lot of activity on board around that time, and we were seen off with cheers. We sailed to Cuxhaven where we dropped anchor in the evening, and the gentlemen who had sailed with us were put ashore; Herr Boas[6] was among them.

> *Minden,[7] 25 June. Last week our fellow-citizen, Herr Dr Franz Boas, accompanied by only one servant,[8] set off on a research trip, expected to last 18 months, to the arctic regions of North America, in order to study the geographical, ethnographic, and meteorological aspects of these regions that are still not revealed to science. A ship fitted out by the Geographical Society, that will be evacuating the members of the meteorological station on Labrador,[9] is taking him to his destination. Dr Boas intends staying among the Eskimos for quite a long time, and taking part in their migrations. The most renowned scholars attach great hopes for rich scientific results from this expedition. We wish that these hopes are realized and that the young researcher will return home safely.*

*Thursday, 21 June.*
We lay in port all day, waiting for a fair wind that will let us put to sea. The ship's crew consists of six men: Captain Mahlstädte,[10] Mate

---

again in September 1883 (Neumayer 1891:41-43, plate opposite p. 46; Deutsches Schifffahrtsmuseum).

5. The ship's cook, Adolf Lange, from Magdeburg.

6. Meyer (also Meier) Boas, Franz Boas' father.

7. *Minden-Lübbecker Kreisblatt*, Tuesday, 26 June 1883. Franz Boas' research trip was also publicized internationally through his father's contacts, in *The Jewish Chronicle* (1883) and in the *Archives Israëlites* (1883) as *"the first Jewish traveller to the Polar regions."*

8. Wilhelm Weike.

9. What is meant is the German polar station at Kingua (Qingua), Cumberland Sound, Baffin Island; in 1882-83 the German Polar Commission did maintain a one-man weather station at Nain, Labrador (Neumayer 1891; cf. Müller-Wille 1998:85).

10. A. F. B. Mahlstede.

Wilh[elm] Wenke, carpenter F. Carl Johansen, from Kiel, cook Adolf Lange from Magdeburg and two seamen, Anton Andresen from Sweden and Wilhelm Wincke, from Rostock.[11]

*Friday, 22 June.*
I was wakened at 1:30 because they were weighing anchor; but the wind was not favourable for us and hence we cruised around in the vicinity of Norderney, where we saw very many fishing boats, but no large ships.

*Saturday, 23 June.*
Our voyage has not made any real progress; rather we regressed. Until noon we were cruising around in the vicinity of Helgoland, until finally the wind changed and we made progress. We were moving very slowly and hence in the evening we could still see the Helgoland light. Since the sea was so calm, we even tried fishing.

*Sunday, 24 June.*
With a somewhat favourable wind we made quite good progress today, but it was a marvelous day, as warm as I could never have hoped at sea. I spent most of the time fishing; we caught so many fish that they have been on the menu twice, and I have also learned to steer.

[Franz Boas noted: *Since yesterday I have been giving Wilhelm instruction in English; I hope he will have learned something before we arrive over there. So far he is doing quite well; he is able and willing, and thus I am rally satisfied with him.*]

*Monday, 25 June.*
Today we made better progress; until evening we were making quite a good speed—seven knots. Then it became quite lively, with the ship rolling constantly from side to side. I lay in my bunk, but due to the constant rocking I got up again. There could be no thought of sleeping.

[Franz Boas stated: *I have just been teaching Wilhelm some more English. But he has a frightfully hard head, which it is difficult to get anything into. But that is not surprising, since he really has never learned anything.*]

---

11. Thus there were three people with the Christian name "Wilhelm" on board, whose surname, moreover, also began with W – Weike, Wenke and Wincke.

*Tuesday, 26 June.*

The morning was overcast and rainy with a very strong wind; in the afternoon it cleared up, but how wonderful the sea looks with a strong wind blowing! The waves come roaring along as if they want to send the ship to the bottom, but before you know it, the ship is on top of the wave. Our days are getting steadily longer; it was after 9 o'clock when the sun set.

*Wednesday, 27 June.*

This morning we left the North Sea with a fair wind, and were heading along the Scottish coast. The sheer cliffs rising from the sea are wonderful, and here one can see high mountains, such as I have never seen in Germany, and large numbers of birds flying to and fro from their nests.

*Thursday, 28 June.*

Early this morning we saw the last islands of northern Scotland;[12] the ship was making heavy weather. The wind was blowing from the side and hence the ship was lying over to one side, and as a result the waves were constantly sweeping the deck forward. At noon, at mealtime, I had a plate of bean soup in front of me, and before I knew it this good soup was all over my clothes. When I got clean again they were pumping water out of the ship. I took a hand at the pump, but it was not long before a wave broke aboard and I was soaked from head to foot.

*Friday, 29 June.*

It is scarcely credible that the storm can spend itself in one night like this. This morning the weather was the most beautiful it could be; one might even have said it was a calm ocean. I've developed the greatest admiration for the gulls and puffins;[13] they cruise around the ship so adeptly and watch for anything thrown overboard, and swim along astern of us. It was a very beautiful evening; the sun set magnificently at 10 o'clock local time, 11 o'clock Hamburg time.

---

12. The islands of Lewis and North Rona.
13. North Atlantic sea birds: gulls or kittiwakes (*Rissa tridactyla*); divers or puffins (*Fratercula arctica*) of the *Alcidae* family.

*Saturday, 30 June.*

As we came on deck this morning the weather was superb; the water was as smooth as a mirror and until noon we had a totally clear sky, until all of a sudden a large halo formed around the sun; our captain told us that this was not a good sign; I don't like the sound of that. We also saw some *Braunfische*[14] that are one and half metres long, with a pointed head; the latter looks trunk-shaped. We could not observe them clearly since they just barely come out of the water to get air. It happened just as the Captain said it would; the sky clouded over, and it also started to rain. But the wind was still fair for us, and hence the ship was still making five knots. Since I do not possess any instruments, I cannot make any more precise weather report. We've also just had to look after our revolvers, since they were starting to rust from the sea air, and then I learned some more English.[15]

# July 1883

*Sunday, 1 July.*

The sky was heavily overcast, and ultimately it started to rain, but we had a fair wind so that we were making seven and eight miles per hour, nautical miles, of course;[16] if it continues like this we should soon arrive. When one is on board ship one cannot easily distinguish Sundays from other days; it is not like on shore. The seamen always wear the same clothes; only dinner is somewhat better than usual; we get pudding.

*Monday, 2 July.*

I have designated Monday as my regular laundry day, and before I started anything else, I took care of the laundry. The weather was not very pleasant, and hence one didn't spend much time looking around

---

14. Porpoises (*Phocoena phocoena*).
15. Franz Boas gave Wilhelm English lessons, so that he could communicate on Baffin Island with Americans and Scots, as well as with the Inuit who had picked up some English from the whalers.
16. Nautical mile = 1852 m.

on deck; we were enveloped in fog all day. Around 7 in the evening one could barely see a ship's length, it was so thick. But ultimately the fog broke up so that the sun was visible around 9 o'clock again; 9 by our time and 11 p.m. by Hamburg time.

*Tuesday, 3 July.*
The thick fog lasted until noon, when the wind changed and the weather became quite pleasant.

*Wednesday, 4 July.*
Changeable weather all day: rain, fog, and sunshine. A seal[17] came quite close to us; it must have strayed from land.

*Thursday, 5 July.*
Still foggy.

*Friday, 6 July.*
The weather has changed. We've got quite a good wind, so that we can stay on course. The air is becoming steadily colder. With these short waves the ship's movements are quite unpleasant.

*Saturday, 7 July.*
Nothing.

*Sunday, 8 July.*
Foggy weather, but a fair wind for us until evening, when it started to rain and the wind strengthened. At 8:45 a rope broke on one sail, so that it had to be furled. Due to the foul weather we went to bed early, but we could not sleep. Around 10:30 p.m. the wind became even stronger until finally we became aware that there was a lot of activity on deck, in order to reduce sail.

*Monday, 9 July.*
The gale became even stronger; one wave after another broke on board. One could not sleep with all the racket; then there was some activity

---

17. Ringed seal (*Phoca hispida*).

on board again, and I got dressed too. I had some things for my Herr Dr, since it was his birthday.[18] I handed them to him; he looked at the clock and it was 3:30 a.m. and the storm was raging violently. This lasted until around 10 o'clock.

*Tuesday, 10 July.*
Land was sighted; it was Greenland. Now we again knew the direction we should be heading. A new course was set, and we thus emerged from the storm. The ship was running at ten knots; until noon it was calm. We fished for gulls[19] and were astonished at the Greenland [mountains],[20] with their glaciers and snow.

*Wednesday, 11 July.*
In the morning we heard drift ice approaching from a distance. The noise that the ice makes sounds like a train approaching; besides there were icebergs in the vicinity. They look very beautiful; they were about six metres from the ship. At noon a whole field of drift ice, ten miles wide, lay astern of us; we had come through the extreme point of it, and hence we had encountered few bergs.

*Thursday, 12 July.*
A cool day, so that one's feet were cold from morning to night.

*Friday, 13 July.*
In the morning quite strong wind and rain; in the afternoon the wind dropped and hence it began raining more heavily. In the evening there was a very high sea running; the sky was overcast and it looked like a storm; the sails were furled. But it was not so bad after all.

*Saturday, 14 July.*
Nothing.

---

18. Franz Boas turned 25.
19. The seamen cast with fishing rods for the gulls that circled the ship, and that would pounce on the bait fastened to a hook, and were thus caught.
20. Greenland/Kalaallit Nunaat.

*Sunday, 15 July.*
We became blocked in the drift ice, and hence in the evening we had to head back, to avoid becoming totally beset. It had become a very fine day, and it was a magnificent sunset, such as one never sees on land; repeatedly the sun's rays came through the icebergs; it was 10 o'clock as it set.

*Monday, 18 July.*
Ice and fog.

*Tuesday, 17 July.*
The ice is still with us; while we make progress during the day, we head back again at night, the ice is so close-packed against the coast. We've already seen the land[21] but there can be no thought of reaching it. It went on like this until late in the evening; then it became foggy. We then had to head further out to sea, so that the ice would not cause us any damage.

*Wednesday, 18 July.*
Continual rain and fog.

*Thursday, 19 July.*
Last night we had quite a strong wind and quite a high sea; in the morning it became quieter. Before noon we had a storm with heavy rain, and due to the advancing fog and rain we are still drifting around in an open channel.

*Friday, 20 July.*

*Saturday, 21 July.*
Nothing on Friday and Saturday.

*Sunday, 22 July.*
The fog has cleared somewhat; it has been quite clear weather. We are surrounded by drift ice; twice today we've run through some ice. We are about 60 miles from land, just as far as on July 16.

---

21. Baffin Island / Qikiqtaaluk (the huge island).

*Monday, 23 July.*

*Tuesday, 24 July.*
Nothing on Monday and Tuesday.

*Wednesday, 25 July.*
Due to the bad weather we have had to head back out of the ice. The fog is so thick that one can see only a few ship's lengths. In the evening there was a knock at our cabin door; we went on deck. There was a seal close to the ship, but it quickly departed when it spotted us. We'd been back below for less than an hour when there was again a knock. There was a large iceberg ahead and we had to change course to avoid it.

*Thursday, 26 July.*
During the night of the 25th/26th we had the first frost, with persistent fog; the sun did not show itself at all.

*Friday, 27 July.*
A beautiful summer's day, such as we have not seen for a long time. The temperature was only 6°, but we had the impression that it was 20°, as compared to other days. It was also quite calm until evening, when it began to rain.

*Saturday, 28 July.*
Today it was so cold that it was fall again, as compared to the 27th, with a strong wind and high seas. 38 days on board ship up until the 28th.

*Sunday, 29 July.*
A strong wind and cold too. We have been sailing constantly along the ice edge, to see whether we can push through anywhere. But there were no openings anywhere, and hence we had to head back out again.

*Monday, 30 July.*
During the night of 29th/30th there was a very rough sea. In the morning we were enveloped in fog and it was also very cold; around noon the weather cleared again and we headed back towards the ice. To be on board a ship and unable to make any progress, is a tedious matter; today we are no further than we were on the 15th. But in the evening we sighted

land and I thought we would reach it and stayed on deck until 12 o'clock.[22] Then the ship hove to and I went to bed. This evening I saw stars for the first time since leaving Germany.

*Tuesday, 31 July.*
Nothing.

# August 1883

*Wednesday, 1 August.*
Strolled around.

*Thursday, 2 August.*
Strolled around.

*Friday, 3 August.*

*Saturday, 4 August.*
Nothing.

*Sunday, 5 August.*
It was calm on August 1 and 2 and hence we lay almost quietly. We could still see the land. On the 3rd there was somewhat more wind off the land, so that the ice slackened. We had to let ourselves be driven further and further away; this continued until noon on the 5th. Then the wind became stronger, so that we had to run back even more. We were about 100 miles from land and we were running through drift ice all day; so we lost the land. We tried to get closer, but in some places the ice was close-packed, so that we repeatedly had to retreat.

*Monday, 6 August.*

*Tuesday, 7 August.*
Nothing.

---

22. Midnight.

Franz Boas (right) and a seaman on the *Germania* off the pack ice at
Cumberland Sound (Baffin Island), August 6, 1883 (Photo: Wilhelm Weike;
*American Philosophical Society*)

*Wednesday, 8 August.*
On the 6th and 7th there was still quite a strong wind, but we had to look for open water. In the evening of the 7th we ran into fog, which persisted all day on the 8th, and the wind died down, which makes for jolly travelling here; mostly we just sleep.

*Thursday, 9 August.*
Nothing.

*Friday, 10 August.*
The fog persisted until the 9th. On that day there was a strong wind, and with it the ice moved over to the west shore;[23] there was a very high sea running and in the evening it started to rain.

*Saturday, 11 August.*
We had clear weather again and headed towards the land again; there was no ice in sight ahead. It was like this until 3:30 p.m. when we were back in close ice again. We then ran back until 5:30 and then headed in another direction, but the ice was close-packed there too. At 7 we had to turn back again, and at 8 o'clock we took in three sails, and swung back again.

*Sunday, 12 August until Saturday, 18 August.*[24]

*Sunday, 19 August.*
On August 18 we made quite good progress towards the Sound; it appeared that we had an open channel, but at 8 p.m. we had to turn back, since everything was choked with ice again. On the 19th we didn't get even that far; the ice had become slack, and we had to haul off; in the evening the ship was laid on the port tack.

*Monday, 20 August.*
This morning we were heading towards land; we ran into drift ice but there was so much open water among the ice that we could keep moving. Just as on the 18th we made some more progress, but at noon we

---

23. Of Cumberland Sound.
24. Wilhelm Weike made no entries in his journal for these days (cf. Franz Boas' daily entries in Müller-Wille 1998:63-66).

again had to retreat; we couldn't go any further forward, and also it had fallen calm which was to our detriment. In the afternoon there was quite a strong wind again, but we again couldn't make progress. What a large number of seals we are seeing among the pack ice!

*Tuesday, 21 August.*
On the evening of the 20th a fog bank had already appeared on the horizon; hence we had to get clear of the ice. On the 21st it rained all day and at the same time the fog was quite thick. It would clear up a little, but would then become even thicker a short time later. At 12 midnight the ship hove to on the port tack. There was quite a strong wind; we went over onto the other tack a few times, and we almost ran into an iceberg.

*Wednesday, 22 August.*
This morning we were making for land; we were travelling through drift ice all morning, until we reached the position where the wind failed us on the 18th and 20th of August; we hadn't got much further when it fell calm and the wind changed direction. We were now more off the west shore of the Sound, and now we headed for the other shore, but there it was still full of ice. At 8 o'clock a boat was launched to fetch a log of driftwood that was drifting around among the ice here.

*Thursday, 23 August.*
It was a very fine day—very warm. But there was no wind. If we had a wind for 15 minutes, it would then fall calm again for a few hours. We were lying just off the ice, but it was so slack that we could have got through it if the wind had not left us, and hence we had to steer clear. At 10 o'clock aurora was seen.

*Friday, 24 August.*
The third day that it has been calm; it was very warm again. Twice we've been lumbered with a stream of ice, so that we had to take boat hooks to fend it off, to prevent the ship from becoming beset, since there is no wind. There was a very beautiful sky as the sun sank into the sea; one doesn't see anything so beautiful on land.[25]

---

25. Between pages 34 and 35 of the journal's copy there is an unnumbered page with the following notes inserted for 22 to 25 August inclusive.

22 [August]. Observations and we would have liked to go to Cape Mercy,[26] but this didn't happen.

23 [August]. Picked up some driftwood, seaweed and blades of grass; roots and…

24 [August]. the driftwood has been eaten by the rats, but today we got some replacements when the current drove the ice against us; some other flotsam came with it: a green spruce branch–green, with cones.

25 August. Hr. Dr Boas took many bearings on the land today.

No. 1. Rock from Kikaton,[27] 29 August 1883.

No. 2. " " " , 31 August 1883.

No. 2 [3]. " " " , 31 August [1883].

No. 4. Mussel shell[28] from the beach at Kikaton, September 1.
Looked for shells on Kikaton, at noon at low tide on September 3, 1883.

### Saturday, 25 August.
Today, with quite a strong wind we got into the Sound; but then the wind died and hence we have not made much progress. We were sailing through drift ice all day, but not so much that the ship was brought to a standstill. We received various impacts, but all went well. The sun set at 8 p.m., when it sank into the sea.

### Sunday, 26 August.
We had fog and quite a strong wind all day; the ship received quite a few impacts from the drift ice; many a ship could not have stood it; they would have been in a thousand pieces. And it was very cold; there was ice dropping from the rigging all day; if it had been clear we could have dropped anchor today; the anchors were made ready at noon. 69 days on board ship, from Hamburg to Kikaton, 1883.

---

26. Uibarun.

27. Qeqerten, the first Inuit place name recorded by Weike; he wrote it as his German ear heard it. The spelling of the official name is Kekerten, the way Scottish whalers heard and wrote it.

28. *Mytilus edulis.*

[Franz Boas wrote to his parents and sisters: *Today I will tell you only that we've always been totally cheerful, that Wilhelm and I have become round and fat, and that we are looking to the future with glad hopes.*]

*Monday, 27 August.*
The night of the 26th to the 27th was a very bad one; there was quite a strong wind as well as dense fog and the drift ice was constantly ramming into the ship so that we could not sleep. All day long we were in fairly open water, but still with thick fog and very cold. The ship lay to the port side almost all day; but there was always a strong wind; in the evening the sails were furled, and the ice was dropping from aloft the whole time.

[The journal continues on August 28 after the letters of July 6 until August 26 1883.]

# About sea and ice – Letters from on board the *Germania*[1] (July 6 to August 26)

Friday, 6 July 1883.

In the hope that these lines will reach you[2] in good health as we are here too. We are enjoying better health than on land. I have become big and fat and Herr Dr is also very well now.[3] If you saw me eating now, then you would say I was starving and very sick; I'm not letting that happen. It is even not so bad as it all was made out to be for such a long time. Waves do come aboard, certainly, when one is standing on the forward deck, but that is not so bad at all, even if one gets soaked from head to foot. One can soon put things to right, simply by getting changed, so it is no great problem. There's even an advantage to it. When I get up in the morning and see that there is a wind blowing, I don't bother washing. I know I'll be getting a shower. It is entertaining for the others when one gets baptized. The best thing is at noon, at dinner; just when one thinks one's spoon is full, the whole mess lands on the table. Occasionally one spills on someone else. Herr Dr eats with

---

1. Between July 8 and August 26 Wilhelm Weike wrote several letters that he sent with *Germania* to Minden on September 16 and which, one must assume, were addressed to the domestic staff of the Boas family. In these letters he summarizes the events during the last weeks of the crossing. The first letter is in Weike's original handwriting; the second and following ones, from September 8 and 25 are hand-written copies that were made by the Boas family in Minden. Weike's letters from Baffin Island were later typed out by Franz Boas' eldest daughter, Helene Boas Yampolski (1888-1963). In the German edition, the editors corrected the texts of the letters in terms of grammar and spelling and dialect expressions were retained.
2. Mathilde Nolting and Linna (also spelled Lina by Boas, surname unknown), maids in Meyer Boas' family household in Minden (see also Franz Boas, September 29, 1883).
3. Wilhelm Weike always underlined the abbreviation Dr in his letters.

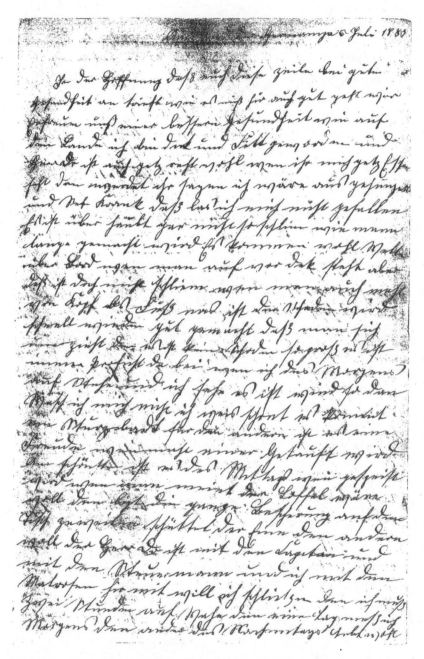

First page of the letter by Wilhelm Weike to Mathilde Nolting written on the
*Germania*, July 6 1883 (*American Philosophical Society*)

the captain and the mate and I eat with the seamen.[4] I will close now, since I have to be on watch for two hours; one day I do this in the morning, next day at noon.

Farewell.

Sunday, 8 July.

I must share with you some minor details as to how things have gone with us thus far. We've spent the week fairly quietly, and I had thought out my plan very well as to how I wanted to surprise Herr Dr.[5] I had got everything organized. It was July 8. Overcast and foggy weather, so that one couldn't spend very long on the forward deck. At 8:30 Herr Dr had already gone to bed and I was standing forward on the ship with Anton[6] and we were singing songs from home, when all of a sudden there was a clattering up on the mast. A rope had snapped on the sail. So then Toni had to go aloft and I went to bed. It was not long before the ship heeled over and everything that had been on the table was lying on the floor. And so I got up and cleaned up the mess again; it continued like this until 12:30, when it got even worse. It went on like this all night. Just as we thought it was getting somewhat better, the waves would come thundering in, as if cannon-balls were hitting the ship, and then the waves came roaring on board and into our cabin. We had already commended our souls; and it went on like this until there were some signs of life on board again. Then I got up, and congratulated Herr Dr. I had lashed everything securely on the table. Then Herr Dr wanted to see what time it was. It was not yet 4 o'clock. Then Herr Dr said: "An early birthday gift." Ah, and Herr Dr was so ill. I didn't want to go back to bed, since I couldn't sleep. When I came on deck, the entire crew were tackling a sail and lashing it. I crawled immediately into the galley. When the ship heeled over, the waves roared on board and filled

---

4. A. (August) F. B. Mahlstede and Wilhelm Wenke; Anton Andresen (Schwede), F. Carl Johansen, and Wilhelm Wincke. The cook Adolf Lange thus probably ate in his galley.

5. It was Franz Boas' 25th birthday on July 9.

6. The Swedish seaman Anton Andresen also known as Toni.

the entire deck, so that the waves towered over the ship. That was nothing yet. Every minute I found myself thinking, she's sinking now. Then the sailors came and sat down at table, but nobody could persuade me to eat. I drank my mug of coffee, and then I was finished; and so it went on until around 9:30. Then, all of a sudden, there was a shout "Land in sight!" And then the ship was set on a different course, since up till then we didn't know where we were. This was our first sight of Greenland, and now all was well. The ship was making ten knots. I wanted to give Herr Dr the good news, but everything was lashed tight with canvas, so that one could not get in or out. Then it became calmer, and the canvas was removed, so that I could get to Herr Dr and see what he was doing. Herr Dr was really seasick; the whole cabin looked a mess. Herr Dr had never been so seasick before. I quickly fetched a bucket and started cleaning up, in order to get things back in order. Then Herr Dr said: "A great birthday, Wilhelm." Then Herr Dr got up at noon, and, as usual, Wilhelm was not seasick. I have a strong stomach; what goes into it, doesn't come up again.

Since July 11 [Wednesday] we've had fairly good weather, until the morning of the 15th [Sunday]. On the 15th we encountered pack ice, and couldn't get any further. We were about 100 miles from land,[7] but we had to turn back again, since there we encountered icebergs, such as you wouldn't believe. At times they rose 300 feet above the water, 200 feet long, 300 wide, and they brought such bitter cold with them, that one got a really red nose. I've often longed for my bed, and thought of Minden. When Herr Dr is in the Captain's cabin, I'm sitting so alone by the fire; and most of the time the weather is foul, so that I can't go on deck. On Sunday the 22nd [July] I soled Anton's boots and patched boots for the others. On the 23rd [Monday] I did a general laundry and in the evening I played solitaire. Then Herr Dr came along and said: "Why are you playing cards all alone?" And then he taught me to play "skat," and then the mate came along and the card game took off.

At noon [on Tuesday, July 10] I got myself a couple of good platefuls of pea soup, and then I felt as if I had no more worries. In the

---

7. Baffin Island, off Cumberland Sound.

afternoon we "fished" for gulls until we caught six; we killed and plucked them and then we felt great. In the evening we were admiring Greenland icebergs that towered up like church steeples and shone like you wouldn't believe. We were only 25 hours from them;[8] but it looked as if we were quite close to them and hence we slept well through the night. So don't you worry. The Good Lord looks after his own. He knows the dangers and looks after them and us. And our many greetings to Herr and Frau Boas and Frl. Toni, Frl. Hedwig and Frl. Anna,[9] and tell them they don't need to worry about us. We'll yet manage, as long as we remain healthy. I shall get along well with Herr Dr, in both good days and in bad. And I extend my best thanks for the letters that were with Herr Dr's letters. It is quite remarkable: We have three men on board here, who have the same initials. The first one is Wilhelm Wenke, the old seaman Wilhelm Wiencke [Wincke] and Wilhelm Weike, and three men named August.[10] And then we have eight concertinas; if one stops playing another one starts up. Many thanks to Frau Boas and Frl. [*Fräulein*] Hedwig for the fine cake; it tastes superb. Yesterday evening, we were bothered by an iceberg that was heading for the ship and was reported by the watch officer. And then the ship had to go about. Once that was over, until 11:30 we sang Minden soldier songs,[11] and then we crawled into our bunks. On the night of the 25th to the 26th [Wednesday to Thursday] we had the first frost, but it has already melted.

7 August [Tuesday]. Being on board ship is like being in a real prison. We are just idling along. On July 30 [Monday] we thought we were approaching land. We stayed up later than usual. It was 12 o'clock when I went to my bunk. Herr Dr still stayed up. In the evening I saw the first stars since we've been at sea. The sun sets somewhat after 9 o'clock; it doesn't get completely dark.

---

8. This means about 200 km away; *Germania*'s average speed was five to six knots.
9. Franz Boas' parents Meyer (1823-1899) and Sophie (1828-1916), sisters: Antonie (Toni) (1855-1935), Hedwig (Hete) (1863-1949), Aenna (Anna) (1867-1946) (Boas, N. 2004: 291).
10. August was one of the Christian names of Captain Mahlstede and two others.
11. It can't be established what marches or marching songs were presumably popular in Minden at the time, but see Letters from Qeqerten, September 9, 1883, with respective footnote.

26 August [Sunday]. We've now come so far that we are in the Sound, but yesterday it was calm and today there is a wind, and it is so foggy that we're not making much progress. And so cold that there is ice hanging in the rigging all day. Today we've been on deck little or not at all. Today it is a letter-writing factory here.[12] We are enjoying good health here. I'm becoming fat. Initially I was quite modest at mealtimes. Then the old seaman[13] said: "You ought not to be!" Since then I've been eating everything that's put in front of me, and I'm looking very well; this keeps up my strength, and I don't need to do much here. I will close with this. Greetings to all in the Boas family.

---

12. Boas and Weike hurried to write letters that were sent back to Germany with *Germania* on her return.
13. Wilhelm Wincke.

# Among Inuit, whalers, and polar researchers (August 28 to September 16)

*Tuesday, 28 August.*
The fog had cleared somewhat and hence we could head for land with a fair wind. It was around noon when we spotted a boat; it was a whaleboat that was approaching us. They had been out hunting and had seen us, and so we arrived safely at 2:40, when we dropped anchor. We were towed by the whaleboat and an Eskimo boat[1] and one manned by our own men to the point where we could anchor, and then the Eskimos remained on board for a while. There was a really beautiful child among them, and three times we heard shouting and the barking of dogs from shore!

*Wednesday, 29 August.*
This morning I set foot on the land of the Eskimos for the first time. We had to bring our things ashore. We had to carry the first boatload up immediately, and since the tide was rising we carried three boatloads only far enough that our things would stay dry, and hauled as much as possible there at high tide, since otherwise we'd have to carry it too far. It was heavy work, carrying everything up, because one was always trudging up-hill, and we had to clamber over rocks, and then back down again. But there was a terrible number of dogs there that looked very sad, because they don't get enough to eat.

*Thursday, 30 August.*
There was a strong wind and a rough sea. We had to bring boxes ashore but could not load many in the boat. The Eskimos helped us carry everything up, and three men had to stay on board to load the boat,

---

1. I. *umiaq*: An open skin boat that can hold up to twenty people with their equipment. In Greenland it could be rowed only by women, but in the Canadian Arctic, by contrast, also by men.

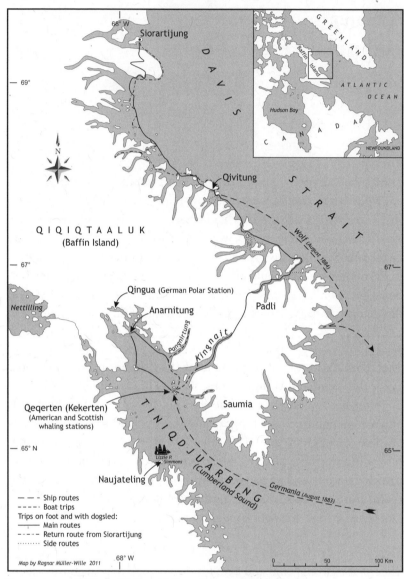

Travel routes of Wilhelm Weike with Franz Boas on Baffin Island, 1883-1884
(Cartography: Ragnar Müller-Wille; Boas 1885a, Plate 1)

while two rowed the boat. It was a little after 4 o'clock when we brought the last boatload ashore, and then I stayed on land. An old Eskimo to whom I'd given a few pipefuls of tobacco on August 29 was so friendly when he spotted me. He came over and shook my hand, and then until 7 o'clock I was a guest in Mist (…)'s house.[2] It is very clean inside; I hadn't expected this.

### Friday, 31 August.

At 5:30 a.m. we were wakened for coffee; when we had finished we brought our bags ashore; these were the last things we had on board. Around 8 o'clock we went back out to the ship for breakfast; afterwards we tidied up in the hold; after the meal we had our first rest. Then, until 4 o'clock we were putting everything in order on deck; then the Captain[3] went ashore with Dr Boas and myself; first I had opened a box on shore to get a compass out of it, then we went along the shore by boat to the tip of the island since Herr Dr B. wanted to make observations there. It was a very arduous trip; then we sat up on a rock, and then later we were in a deep gully. Once we had finished the observations we climbed the mountain and looked for plants.[4] Thus we got back to Mist. Mössd's[5] home at 7 o'clock. Then I made the rounds of the Eskimos with Anton Andresen[6] and visited them in their huts. It looked quite miserable there; we visited one woman who had a one-year-old child.

---

2. Mr. James S. Mutch, in charge of the Scottish whaling station.
3. Mahlstede.
4. During their stay Boas and Weike accumulated a collection of 44 species of flowering and non-flowering plants and 32 species of lichens, which were later identified by Hermann Ambronn (Jena and Leipzig) and Berthold Stein (Breslau) in Germany (see in Neumayer 1890:97-99). H. Ambronn (1856-1927) was a younger brother of Leopold Ambronn, the deputy leader of the German Polar Station in 1882-83, and also Boas' fellow student in Heidelberg in 1877.
5. Mister Mutch, the Scottish whaler.
6. The Swedish seaman on board *Germania*.

# September 1883

*Saturday, 1 September.*

Around 9 a.m. we went ashore; then Dr Boas first photographed *Germania* from the beach, and then took two photos of the station.[7] Then we opened boxes and unpacked things until 11:45, then we set off to make observations. We had to climb over hills; the sun was shining very warmly so that a couple of drops of sweat fell at every step, and then we didn't know at all where we should be going. At 12:20 we came to a spot that was quite suitable.[8] We lingered there until 1:10, then we started back. We got back to the ship at 2:15. Then we had lunch. At 4 o'clock we went back ashore and Dr Boas took more photos. Then we stayed at Mr. Mosch's[9] and I visited Natukali.[10] We got supper on shore and returned aboard around 9.

*Sunday, 2 September.*

Today we marked Sedan Day.[11] We spent the morning on board ship, and at lunch we had fresh roast reindeer.[12] After lunch we were rowed ashore; there we first visited the Eskimos. After an hour Anton Andresen had to go back aboard to fetch the cook.[13] Then I went with C. F. Johannsen[14] to the cemetery, where only men from the whaling ships lie buried. The grave markers are made of a post with a board fixed to it, and carved into it are the man's name and when he died. On the way back we also came across Eskimo graves that lie on the ground and are covered with rocks.

---

7. These photos did not survive.
8. Locations where Franz Boas could make observations to determine time and his position.
9. Mutch's.
10. Nuktukarlin, the first person Wilhelm Weike mentions with his Inuit name.
11. The German day of remembrance for the victory over France at Sedan on September 2, 1870 that was celebrated from 1871 until 1918.
12. Wild reindeer (*Rangifer tarandus groenlandicus*) known as "caribou" in North America, an Algonquian word; the Inuit word is "tuktu."
13. Adolf Lange.
14. Carpenter F. Carl Johansen.

The German Polar Station at Qingua (Kingua) at the north end of Cumberland Sound seen from the west, 1882-83 (Neumayer & Börgen 1886, Vol. 1: XX)

*Monday, 3 September.*

I got up at 5:30 a.m. and worked on board ship until breakfast, after which we went ashore around (…) o'clock and photographed the country from up on a hill; it was soon noon, and then I built a cairn in order to find the location again. Then we looked for more plants; it was already after 12 when we came back aboard. Then we were at work and stayed on the ship for a while and at 2 o'clock went back ashore and took more observations. In the afternoon I had more time and I searched for small insects. While we were up there, a boat arrived from Kingawa[15] that brought a letter[16] for the Captain.[17] In the evening I was busy at the station, after which I was wandering around by the water, until Mister Rosch's[18] eyes[19] invited me into his home. I went in and he said that he

---

15. Qingua, the northern end of Cumberland Sound and the site of the German polar station during the Polar Year, later also called the First International Polar Year, 1882-1883.

16. From Dr Wilhelm Giese, leader of the German polar station.

17. Mahlstede.

18. Mr. John Roach, captain of *Lizzie P. Simmons* out of Montréal (Québec, Canada), married to an Inuit woman, and active as a whaler in Cumberland Sound since 1876.

19. What is meant is a non-vocal communication, since on his arrival Weike could not speak English.

could understand German; I was so happy to find somebody to whom I could talk.

*Tuesday, 4 September.*
I got out of bed at 5:30 and had some coffee. The ship's crew then fetched a boatload of water; in the meantime I was cleaning in the cabin. When they returned I helped to haul the water on board. Then we had breakfast, after which I went ashore with Herr Dr Boas to collect plants, but we did not go very far and came back aboard at 11:30. We stayed aboard until around 3 o'clock and I was supposed to go back with him, but nothing came of this. And then I went with the other boat to fetch more water. We got back around 6, and then we had to unload it, during which time Eskimos came aboard, who were to return to Kingawa; they started back at 7:30.

*Wednesday, 5 September.*
I got up at 5:30 a.m. and went ashore with the boat to get fresh water. We returned around 8 o'clock; the boat in which Herr Dr B. and six Eskimos were to travel to Kingawa was lying alongside the ship. They set off between 8 and 9 o'clock. Once we had unloaded the water from the boat I washed some things and tidied up in the cabin.[20]

*Thursday, 6 September.*
Today I was scouring and scrubbing and washed everything, so that when the party[21] comes aboard we'll be able to leave. At 5 o'clock news arrived that there was a ship[22] in sight; the flag was hoisted. But the ship did not come into the harbour. At 8 o'clock we went ashore again and visited the Eskimos again; at around 9 o'clock we came back aboard.

*Friday, 7 September.*
When I came on deck at 6 o'clock, the ship was off the harbour; it dropped anchor at 7 o'clock. But it was not a steamer.[23] There was a

20. From now until September 10 Wilhelm Weike was alone on board *Germania*, without Franz Boas, and looked after unloading items of equipment and provisions.
21. What is meant here is the personnel of the German polar station.
22. *Catherine*, supply ship of the Crawford Noble whaling company from Dundee, Scotland.
23. *Catherine* was a brig, i.e., a two-masted sailing ship.

strong wind and at 8 o'clock we dropped the second anchor. I would have liked to go ashore, but no boats were launched due to the strong wind and hence I rummaged about on board.

*Saturday. 8 September.*

During the night of 7th to the 8th it snowed; there was ice lying on the deck and again, because of the wind, no boats were launched, and hence this morning I had to polish the kettle and clean the dishes for the party. At 12 noon there was a heavy fall of snow, so that at 2:30 we had to shovel snow off the deck; at 5 we shovelled snow again and around 6 o'clock the chains were still being chiselled out.[24]

*Sunday, 9 September.*

On the night of 8th/9th there was a strong wind; the water on deck had frozen and new ice had formed near the shore. In the afternoon we went ashore and visited the Eskimos; in the meantime visitors from the Scottish brig were on board *Germania*. We came back aboard at 6 o'clock.

*Monday, 10 September.*

At 7 o'clock I had to go on deck to help weigh the anchor and then we worked until breakfast. At 9 o'clock I went ashore to collect plants. There I encountered a wild rabbit[25] and 15 ptarmigan.[26] But I didn't have a gun with me and had to watch them fly away. At 2:30 I came back aboard. The port anchor was completely weighed. Dr Boas came back from Kingawa a little before 7; later the captain from the Scottish brig[27] also came aboard and then we received letters; that was an evening for celebration. I couldn't sleep for excitement.[28]

---

24. Meaning unclear, it probably refers to the anchor chains that were frozen in and had to be freed.

25. Weike used both "rabbit" and "hare", which are different species; this animal was the arctic hare (*Lepus arcticus*), which should be differentiated from the European snow hare (*Lepus timidus*).

26. Rock ptarmigan (*Lagopus lagopus*).

27. Abernathy, captain of the *Catherine*; his Christian name is not known.

28. Mail from Minden that had been sent by the Boas family to Aberdeen to be forwarded.

*Tuesday, 11 September.*

During the night the ice was drifting quite strongly into the harbour, and hence at 1 a.m. the port anchor was dropped again. During the day there was quite a strong wind and dismal weather; we did not leave the ship, but were sorting plants. In the afternoon I did laundry and then wrote letters and did a general clean up. I put on clean underwear and bathed naked.

*Wednesday, 12 September.*

There was a strong north wind so that the ice was constantly driving into the harbour; by evening we were quite beset aft. I could not go ashore today and tonight will be the last one that I'll sleep on board *Germania.*

*Thursday, 13 September.*

When we came on deck in the morning Captain Rosch's ship was in sight.[29] Now we had a lot to do, and we had to move ashore and get our last things ashore as soon as possible, because we were still to receive things from the party [from Kingua Fiord]. The gentlemen[30] were delighted to get aboard a ship again. During the night the ice had moved into the harbour even more and hence it was difficult to get aboard through the ice. Throughout the day there were all kinds of different people in the boat: Americans, then British, and then again Germans; it was great fun. The best time was in the evening; a boat had come ashore from each of the three ships, and we gathered at the American station. There we had a concert in the evening; the carpenter[31] from the Kingua party played a concertina. To it we sang sometimes in German, sometimes in English. It was late when we broke up. We first visited all the *tu(b)iks,*[32] and then I headed for my new sleeping place. I had to lie on the floor in the room; having laid down a mattress and a blanket.

---

29. The American whaler *Lizzie P. Simmons,* owned by the C.A. Williams Company, New London, Connecticut (USA); according to Franz Boas the crew consisted mainly of Americans. Among them were a Jew and a "mulatto" as well as two Germans, Fred Grobschmidt (German-American born in Memel [Klaipėda, Lithuania], emigrated to the U.S.A. in 1869; in 1883-84, first mate on board; also used as surname "Sherman") and Wilhelm Scherden, the second mate.

30. The members of the German polar station.

31. Either Albert Jantzen or Richard Weise.

32. I. *tupiq*: an Inuit caribou-skin tent. This is the first Inuit word that became a regular component of Wilhelm Weike's and Franz Boas' German vocabulary.

*Friday, 14 September.*
I had quite a fine night, sleeping on the smooth floor. I didn't have much sleep; it was 6 o'clock when I got up and had a coffee at the station. Towards noon I went aboard *Germania;* in the afternoon we were still going from shore out to the ship. Finally we raised our flag; we used our boat-hook as a flagstaff.

*Saturday, 15 September.*
We still had a lot to do today, and hence there was still a lot of toing and froing between the ship and shore, for we were still transporting all our things to the American station. Something happened in the evening; we had been ashore and had a case of rum on board, which a gentleman was to take to the ship. Herr Boas wanted to send the case out to the ship by boat, but because the other gentleman did not grab it right, the boat was pushed off and the boat capsized and Dr Boas fell into the water, along with the case of rum, followed by myself. In distress I grabbed the boat with one hand and stayed with the boat. Herr Dr B. swam to the ship; I had to fish the case out and thus I too got aboard. I stayed on board for the night.

*Sunday, 16 September.*
Things began early; in the morning anything went: red wine, champagne, and everything mixed up together. Around 10 *Germania* put to sea; seeing her depart was not so pleasant, since I was losing first the friends I had made on board ship, and then the acquaintances whom I had made on board and on shore. When the *Germania* departed those were almost the last Germans whom we would see; there were just two Germans left on board the American ship.[33] We stayed on board the ship for the afternoon and got pretty drunk again. As the *Germania* was just departing I hoisted our boat's flag three times, and that was it. At Captain Rosch's we got drunk again; when we arrived we got a meal immediately, and so we remained on board until evening; afterwards we went to the station and went to bed early, because next day we planned to be travelling.

---

33. Fred Grobschmidt and Wilhelm Scherden.

Scottish whaling station at Kekerten Harbour, looking north, with (left to right) *Catherine, Germania* and *Lizzie P. Simmons*, September 13-15, 1883; retouching, notes and place names by Franz Boas (Photo: Franz Boas; *American Philosophical Society*)

Kekerten Habour, 101 years later on August 5, 1984 (Photo: Ludger Müller-Wille)

# Boat trips and hikes
# (17 September to 22 October)

*Monday, 17 September.*
Nothing came of our plans to set off, since we had a foul wind and hence we remained at the station. In the morning Dr B. made observations and we got up so early that we could still cook something. I had finished cooking, but we had to eat at Mr. Mosch's and hence our meal was left untouched. In the afternoon we built a cairn up on the hill, and afterwards we filled more shells. There was still a strong wind so that the sand was blowing quite badly; we are happy that we've made such progress. I had not slept particularly well for the last few nights.

*Tuesday, 18 September.*
There was still a very strong wind, so we could still not get away and we had to stick around the station. At noon, at low tide, we went looking for mussels and sea creatures and preserved them in alcohol. Around 4 p.m. we went in our boat[1] to the other side of the harbour, and built another cairn. There we found two seals and two rabbits, but we didn't have a gun.

*Wednesday, 19 September.*
When we woke this morning it was so foggy that we couldn't go travelling, and hence we had to stay here again. Semi[2] came this morning, but he had to leave again. In the morning Herr Dr B. made some more observations and in the afternoon we climbed a hill and built a cairn there. It was just low tide and hence we ran through the east side of the

---

1. *Marie*, the rowing and sailing boat that Boas brought with him from Germany, and had named after his fiancée Marie Krackowizer (1861-1929).
2. Jimmy, as he was called by the American and Scottish whalers, but whose real name was Ssigna (ca. 1848 to 1898). Between September 1883 and May 1884 he was employed by Franz Boas as his Inuit assistant and companion; Weike wrote his name as "Semi", "Simi" or "Singna(r)."

Qeqerten [Kekerten] Archipelago in Cumberland Sound, 1883-1884 (Boas 1885a, Plate 1, Inset IV)

harbour to get there sooner; the water was knee-deep in places. When we came back we went aboard the brig again and drank tea.

*Thursday, 20 September.*
This morning we finally got away somewhat after 7 o'clock. As we set off we had to row across the harbour; once we were out of the Kikatons we set sail; we had Simi and his boat. Ultimately the wind abandoned us and hence we had to row; after two and a half hours of work we finally arrived; we landed and cooked something. After our meal we climbed to the top of the small island and Dr B. measured the height, and then we landed on the other side, and then travelled back to the former location on Kikaschuk[3] Island where we pitched our tent for the night. This consisted of the boat's sail, and then we accommodated ourselves next to each other on the ground, with a rock as a pillow.

*Friday, 21 September.*
Got up at 5:30. Made coffee and then made preparations for pushing on. Around 8 o'clock we travelled on from Kikkertaktusdak[4] to Kinnid Haber[5] where we landed around 12 o'clock. We had a good time since we were able to sail, and had to row only a little. Once the boat was hauled up, we cooked something, and after the meal we set off inland on foot. We first climbed over two hills; between the two there was a large freshwater lake. We walked around it and came to the second hill where we had a wide valley before us. Through it flowed a river with

---

3. Qeqertaping.
4. Qeqertuqdjuaq.
5. Kingnait Harbour, the whalers' anchorage on the north side of Kingnait Fiord.

three waterfalls. We had a fine view from the hill. We climbed down
into the valley and walked on to the waterfalls and then through some
bogs, until we had to start back. On the return trip we crossed a rapid,
where I fell into the water, and hence I had to run on with wet feet and
legs. We then lost our way, and hence we had to go through the water
again, and thus we got back to the harbour around 6:30. Singna[6] had
already pitched a *tupik*, and then we cooked and ate and then we lay
down on the ground and slept.

## Saturday, 22 September.

We got up at 6 o'clock and made a fire with heather[7] and with it brewed
our coffee. Once we were finished we hauled the boat ashore and then
headed inland. We took a bag with something to eat; Singna also went
with us. We again walked up the valley, to follow it further; we could
not climb the hills due to the dense fog. We came to a fourth waterfall
and so we pushed on until noon. Then we had a fine meal: bread-and-
butter with water, and while we were eating, it began to snow. One can't
carry very much; we were quite happy to be hiking like this; we occasionally used our rifle as a walking stick, since one has to take a gun
along. When we had finished our meal, we went hunting but encountered no game. Singnar finally spotted a rabbit on the other side of the
water, and then we went down the hill and through the water. But we
were unable to follow Singnar, it was so steep on the other side, and hence
we had to go back through the water to the side we'd started from. When
we were back over there, I misunderstood Herr Dr and climbed the hill,
where I looked around. There was nobody in sight and hence I went to
the site where we had eaten lunch. When I got there, Herr Dr was lying
asleep; I sat down near him until he woke; Singnar was still missing. We
wanted to head back and so we fired our rifle to give him a signal, but
he did not appear, and hence we started back, leaving his tin can behind.
And we ran through the snow so that he could tell where we had been.
I had found a caribou antler, and we took it with us; I carried the food-

---

6. Ssigna (Jimmy).
7. In the German version this heather was incorrectly called lichen *(Cladonia rangif-
erina)*; William Barr provided the correct identification for arctic heather *(Cassiope
tetragona)* (see also Boas' plant list in Neumayer 1890:98).

bag and Herr Dr carried the antler. We stopped at an open spot and then Singnar suddenly arrived. He had gone back on the other side. And so we proceeded; we still had a good distance to travel to Kinnid Haber, where we arrived around 7 o'clock. Then we cooked a meal; we had shot a bird the day before and we made an excellent soup. It tasted great after our long hike and afterwards we lay down to sleep.

*Sunday, 23 September.*

We got up at 6 a.m. and brewed our coffee, because we wanted to start back. It was high tide at around 9 o'clock and hence we were able to leave; we had to row for a while initially and then we set sail; the wind was light at first but then it became stronger, so that we had to reduce canvas; at the same time there was quite a heavy groundswell, so that the boat was rolling from side to side. Finally it became quite calm again, and therefore we had to row. Around noon we landed to cook something; this did not take long and we were soon finished. After our meal we pushed on; we wanted to spend the night on Kikkatakschuak,[8] but the swell was so high that we could not stay there and hence we had to continue to Kikkerton. There was no wind and therefore we had to row. Hence we were not making much progress, and still had a long pull ahead of us, and therefore kept on into the night. My arms were soon ready to give up and I was delighted when Herr Dr said that we ought to have something to eat. We still had some cold coffee from noon; we shared it and had some bread-and-butter, and then we continued rowing. There was still no trace of any wind, and it was impossible to see if we were on course, and so we continued through the night. The sweat was running from our brows and not a word was exchanged; occasionally one of us would let out a groan, but then a deathly silence descended again. I was sitting forward in the boat, Herr Dr in the middle and Singna at the tiller. Finally a light breeze came up and, at long last, around 11 o'clock we reached Kikkerton harbour. We were quite glad to be there, having first been sweating so much and then frozen to the point that one's teeth were chattering. When we arrived there were natives[9] there, who helped us carry our things up to the house.

---

8. Qeqertuqdjuaq.

9. As an ethnic appellation for the aboriginal population Weike used either "Eskimos", or generally "Eingeborne" [natives] or "Fremde" [foreigners].

*Monday, 24 September.*
It really felt good to sleep on a mattress again. We got up at 6 o'clock and got our things in order again; they really needed it as much as we; at noon we had roast seal, which tasted really good. In the afternoon we were unpacking boxes again.

*Tuesday, 25 September.*
Today we had a lot to do again because the Scottish ship was about to leave and Herr Dr was travelling with her to Warham Island[10] where she was to load more cargo;[11] Herr Dr would then come back from there. Around 3 o'clock we went aboard to escort the ship out; almost all the natives came with us. The ship was towed out of the harbour by the boats; there was little wind, so progress was slow, I had to eat supper on board ship one last time, and came back ashore around 7:30 p.m. Now I was entirely alone at the station, and was master of the house. In the evening I fitted up my bunk.

[The journal continues on September 26 after the letters of August 28 to September 25, 1883].

---

10. Miliqdjuaq. Weike was now alone at the station from September 25 to October 4.
11. Oil from sea mammals (whales, walrus or seals).

# From an alien world–
# Letters from Qeqerten
# (August 28 to September 25)

### On board *Germania*[1]

Arrived here in [Qeqerten] harbour on August 28 [Tuesday]. We dropped anchor at 2.26. Everything looks good here. High hills all around. I've already been working very well with Herr Dr.

On September 2 [Sunday] I visited the English cemetery. The Eskimos bury their dead on the ground and cover them with rocks; one can see the half-rotted corpses lying there or else simply bones.

On September 5 [Wednesday] Herr Dr travelled by boat with Eskimos to Kingawa[2] and I remained on board and did laundry and cleaned things up. Oh, how I would have liked to go with Herr Dr, for I always thought that these are strange people.

On September 6 [Thursday] we had a lot of fun on shore. We were visiting an old Eskimo, Natukali.[3] He is my friend. When I'm on shore I visit him and I loaf. We communicate quite well. I like the little children best. They are quite white, but after a few years they become brown. The old women are as wide as they are tall. They smell quite badly, too – and how!! They are very friendly, one has to give them that. I'm sure you've celebrated Linna's birthday well.[4] Now Herr Dr has come back, so I have to polish his rifle and revolver. On the 8th I had to polish our kettle and shovel snow. Went to bed at 8 o'clock and got up again at 12.

---

1. Wilhelm Weike wrote this letter on September 13 and, on September 16, sent it with *Germania* to Minden via Hamburg. With a view to clarity the editors have divided the unbroken text of the letter into sections (paragraphs) that are organized by date.
2. Kingua (Qingua), the German polar station during the Polar Year 1882/83.
3. See September 1, 1883.
4. Linna: a maid in the Boas household.

9 September [Sunday]. Was on board ship all day.[5] Herr Dr was on shore today and came back around noon. He would have liked to come back aboard earlier, but this did not work out. The beds that we brought with us are a totally useless piece of furniture. We can't use them. We sleep on a mattress and cover ourselves with a woolen blanket. This gives us a good sleep. Linna does not need to worry that we are dying in filth, since there are no women here. I'll handle things just fine just like in Minden believe me. I'm sure, Frau Boas, too, sometimes also thinks: "I wonder what it is like there now." Even if I have to steal the water, I'll get the laundry done. Greetings to Frau Boas. Oh, I hope Frau Boas is not having any unnecessary doubts. I'll look after Herr Dr as only I can. Herr Dr always says: "Wilhelm, your time as a recruit is over; you've now become a sergeant." We're always singing *"Wir treten an die Heimatreise"* to the tune of an Eskimo jig.[6] Frau Boas certainly does not think that we'll get along well together. We'll be struggling bravely and we'll stick together. The greatest thing is when the Eskimos get some tobacco, when it is shared out. Mother gets some, and father, sister and brother get some, since smoking is their favourite pastime. As soon as the children can hold a pipe, they have to smoke too.

Today [September 13] I visited the woman who is making our clothes. They are very skilful; their stitches are as fine as if sewn with a sewing machine, and they tan the leather with their teeth.[7] Now I must close, since we have to leave the ship today and I still have a lot to pack.

---

5. Franz Boas' relatives: M. Boas, kin and first name not known, and Willi Meier, his cousin, mother's brother's son.

6. At the time of the German edition this song was not yet identified. It is a 19th century reservists' song of an unknown author that was sung at discharge; here Weike took the third line from the song's first verse *"Bald scheiden wir aus diesem Kreise / und legen ab den Ehrenrock / Wir treten an die Heimatreise / mit einem Reservistenstock."* [Soon we'll leave this circle / and take off the honoured uniform / We are now homeward bound / with a reservist's stick.] (von Nida 1893). Jig: a folk dance to music played on a concertina or fiddle/violin. The Inuit adopted this dance from the Scottish whalers and nowadays consider it part of their own cultural heritage.

7. It is not "tanning" that is meant here, but rather Inuit women chewed the dry leather with their teeth, so that it was soft and flexible in order to work it and use it. This put a heavy strain on their teeth and resulted in dental problems. Men never took part in this task.

Greetings to Herr and Frau Boas. Fräulein Toni, Fräulein Hedwig, Fräulein Anna, and Herr M. Boas. Herr Meier must be back there again.[8] To Fräulein Lütge and especially to her father.[9]

I had not suspected that our quarters [at the Scottish whaling station] would be so fine; I'll be able to arrange everything so well here. Previously three Scots lived here; two have left and only one [James Mutch] remains; he has lived here for ten years. Again, a thousand greetings to Frau Boas; she ought not to fret too much.

[Tuesday] 18 September 1883.[10] In the hope, that these lines will reach you in good health, as they leave here. We are as healthy as fish in water. But you will have received our letters with *Germania*; those last few days on board the ship were chaotic. I was here one minute and there the next.

I had to vacate the ship on September 13. Herr Dr remained on board. I was brought ashore in the evening to the sound of music, and then we went to the American station, where a concert was being held. It was a very merry occasion. I didn't get to bed until 12. I had to arrange a bed on the floor. But I couldn't sleep.

In the morning [September 14] when I got up, I first went to the station, and then Herr Dr came and took me out to the ship. I ate and drank there and stayed there till evening, then I had to be going again, so I left early. But then there was music again. Later there was a lot of merriment again, and things were topsy-turvy. Then I had to play the triangle again. But I went straight back to the house, as did the others. When they left, the place seemed dead. The men from three ships amount to quite a crowd. I was among Englishmen, Scots, Americans, Italians, and God knows what other nationalities there were here.

In the morning [September 15] Herr Dr fetched me from shore again since we still had some things on board ship; these were

---

8. Franz Boas' relatives: M. Boas, kin and first name not known, and Willi Meier, his cousin, mother's brother's son.
9. Bertha Lütge, the Boas family's seamstress, and her father, Herr Lütge.
10. Wilhelm Weike wrote the two following letters on September 18 and 25 on shore at the Scottish station; he gave them to Franz Boas on September 25, and he sent them via Aberdeen to Minden on board *Catherine* on October 3.

now brought ashore, and so the confusion continued. In the afternoon we practically had a joy ride, and hoisted our boat's flag. Nonetheless, in the evening things would have almost gone wrong for us. I stayed on board for the night and slept on a couple of sea chests. It was a totally wretched night; all preparations were then being made for the ship to depart.[11]

[September 16]. Now we had everyone on board from all the ships and there was some serious drinking. Finally I was invited to join the men belonging to the [Kingua] party.[12] I was treated to slices of corned beef, and to red wine, and we even had two bottles of champagne. At 10 o'clock *Germania* got under way. Our boats towed along astern, and thus we headed outside along with her. When I will return [home], I don't know. I sat in the small boat astern of her and waved the small flag three times,[13] and then we went back again. We had wanted to make a trip that day, but it was now too late, and hence we stayed on board the American ship.[14] There were still two Germans on board,[15] and we were welcomed in very friendly fashion. We ate and drank and we knocked back a couple of bottles of red wine. And so we returned to the house in the evening and went to bed early, because we wanted to start travelling next morning.

We lay down on the floor close to each other but next morning [September 17] the wind was so strong that we could not travel and hence we organized our things somewhat, and in the afternoon we were up on the hill and built a cairn. It was all we could do to keep from being blown away by the wind. But we were sweating as we worked. When we were finished we went back to the house. I'll get along better with Herr Dr than I expected; otherwise our relationship is just as at home. In the evening I went to the Am[erican] station. There was nobody there who could speak a word of German. And yet I communicated well with them. There

---

11. *Germania.*

12. The 11 members of the German polar station.

13. What is meant here (and later) is the flag that Boas' fiancée sewed for him and embroidered with her name, "Marie" (Boas in Müller-Wille 1998:141).

14. *Lizzie P. Simmons.*

15. Fred Grobschmidt and Wilhelm Scherden.

is a blind Eskimo here, who was brought in. He plays the concertina and thus we made music with two instruments. I went back home to the house with Boy.[16] I get along well with him, but he's leaving with the ship.

18 September [Tuesday]. We slept well. In the morning Herr Dr woke me from such a wonderful dream. But the wind was even stronger so that we could not get away, and hence we had to stay at home. Around noon, at low tide we searched for mussels and sea creatures and preserved them; it's quite funny when they are given a *Schnaps*, alcohol, and die in it. In the afternoon the wind dropped, and hence we went across to the other side of the harbour in the small boat and built a cairn; we encountered two wild rabbits there. But we didn't have a gun with us. On our return we hauled our boat ashore, and thereafter I preserved some more creatures, and while so doing I was thinking a lot about Minden. Boy said I should go with him to the other station, but I preferred to do some writing. But then I'll probably want to go to bed, since if it stays like this, we'll be leaving tomorrow. If I don't return before the brig heads homeward, fare well to everyone. We can't determine when we'll be returning. I didn't know that the gentleman had promised to go to Minden.[17] I've only just heard that, otherwise I would also have sent greetings by him. Herr Dr has probably looked after this already. There was somebody else on board the ship who was just like us. I've said goodbye to different people four or five times. Many thousand greetings to Herr and Frau Boas and to the Fräuleins.[18] They shouldn't worry unnecessarily. We are healthy and happy. It's a wonderful thing, just to be patient and to hope for God's help. Now I shall close, since time presses. Just one last assurance that we are healthy and happy. And once we've completed our trip safely, we will make the rounds in Minden. Goodbye to you all, until we've the pleasure of seeing

---

16. Boy, probably the nickname of a young seaman on board the *Catherine*.

17. This refers to Leopold Ambronn (astronomer in Hamburg and Göttingen; 1854-1930), deputy leader of the German polar station (also see note above). At Boas' request he paid a visit to his family in Minden in October 1883 and delivered letters and documents (Franz Boas/Hermann Ambronn, Minden/Heidelberg, 2 May 1883).

18. Franz Boas' three sisters.

each other again. Heat [your house] well, you promised us that, so we can feel it here.

Kikkerton, [Tuesday] 25 September.[19]

Dear Mathilde.

We've returned safely from our little trip. We set off on the morning of [Thursday] the 20th [September]. We had a native[20] with us, as well as his boat, which required two men to row it. Once we had left the Kikkertons we set sail, and we made good progress as far as Kikketaschauk.[21] Off the point the wind died and we had to row; this lasted for two and a half hours. It was not easy. We sat on the rowers' benches, repeatedly glancing over our shoulders, to see whether we were approaching the landing place; and thus we got there at noon. There we brewed some coffee and had something to eat, and then we climbed the hill. Ultimately I had to use my rifle as a walking stick as my legs were giving way. And when we reached the top the sweat was streaming down our faces. Herr Dr had two black streaks, one on each cheek; it really looked great! When we got back to the boat, the wind was foul, in terms of pushing onwards, and hence we had to stay there. We rigged a tent using our sail, and brewed some tea, and then lay down on the ground. We had a woolen blanket in which we rolled ourselves up, and then we went to sleep. At times we were so cold that our teeth were chattering, but we were tired enough to be able to sleep and so we slept until [Friday] the 21st [September].

We were up again at 5:30 in the morning and brewed our coffee and then we pushed on. After we had been rowing for a while we were able to set sail and we continued like that. Our rifles were lying on the bench beside us, and so we fired at seals. But they are very difficult to shoot. They barely stick their heads out of the water, and then dive under again. But we did manage to kill one

---

19. One copy of this letter begins "Dear Mathilde;" there is no addressee in other copies. It appears that Wilhelm Weike sent one copy of the letter to Mathilde Nolting (1858-?), maid in the Boas household and his future wife, and, as with the previous ones, one copy to the domestic staff.

20. Simmi (or Jimy): Jimmy or Ssigna (or Singar).

21. Qeqertuqdjuaq.

bird, and thus we reached Kinneit Haber[22] at noon, and there, for a change, we brewed some coffee. When we are travelling, the story is: "Coffee, for thee I live, for thee I die." Once we'd had our coffee we headed inland. Simmi stayed with the boat, while Herr Dr and I headed off. Once we had climbed over a hill a large fresh-water pond appeared before us, and beyond it a second hill that we also climbed. Then there was a second valley before us, with a river flowing down it, with three waterfalls. We sat down and admired the beautiful scenery. Finally we climbed down the hill and walked to the waterfalls. Then, ultimately, we started back. We crossed the river at a point where there were some large boul-ders. We jumped from one boulder to the next. I fell blithely into the water. Thereafter walking was even less pleasant since every-thing was wet. My fur stockings were slipping from side to side, and then we got lost, and had to get across the water again. Thus we arrived back at 6:30. I first changed into something dry, and then we brewed coffee and we crawled under our blankets.

Next morning [Saturday, 22 September] we got started at 6 o'clock. We hauled the boat ashore and then all three of us started hiking. We took some bread and butter with us in a food-bag that we took turns carrying, for when one is hiking with one's rifle and the shells for it, one already has quite a load. One moment one is on top of a hill, and the next one is in a bog. We reached a fourth waterfall, then hiked on to a meadow, where we stopped and ate our bread and butter and drank a mug of water with it, and it began snowing again. After our meal we tried hunting again, and to do so we separated. I climbed a hill and looked around but there was nobody to be seen, and so I went back down to the meadow where we had left our things. When I got there the Herr Dr was lying sleeping. Only Jimy was missing now. We fired our guns as a signal to him. But he didn't appear. So we went back and ran around in the snow so that he would see where we had been, and then we hiked on until we stopped again and rested. Then he sud-denly appeared and we all pushed on. Back at our campsite we cooked some bird soup.

---

22. Kingnait Harbour.

Next morning [Sunday, September 23] we set off again at 6 o'clock. We had to get back home. At first we had a fair wind, but then it strengthened so that we had to reduce sail, and then it fell calm and we had to row. This continued until noon, when we went ashore to brew some coffee, and then we continued rowing until it was dark—but still no wind. Without landing we ate some bread and drank cold coffee with it that we had kept from lunchtime; this provided a little relief, and then we pushed on. We didn't exchange a word in the boat, and one couldn't see what one's oar was doing. My arms had long since refused to obey, but I didn't want to admit that I was exhausted. Finally a breeze arose and thus we reached the harbour at 11 p.m. We'd been rowing all day on Sunday. In the morning I was singing the beautiful song "Warum denn gerade heute." [Why today, then?][23] But this did not help at all. These will probably be the last lines for now. Many greetings to all, until we happily meet again.

Wilhelm.

I forgot one thing. Yesterday I put on my first Eskimo boots, and hung my others on a hook. A woman helped me with this and then she said "So muh jif ein Kiß."[24] When I didn't want to, she tried to stick me in her hood. Then I tried to get up on a box, when she ran off and jumped onto Bob's[25] back and he had to carry her around.

[The journal continues]

*Wednesday, 26 September.*
It was very windy last night so that initially I could not sleep, and then I overslept somewhat. At noon Singnar and I were to build a cairn, but he was unable to, so I went off on my own, taking my gun with me; this worked out well; since I ran across two ptarmigan. They were my

---

23. This song could not be identified.
24. Here Weike is trying to reproduce the sentence that the Eskimo woman uttered in her pidgin English, as he heard it with his German ear: *"So (now you) must give me a kiss."*
25. Bob, an Inuit man at Qeqerten.

first kill and I was really delighted at this. While I was up on the hill where I planned to build the cairn, I spotted a white patch, resembling snow; I took the telescope that Herr Dr had let me have, and I saw that it was a rabbit. I headed towards it and shot it: so I had a second kill. In the evening I prepared the ptarmigan.

*Thursday, 27 September.*
There was a persistent storm during the night that continued today too. When I got up at 6 o'clock, it was cloudy; once I'd had some coffee I went to find Singnar, to see if he was ready to come up the hill, and thus we set off somewhat after 8 o'clock. The wind was cutting through one's clothes. It was impossible to build a cairn up there, and so I recovered my pick-axe that I had left lying there yesterday, and we went home. The snow was driving so that we could not see, and there was no possibility of shooting any game; one couldn't have seen the target, the snow was driving so thickly in one's eyes. We got back to the house a little after 11 o'clock.

*Friday, 28 September.*
The wind raged all night; in the morning it died away; I prepared my meal and then I went up the hill. I had the pleasure of seeing the dogs storming a *tupik*. The door was not tightly closed and all the dogs that could went inside, until the natives returned and positioned themselves with thick clubs at the entrance, and thrashed one dog after the other until they had all snuck out. I got back from building my cairn at 6 o'clock. On the way back I met another native who had been out hunting, and we returned home together. I was barely back at the house when Singnar arrived and tried to tell me something very vehemently, but I could not tell what he meant. Finally he made me understand that the *cunis*[26] had stolen some butter from us. On seeing that I had understood, he went off quite happily, and hence I prepared my evening meal, which was the leftover from lunchtime. I had now eaten my peas three times, since that is what I had this evening; I couldn't even wait until they were hot.

---

26. "Cooney," the general term used by the English-speaking whalers (Scots or Americans) for Inuit women (Ross 1985; see also Müller-Wille 1994:276).

*Saturday, 29 September.*

During the night it had snowed quite heavily. Once I had had a coffee I went to Singnar's since he was to come with me to help me build cairns. When we were ready to go, it might have been a little after 8 o'clock, and just as I had closed the door, the *cunis* came, wanting to get bread; I sent them away until I came back. Once we had finished the first cairn Singnar said that it was named Wullem.[27] Then we built a second one, after which we went hunting but encountered no game, and hence I got back at 1:30. Then I fed the *cunis*, and then I ate, myself. In the afternoon I stayed indoors.

*Sunday, 30 September.*

This morning after my coffee I had a general shave and bathed thoroughly. Thereafter I climbed the hill and watched out to see whether the boat was coming back yet. While I was up there it began to snow, and I didn't stay any longer; on my way back I saw some natives on the other side of the island. I went over to them; they were collecting heather that they use for bedding and also as fuel. In the afternoon I was at Singnar's; towards evening a boat arrived. Everyone started shouting on spotting the boat. I was in Singnar's *tupik* when the boat came in sight. When Singnar heard the shouting he said it was undoubtedly a boat that was returning from shooting *tuktu*.[28] But then they did not land immediately; they first landed on a small island, and arrived only in the evening. Then everyone who could ran down to where the boat landed. Before you knew it a *tupik* had been erected, and their dwelling was ready.

[On September 29 Franz Boas wrote to his parents and sisters: *Moreover Wilhelm has told Mathilde and Lina*[29] *(to whom you must extend numerous greetings from me too) that he has never been given so much coffee in his life before, as here. We get coffee morning, noon and evening.* He continued: *Although I am delighted to get to know a new part of the Sound,*

---

27. He meant Wilhelm Weike; the Inuit built cairns for driving game or as signposts; they are called *inuksuk* (=like a person). This cairn probably resembled Weike!
28. Caribou (*Rangifer tarandus groenlandicus*).
29. Mathilde Nolting and Lina (last name not known), both of whom were employed in the Boas household.

*I do not enjoy leaving Wilhelm alone for so long at Kikkerton. The American schooner* [Lizzie P. Simmons, *Capt. Roach*] *has left now too, and he is the only white among the Eskimos. He has to distribute their daily rations and look after them in every way. This would not be so bad if he understood English, but as it is I am rather anxious.* Later he noted: *Wilhelm is also reliable.*]

# October 1883

### Monday, 1 October.

Today there was more snow lying and it was still falling when I got up. Given the weather, I wanted to stay indoors, and then Jack's *cuni*[30] came and we did some thorough cleaning, scouring and scrubbing everything; at the same time I was making an excellent bean soup, to which I added barley and lentils; and then I cooked my rabbit. This made an excellent meal. After eating I washed linens and stockings; once I was finished, I couldn't stand to be inside any more and had to go out. Hence it was not long before I had my gun on my shoulder and my cartridge bag strapped on; then I lit my pipe and went off up the hill to go hunting. When I had got up there I spotted a rabbit; I had to climb up another slope to reach where it was sitting, but as I got closer it ran off. I never got close enough to fire, and hence I was chasing around after it until it got dark, and so I had to start for home empty-handed. When I got home and took my stockings in, they were frozen stiff, since it had been freezing during the day. I soon had a fire lit and my excellent bean soup was soon hot, and I also made some tea.

### Tuesday, 2 October.

This morning Captain Rosch's [Roach's] ship weighed anchor, and, with a fair wind, was soon out of the harbour. When I was finished with everything inside, I went up the hill and looked out for the boat, getting back only in the afternoon. Then I made a handle for our axe. By 8 o'clock the windows were already frozen up, and one could see frost-

---

30. Hannibal Jack's wife.

flowers on them. In the evening another three families of natives arrived by boat. They had soon pitched their *tupiks*.

*Wednesday, 3 October.*
At 8 o'clock this morning I set off again to watch out for the boat. At the water's edge I saw an open area with a good growth of grass that I felt I had to visit. Once I was there I didn't want to go back the same way, but rather to climb up by a rock face; initially this went well. But when I was part way up, going any further looked unpromising, and I couldn't go back down either; below me I could hear the surf raging, and turned my gaze upwards, where I could probably find a way up. There was no help for it; I began climbing merrily; the sweat was running off my brow but I persisted, and after I'd been climbing for almost an hour I reached the top after enormous effort and in streams of sweat. It was lucky for me that the moss was frozen fast to the rocks; otherwise I would indubitably have fallen. From the top I looked back down one last time, then I pushed on; I was inexplicably thirsty. I didn't want to eat snow, but I knew the direction in which a pond lay and headed for it, but when I reached it, it was frozen. I dragged a few big stones to it, and smashed the ice, and scooped up the fresh water in my hands. The ice was already a couple of inches thick. Once I had quenched my thirst, I headed onwards and got back home around 2:30. I wanted to take the weight off my feet as soon as possible as they were hurting me so badly.

*Thursday, 4 October.*
Because of the foul weather I stayed at home and worked at things there. It was around noon when Herr Dr Boas walked in the door; I had just swept the house clean again, and was busy filling shells since I wanted to go hunting. I was really happy to see him again; in no time at all I had a meal ready. Once we had eaten we unpacked boxes.

[On his return Franz Boas breathed a sigh of relief: *Wilhelm is in good health; he has erected a cairn and has shot a rabbit and two ptarmigan.*]

*Friday, 5 October.*
This morning things were different from the way they have been up until now; then I had slept until the coffee was ready; but now I had to get up and make it. I got up a little after five; I had to brew coffee for

the Mo-Eskimos[31] and then for us; but I made good progress at this. During the morning we had our hands full, stowing away the things that we had unpacked yesterday. I cooked more for my noon meal. After the meal I had to clean guns until evening, they were in such a foul state. We had got one from Kingawak[32] that had been used by Eskimos.[33] For a year it had been covered by sealskins; it was not much fun trying to get it clean. In the evening I was in difficulties again; I was supposed to prepare dried fish[34] that had been soaking and didn't know how to begin. Mö[35] had shown me a frying pan; I went right to it and fried the fish in some butter, although I was dubious as to how it might turn out. When we had sat down at table, I was waiting every moment for some strong reaction, but it tasted very good.

[Franz Boas remarked: *Arrived here at Kikkerton safely at noon where I found Wilhelm in good health. I am very happy with his performance during this period; he has carried out all his tasks, looked after the Eskimos and the house properly; nor has he been extravagant with the food and has employed them well. -- Mutch wanted to have one of Wilhelm's pipes and to give him a rum for it.*]

## Saturday, 6 October.

This morning I got moving early; I got up at 5:45 and made coffee. After our coffee we got organized for setting off; by 9:30 we were finally ready to leave. There was a fair wind and we could set sail immediately. The boat's[36] crew consisted of five men, Herr Dr, myself and three natives;[37] as we got under way we ran into thick fog so that we could not see very far; towards noon it became somewhat clearer, but we had persistent

---

31. This is what Weike called the Inuit who worked for James Mutch at the station or as whalers.

32. What is meant is the German station at Kingua.

33. Oqaitung (whom Weike usually called Ocheito) and his family who in 1882-83 were employed by the German station as a "local work-force" for hunting and fishing, and who lived near the station; the Germans referred to him as "our home-Eskimo" (Ambronn 1883:352).

34. Stockfish: fish, usually cod (*Gadus morhua*) that is salted then dried.

35. Mutch.

36. One of the whaleboats belonging to James Mutch.

37. Ssigna, Yankee, and Nachojaschi.

snow. At noon we landed on a small island[38] to brew some coffee, but we did not have fresh water and had to melt ice to be able to make coffee. At noon the temperature was 1°. Once we'd had our coffee we pushed on, but there was no wind and we had to row. We were hunting seals as we went along, but due to the waves we were experiencing, we had little success at shooting. One of the natives[39] shot one. We were really happy at getting it aboard! With only a few backstrokes the boat was making a terrible speed. Once the seal was lying in the boat, we pushed merrily on; we stopped at another island and got some fresh water, since the natives said that where we planned to spend the night there was none. We arrived there in the twilight; but were able to find only a poor site for our night's camp. We soon had a fire going, using partially seal blubber for fuel. All five of us slept in one *tupik* that was pitched on gravel and ice. When we were finally in our sleeping bags it was a pleasure, we soon fell asleep.

*Sunday, 7 October.*
I had a really good sleep, but by around 10 o'clock it was already damp under me, but the water did not come through my sleeping bag. We got up at 5:45 and made coffee. Then we made the pleasant discovery that the meat we wanted to eat with our bread was frozen solid, so that one couldn't get one's teeth into it. It was good for our teeth, first ice and then hot coffee! But we managed to finish it and set off at 7:30. There was no wind and we had to row; for a while we had gusts, and hence we stuck closer to the coastline, until we got into the fiord.[40] Sinar[41] shot another seal; at 11:45 we landed at a site where we wanted to eat lunch, but there was no fresh water there, and hence we had to row on. Around 1 o'clock we got to where there was fresh water; we'd soon drunk our coffee and then we pushed off again. Towards evening we were rowing through new ice, that was already a few centimetres thick. Around 6 o'clock we reached our night's campsite on a small meadow. Here we

---

38. Tuapain.
39. Nachojaschi.
40. Pangnirtung.
41. Singna (Jimmy).

found old Eskimo huts,[42] such as they built in olden times, but no longer do. This evening we pitched two *tupiks*, because we were too crowded in one. For supper we had seal meat and tea, which tasted good.

## Monday, 8 October.

I got up at 6 o'clock. The natives were already out and about; we lit a fire and made coffee and then we started rowing again. At first the weather was fine, but we soon ran into fog. We were also hunting seals occasionally. In the morning we put ashore and got some fresh water, and then we pushed on; we encountered ice again occasionally; once we'd got some fresh water, we rowed on again. We could see ice along the opposite shore where there were seals hauled-out; the young ice was already sufficiently strong. But we couldn't push through it with the boat, and hence we stopped at the edge of the ice, and then we pounded on it until it all broke up. Absorbed in our seal hunting, we'd quite forgotten that it was already noon, and when we went ashore to make lunch it was already 2:30. We made pea soup with seal meat; this tasted really good after our long row. Once we'd finished our meal it was already getting dark; we could do nothing more, but unload the boat, pitch our *tupik* and make tea.

How beautiful it looks: such a narrow inlet with high mountains on either side, that look more like old castles than mountains. We had pitched our camp under just such a mountain, that one felt quite fearful and anxious.

## Tuesday, 9 October.

Got up at 6 o'clock this morning and packed up our things, because we wanted to start back. But we couldn't get away immediately because it was low tide, and hence we walked further up the valley. It was a little after 8 o'clock when we set off; we thought it wouldn't be very far, and ran until we were quite out of breath. We finally came back down off the slope, because it was now dry where there had been water

---

42. I. *qarmaq*: houses built of turf, rocks and whalebones, located on the Pangnirtung peninsula, where a modern settlement with the same name is located today. These huts date from the Thule period, about 300 to 1000 years BP.

previously.[43] We finally reached the first glacier, that was as wide as the Weser at Minden, and then we reached several glaciers with big ridges of ice and earth. We climbed up a mountain and thought we were on solid ground; but when we investigated it was ice with large rocks on it. In this so-called ice-landscape there were large caves from which water was flowing. I've been in several places in this country, but I've never seen it so rough and ancient. There is permanent snow up in the gullies. We'd probably been running for two hours, but there was still no end in sight. We watched a small avalanche fall onto one of the glaciers. It sounded like loud thunder; a cloud of snow-dust billowed up—quite terrifying. We stopped for a while and then we started back. Now we had to check the time, to determine how far we had gone. We had been running like crazy on the way out, and it was just the same on the return trip. We saw another fox; I tried chasing it, but it was smarter than I. As we got closer we saw that the boat was out seal hunting; we shouted and they came back to the old campsite.[44] It was already after 12; they came ashore and we brewed coffee; this was really refreshing after our long run. After the meal we got into the boat and started back; we had a good wind and were able to sail, and during the afternoon travelled as far as during the entire previous day, i.e., back to the old campsite where the old huts were located. We pitched our *tupik* on the same spot again, but in unloading the boat we had to carry our things a long way, since it was low tide.

### Wednesday, 10 October.

We got moving again at 6 o'clock this morning; we brewed coffee and ate frozen meat with it. After this breakfast we launched the boat; we were able to sail for some time. The wind was initially strong, but it steadily weakened; but we'd covered a fair distance outside the fiord before we had to start rowing. We rowed out around the left-hand cape[45] and looked for a spot where we could go ashore[46] to cook a meal. We again cooked pea soup with seal meat; this is a gourmet meal here.

---

43. Across mudflats at low tide; the tidal range at Pangnirtung is more than seven meters.
44. The three Inuit companions.
45. Alikun.
46. Augpalugtung.

I always looked forward to it; I was busy writing when Herr Dr told me that the soup was ready; I really did justice to it. After our meal we continued rowing—into the wind, moreover, and we got a trifle warm. We stopped at a spot to get fresh water, and then we rowed quickly on again. I was constantly looking for a good spot where we could camp for the night. We finally reached a suitable spot where we could land; it was around 6 o'clock. I was really happy to carry everything ashore. We were busy unloading the boat when Singnar shouted: "Silo, Silo!" [47]—a boat. We all looked in that direction and saw that the boat was under full sail and was heading for the harbour where we had landed. This boat had still not reached land, when a second one appeared. There was much running around. The brother and sister of one of the natives in our boat were in the second approaching boat. I walked over to the spot where the boats landed. When Inki [48] met his brother, he gave him his pipe to smoke; that was their whole greeting. Their arrival was a happy occasion for them as for us too, since they were the first people we had met on our trip. In the meantime our coffee had finished brewing; we drank it, then went visiting. I went from one *tupik* to the next; there was a girl playing a concertina in one of them. All of a sudden a small village of six *tupiks* had sprung up. It boasted music and everything. I smoked a pipe of friendship with one of them. But finally I had to leave. Herr Dr wanted to make observations and I had to help him. It wasn't long before we received visitors around us, examining the instruments. When we were finished they followed us into our *tupik*, and it was soon full. I undressed and crawled into my sleeping bag, and gazed out quite contentedly. But they stayed with us for quite a long time to see what we might offer; they received schnapps and tobacco from us; they were really gasping for a drink. But they hung around for quite a long time; we were not accustomed to staying up so late when we were travelling. Around 9:30 they finally departed, and hence we were able to go to sleep.

*Thursday, 11 October.*
This morning the temperature was -8°. We got up at 6 o'clock; the natives were already on the move. As we were drinking coffee one of the boats

47. I. *sili* (exclamation): "Aha! There's something over there!"
48. Yankee.

departed, soon followed by the second one; our boat was the last of our
naval fleet or hunting boats—call it what you like. It wasn't long before
we overtook them, and stopped rowing and set sail; we had a fair wind
and were making good progress. Suddenly Inki began looking for his
powder bag, but it was missing. We shouted to the other boat, to ask if
they could spare a *kayak*;[49] then Inki went back to fetch his powder bag.
We travelled in company with the other two boats for a while, but then
we had to drop behind to wait for Inki. We had quite a strong wind and
hence we had to tack. This was no fun on a cold night. Eight degrees
below zero is a bit too much, especially in a canvas *tupik*. It was quite
some time before Inki came back; we had totally lost sight of the other
boats. We finally saw him coming; now we had the *kayak* too; this meant
we were always stopping. The sun was shining warmly but when a wave
broke into the boat, the water froze immediately; moreover there was
quite a sea running, so that one was afraid that we were all going to be
overwhelmed by a wave. My feet were so cold that I soon couldn't feel
them. We had reached the spot where we had camped the first night,
but due to the surf we could not go ashore to pick up Inki's seal. Soon
we were in the lee of a small island; we reefed the sail and pushed on
again. We ate some bread and had a drink of schnapps; this was lunch.
I was really happy when the Kikertons came into sight. We soon got
out of the rough seas and into the lee. Now we had problems with our
*kayak*; the plan was to tie it differently to the boat but Nakojaakgasi[50]
let go too early; it dropped astern and filled with water. Now we had
quite a job pulling it to reach the boat, but then it was secured and baled
out. Thus we had a real problem with our *kayak*; our arrival with it was
quite unfortunate and we continued to be unlucky with it. But then we
got safely back to our harbour. When we got ashore there were lots of
natives there. It was a little after 5 o'clock; I had been in the boat for a
good 10 hours and my feet were so cold that I couldn't even stand. The
natives were quite prepared to help and carried our things to the house,

49. I. *qajaq*: usually a one-man boat with a wooden frame covered with bearded sealskin. *Kajak* and *Iglu* (I. *illu*: house) have been permanent components of the German
vocabulary at least since the early nineteenth century. In English, *igloo* appeared in
writings in 1854 and *kayak* in 1757 (Oxford English Dictionary).
50. Nachojaschi.

and we were delighted to be back in a heated room. It wasn't long before supper was ready; Mis=Mo[51] had prepared it. It tasted quite superb tonight.

## Friday, 12 October.

It was a real pleasure to be back in a warm room again and to sleep in a bed. I got up at 6:30; one of the natives had already lit a fire. Once I had gotten organized I fried some seal meat for breakfast, for when one gets back from a trip, one is really hungry, and one eats twice as much as usual. Today there was quite a lot to be done here: packing things on the one hand, while Herr Dr unpacked more boxes. For lunch I cooked Brussels sprouts and fried some caribou meat; this was a real gourmet meal. This afternoon we received some caribou skins, which gave us a lot of work; Captain Rosch was here too. For supper I wanted to make pancakes, but they stayed so long that I didn't get to it and instead I cut up a smoked sausage; when we are at home we live splendidly and very happily. This evening Mi-Mo[52] had a lot of visitors; he gave the Eskimos who had arrived in the boats coffee. The house was so full that one could not turn around. There was a woman there who had a child in her *kolitan*[53] who was quite naked; they are accustomed to the cold from an early age, and they are not so bundled up as in Germany.

## Saturday, 13 October.

It was very cold this morning when I went outside; ice had already formed on the harbour, but it was driven away by the wind again. Ito[54] had again lit the fire and was cooking rye porridge. When it was ready I brewed our coffee, and at the same time I got some soap in preparation for laundry. When I'd had my coffee I opened a can of dried apples; I wanted to make apple dumplings; I had a lot to do and so I went at it in good time. I roasted half a leg of caribou. It was probably about eight

---

51. Mister Mutch.
52. Mister Mutch.
53. I. *qullitaq*: outer fur coat for women with a pocket at the back with a hood, provided with a widening on each side for the legs of the babies and infants that are carried there (I. *amaut*, also *amauti*).
54. Itu.

pounds;[55] it was a good chunk of meat for three men.[56] But I misjudged the oven, it did not roast as well as I thought; the result was a sort of roast beef.[57] But we really enjoyed it. Once I'd washed the dishes I returned to my laundry; I'd finished it by around 3:30 and hung it outside; as I was bringing out the lasts items, the first items were already frozen stiff. Then I had to think about myself, since I had not bathed thoroughly since we had returned, and Herr Dr wanted to set off again tomorrow, and I don't want to go off again like this. We still had a lot to do. Herr Dr was pouring bullets. Once I had bathed I got hold of the guns, since they had not been cleaned either, although they looked quite clean! They had been in a lot of meltwater and salt water and even though they are reamed out with the ramrod when we are out in the field, that's not good for them either. I roasted my caribou leg some more; it was excellent for supper. Once I had washed up I packed away the dry laundry, then packed our travelling bag; it was after nine before I was finished, and then I still had many things to do. When we come back from a trip we are really happy to come into a warm room; but once we've been back for a day, it's the same old story again: if only we could be on our way again! We were to have left today, but the boat was damaged, and hence we had to stay here longer.

*Sunday, 14 October.*
Today we had a Sunday lie-in; it was 7 o'clock when we got up. Ito already had a fine fire going again, so I could make coffee right away. The coffee was already brewed and we were about to drink it when I saw a boat in the water that looked very familiar; it was not long before Singnar arrived to say that he was ready. But Herr Dr said that we didn't want to leave today. This was all right with Singnar; he went s[eal hunt-ing]. It was certainly a pleasant Sunday. For lunch I cooked young peas and roasted a rabbit. This did not involve much work, so I had plenty

---

55. Here Weike used the then usual symbol for "pound;" this appears only six times in his journal; it is replaced by the word written in full.
56. James Mutch, Franz Boas and Wilhelm Weike, who lived together at the station.
57. Weike used the English term here, probably implying, ironically, that the meat was not cooked through, and was still "rare."

of time to put everything in order. But the time began to drag for me in the house; I was delighted when it was noon so that we could eat; I soon finished washing up too, and then I got my kommings[58] out. When Herr Dr saw this he said: "Are you ready?" "Yes!" And then he packed up two instruments and I got my gun. Shells in my pocket, and we were off up the hill. When we got up there, Herr Dr made a couple of observations, but then the sun left us and we had to discontinue. Herr Dr went back to the house, and I went off to do some more hunting. I ran from one hill to the next but couldn't spot any game and finally headed back to the house. I arrived after 5 p.m.; then I had to think about supper again since 6 o'clock was mealtime. I had everything ready and then we were able to eat right on time. Once I had washed up I went outside; I was heading for the *tupiks,* but then I heard the natives shouting over at the American station. I went over there; when I got within sight, I saw that they had hung a bear skin on a frame, with ropes attached to it and were playing at manning a ship. They had a captain and a mate, and all the other shipboard positions. I became the cooper.[59] These were not children playing this game, but there were some among them who were already in their twenties. Thereafter they mounted a "whale hunt." Two men, one large and one small, represented the whale; others grabbed their *qullitaqs* and represented the boats. They split themselves into three groups and headed after the whale; then they pretended to harpoon it; once it was dead, it was brought to the ship, but this was quite a struggle. The whale was still alive and thrashing so much that they let go of their *qullitaqs.* But then there was a lot of shouting and then the fish [whale] had to be attached behind the last "boat" and then, with much shouting, they got under way again. When they reached the spot that represented the "ship" they got a schnapps. The "captain" used a large stone as a bottle, and a small one as a glass, and started pouring; they got small stones to represent tobacco. Once this was completed, they mounted a "bear hunt;" the smaller men became dogs and two

---

58. I. *kamik:* high waterproof boots made from the skin of the ringed seal (upper) and bearded seal (sole).

59. *Kuper* (English *cooper*) was both the nickname and the profession of the Dane, Rasmussen, at the American station; he produced and maintained the wooden barrels for the whale oil.

large men bears and the rest were hunters; and then they ran and raced until they had the bears. Finally they began "ankuting"[60] in the *tupiks*; and then they finished. Such are the pleasures in which the young people indulge, here in this country.

## Monday, 15 October.

Got up at 5:30 this morning and got ready to set off, but there was such a strong wind that we could not leave; the waves were so strong that we couldn't launch a boat; we had to stay in the house. We had enough to do here; there was plenty of work. I cooked the rest of our caribou leg for lunch. Herr Dr unpacked boxes; we had found a can that had a hole in it. It was kale; I cooked it to go with the meat; it wasn't quite first class but we didn't let that stop us and we ate it heartily. We had plenty to do in the afternoon too. At one point I was able to leave; I joined a native in his *tupik*; he was to cut my hair, since it had not been cut since I left home. He got ready carefully; combed out my hair then began cutting, giving me a bowl-cut, as we used to say at home. He cut it Eskimo-style; if only my face were brown, I'd be a real Eskimo. He had scarcely finished when Herr Dr called me again. I was already missed there again. For supper I made hot chocolate; this was a great holiday meal; I made a lot of it, and not too fat. We're living like princes, even if not quite so richly.

## Tuesday, 16 October.

Last night I was frozen to the bone in bed, and just as I was getting warm I had to get up. There was a fair wind and we could depart. Making coffee went smoothly; we'd barely drunk it when Singnar came to tell us the boat was in the water. Now we rushed like madmen to get away; we had to row out from the Kikkertons, and then we continued under sail; at 9 o'clock the temperature was still -4°, but we felt warm. From Kikkerton we headed obliquely over into a fiord.[61] We were able to sail into the start of the fiord, and then we had to row. Taking advantage of an opportunity Herr Dr shot a fox from the boat. At 12 o'clock

---

60. I. *angakkuq*: Inuit shaman. Wilhelm Weike and Franz Boas germanised this word into "*ankuten*" -- to conjure or act as an *angakkuq*.
61. Weike had written *Yorst*, but the copier had corrected it.

Break at Ujarasugdjuling in Kangertloaping Bay with Wilhelm Weike (left) and Inuit companions Nachojaschi, Singnar and Utütiak (order not identified), October 16, 1883 (Photo: Franz Boas; *American Philosophical Society*)

we landed and brewed coffee. Herr Dr first made observations then photographed the head of the fiord, and then us at our noon break.[62] There was too much new ice at the head of the fiord, and we could not reach it. Then we headed south; we started off again at 1:45; the temperature was -3°. Our next goal was Saml Fjord.[63] It was calm at first then there came gusts of wind, which are not uncommon in this area. And at the same time there was a fearsome sea running. At first, while we were in the mouth of the fiord, we were quite sheltered; but with the wind we made good progress up the fiord. When we reached a spot where we could haul the boat up,[64] we made a stop; we unloaded, hauled the boat ashore and then started cooking. The temperature was -8°. Once we'd consumed our evening meal we crawled into our sleeping bags.

*Wednesday, 17 October.*
When I got up this morning our *tupik* was covered with hoar frost; as I stuck my head out of my sleeping-bag I got a face-full of ice. The temperature was -7°, and when I tried to light my pipe, the stem had frozen up; I first had to thaw it out. We pushed on at 7:30. There was thick fog with snow; we couldn't see the sun. Shortly before noon we ran through a tide-

---

62. Ujarasugdjuling.
63. Salmon (I. *iqaluk*). Salmon Fiord/Eqaluaqdjuin.
64. Supivisortung.

race, where we had to row hard to get through. We stopped at 12 o'clock and made Carne pura soup.[65] Our Eskimos looked after the fire and in the meantime I looked for rocks. Once we had finished our soup we headed further up the fiord. We did a bit of seal hunting, but the wind was too strong and we got nothing. Around 4 o'clock we reached the head of the fiord. The boat was left in the water and everyone went ashore to look for fresh water and a campsite. We chopped through the ice at one location, but there was no water below it. We finally found a very small amount of water that we had to scoop up with a mug. Once we had got everything organized, we pitched camp and picked berries, that were as big as blue berries [*Bickbeeren*];[66] they were only just frozen, and one had first to thaw them in one's mouth, but we didn't mind this; we searched for them for as long as we could still see. After supper Herr Dr took some more observations, while I had to record them; we got cold fingers at this, since it was -11°. A day of remembrance.[67]

[On October 16 Franz Boas described this idyll of camp life as follows: *I am sitting in my tent; next to me Ssigna has just crawled into his sleeping bag and Wilhelm is almost snoring already behind us in the corner. In the next tent I can hear Nachojaschi and Utütiak* [Yankee], *my two other Eskimos, chatting, while the sea roars below.*]

*Thursday, 18 October.*
Last night the wind was blowing quite strongly; nevertheless it was not so cold. Once we'd had our coffee, we started back. Due to the strong wind we had to put ashore, and we rigged the sail. But it was not long before we had to reduce sail, since the wind had started to blow so strongly; things continued quite well like this for a while, until we had to furl the sail completely and had to start rowing. But we were not making much progress; we were pulling as strongly as the oars would

---

65. Meat broth cubes.
66. In the German edition incorrectly identified as *Vaccinium myrtillus*. William Barr raised the issue of identification; it was confirmed to be *Vaccinium uligonosum* by William A. Weber in 2009 (also see Boas' plant list in Neumayer 1890:98).
67. It was not possible to determine which kind of remembrance day, most likely private, this was.

stand, but we were barely able to move them. When we thought an oar was in the water, we'd find that it was up in the air; the wind was stronger than we were. To cap it all, a wave came right over us and I was soaked from head to toe; the water immediately froze so that I had icicles hanging from my fur clothing. We were forced to go ashore, but this was no easy task; we tried to get ashore at three locations but were always thrown back by the wind, until we managed to get in the lee of a small headland. But this was not a spot where we could stay; we were looking for a place where we could pitch our *tupik,* so that I could change into dry underwear. This was my morning bath! When we finally got ashore, we had forgotten everything. While I changed, Nakojaschi went looking for another spot for us. But there was none to be found; we all started eating seaweed[68] on shore, like the Eskimos. Since there was no suitable campsite we had to get back in the boat. Initially the wind seemed to have dropped; but we were scarcely properly out on the water when the wind rose again, but now even worse than it had been; we had our work cut out to hang on to our oars. We had reached the other side of the fiord and had to get round a headland, when we were hit by a snow squall that made us think our end had come. We were assailed by a mixture of water and snow so that we could barely open our eyes; my oar flew out of my hand; it flew ahead of the boat, but somebody grabbed it again as it drifted past the stern. We now strained like mad, to get back ashore again. We found an absolutely dreadful place for the boat, as well as for our *tupik.* We had to pitch the *tupik* on a slope, and so that it was not blown down, we first piled heavy rocks inside it, and then some more outside. We lit a fire to cook by, but this was a bad scene; for just as we thought we'd got it burning a snow flurry would come blasting in, and we'd really have to start blowing to get it going again, and while soup was cooking in the pot, there would be ice freezing on the lid. Once it was ready we carried the soup into the *tupik* and ate it there. We didn't leave the *tupik* again, but the Eskimos went off to check on the boat and didn't come back until 10 o'clock. It was "quite a day" as they say; we didn't enjoy it at all!

68. Edible seaweed (*Fucus vesiculosus*).

*Friday, 19 October.*

It had snowed so heavily during the night that we were knee-deep in snow. The Eskimos had had to go out earlier again, to secure the boat, since it would soon be high tide again. I got up at 5:30; they already had water boiling for coffee; then we had our coffee and packed up our things again. But in the deep snow things went very slowly until we'd loaded everything on board; otherwise in the meantime we could have rowed a fair distance. At first we were heading into the wind and at first we were freezing; but as we rowed we started sweating. Herr Dr had the helm while Singnar and I rowed; we were glad when we reached a point where we had the wind on the beam; we did not go very far; we camped at Schubiwisuk,[69] where we had camped the first night. The tide was dropping and hence we were able to throw all our things above high-water mark, and then the boat was hauled ashore at another location. Once we had finished this, we went and shovelled away the snow at a spot where our *tupik* was to be pitched, and then the sun broke through. Then we dried our things. But our joy was short-lived, since it started snowing again and we had to bundle things into the *tupik*. In the evening we had coffee in the *tupik*. As the pot came inside, the fog was so thick that we could not recognize each other. The wind began blowing strongly again.

*Saturday, 20 October.*

Last night was a lot of fun! The wind all but blew us and our *tupik* away! It came close! The wind kept rolling me [against] Singnar, and he would keep pushing me back; we kept this up all night, and got very little sleep. We brought our bread inside the tent and ate it in our sleeping bags. We couldn't brew any more coffee since our firewood was all exhausted. We didn't leave our sleeping bags all morning. At noon we were able to brew coffee since Singnar had gone looking for firewood. Herr Dr was constantly checking the barometer to see if it had risen; but it had risen very little; there was no change in the weather. In the afternoon I went for a short walk. I went up a hill, but I could go no further upright; I then crawled up on hands and knees, until I ended up in knee-deep snow. Singnar and Nakojaschi were out gathering wood; I joined them and then we went back together; I crawled back into my sleeping bag,

69. Supivisortung.

Tent camp near Supivisortung, Eqaluaqdjuin Fiord, with Wilhelm Weike (at tent), Nachojaschi, Singnar, and Utütiak (order not identified), October 20-22, 1883 (Photo: Franz Boas; *American Philosophical Society*)

since that was the best place to be. Singnar also came into the tent and then we had a great concert. Herr Dr started off by singing, then I joined in and then Singnar sang Eskimo songs for us. We took the opportunity to pass a pleasant afternoon. In the evening we were able to brew coffee again as they had gathered enough wood.

*Sunday, 21 October.*
Last night there was again a strong wind, so that this morning there was such a heavy sea running that we could not depart. For breakfast we had nothing hot. After eating, we got up and all went out to look for wood that had to be scrabbled out from under the snow. We found so much that for lunch we were able to make pea soup, which was really beneficial. After this meal we went out. Singar and Nakojaschi went off to look for wood. Janki[70] went hunting. Herr Dr and I first walked along the tidemark; it was exactly low tide, so that one could walk a good distance from our *tupik* to the water, across a surface that was snow-free. But later we headed inland again in the direction in which Singnar had gone; as we got higher up we could see them heading back with their wood; we followed them back. When we got closer, so that they could hear us talking, they looked to see where we were, and looked around

---

70. Yankee.

in amazement when they realized that we were behind them. For when we started out we had taken exactly the opposite direction from theirs. On the way back we found a couple more old Eskimo houses. Once we were back in our *tupik*, I unloaded my rocks that I had collected.

*Monday, 22 October.*
We got up at 6 o'clock this morning. The weather was quite fair, so that we were able to start back since things would soon be looking bad for us: our provisions were nearly exhausted; we were already unable to get our full ration. We packed up our things and then we headed down to launch the boat. It was a real delight to have the boat in the water again. From the point where the boat lay to our things there was a layer of slush; we had to haul the boat through it. Once we'd loaded our things we again set off, to get out of the slush. It wasn't long before we were sweating. There was little wind so that we had to row almost the entire distance out of the fiord. There was snow falling persistently; once we had set the sail, the wind steadily strengthened. I thought it was going to start blowing too strongly; we had already taken a reef in the sail. Singar, moreover, was not confident about putting out to sea; we therefore put ashore again, since the water was starting to smoke. It was 11 o'clock; we peered out as far as we could see to check how things looked outside. But there was no alternative; we wanted to get home and got back into the boat. But it was snowing so thickly that we could not see far; if it hadn't become clearer we would have sailed north past the Kikkertons; we didn't know where we were until it became somewhat clearer. In the morning we had been sailing with the wind, but now it was abeam, this is how much we'd been blown around. We ate lunch in the boat; it consisted of bread and schnapps. As we approached the Kikkertons we had to row and, what's more, into the wind. Herr Dr rowed along with us, as well as Singar; thus we arrived home safely in the afternoon. The Eskimos all came running and carried our things up to the house. We were really glad to be in a warm room again. Mi Mö had prepared supper, and we did very well, for when one comes back there is always a major feed. Once we'd finished supper I had to go over to the American station to see the cooper and to invite him to our place. Then we again had a great concert with the concertina; we always have a merry time of it here!

# Life and death at Qeqerten
# (October 23 to December 10)

*Tuesday, 23 October.*

This morning I was really happy to be in a warm living room. Ito had lit the stove early; I brewed the coffee and we had boiled herring with it. As one looked around, all one could see was wet clothing that we had brought back from our trip. For lunch we cooked rabbit soup and young peas and carrots. Ah, this was the soft life again! Wine on the table and stewed fruit; everything one's heart could desire. Outside there were snow flurries, so that one could not even open one's eyes; as far as possible I stayed indoors; I had quite enough to do there to put things in order again. Even my gun was so bad one would have thought it couldn't reasonably be put to rights again. For supper I had to make pancakes. Herr Dr had wanted to have some earlier, before our trip, but it didn't happen. Even though the pancakes were made from just flour and water, they still tasted good. I made four of them; there was only one small piece left over. Today, too, we got our new sealskin *Colitans* and new caribou-skin leggings,[1] so that we were soon equipped like an Eskimo. At 11 o'clock I headed for bed; it was high time for my eyes were falling shut.

*Wednesday, 24 October.*

This morning I had quite a fright when I looked out from my bunk and saw that it was 7 o'clock. We had gone to bed late and I had had a good nightcap. Ito had already made his coffee, and the water for mine was boiling again. In no time I had the coffee ready and had swept out the room. At 8 o'clock we had had a good drink; there was roast ham, cheese and sausage on the table; I hadn't lived like this in Minden, but this applied only to the situation indoors, since outside it is (…). For lunch I made rice soup with cabbage and mutton. But it was frozen so hard that I could barely get it out of the can. Jönki[2] was here to bake bread

---

1. Weike and Boas later ordered fur pants from the Inuit women of Qeqerten.
2. Yankee.

today. Mi Mo thought I couldn't handle it, since I hadn't seen it done before. In the afternoon I made a housing for our thermometer, although I didn't finish it; I still had to solder the roof and make a door for it. This evening I received new fur pants. When I had to adjust them, Mi Mo said I'd developed a paunch. I had tea on the table on the dot of 6 o'clock, and I soon set about washing up since when there are Eskimos here one of them will always try to do more than the other; beforehand I let them pick at the bones that came from the table; they lick the plates clean, worse than cats.

*Thursday, 25 October.*
This morning I was really lazy; it was 8 o'clock before I crawled out of my bunk; my water was already boiling; Ito had taken care of it; and in no time at all we were drinking our coffee. Now I had to think about lunch; I had to make soup with peas and barley and two ptarmigan. This resulted in a great soup; in the meantime I finished my thermometer housing. The weather was still the same, with a strong wind; we could be glad that we had come back on the day we did; otherwise we would have suffered serious hunger; as we are here now, we are living so much better. For lunch I heated up another can of meat, but because it was so cold I took it out of the can and emptied it into a pot; after it had been cooking for a good fifteen minutes I put it on a dish, but when Mi Mo cut into it, it was still frozen in the middle; it hadn't been on the table for even ten minutes, but it was ice-cold. In the afternoon I was packing things for our next trip; we were now properly warmed-up again; as soon as we have better weather again, we'll be setting off. We received a barrel with 200 pounds of blubber from the American station.[3]

Around 4 o'clock we already had to light a lamp; when I was finished washing up this evening I went to visit Singnar, and thus saw how the Eskimos play cards. He was playing with his wife; it was exactly like the Black Peter that we play at home.[4] The cards they had could barely be identified any more, they were so dirty; I watched for quite a while; he was shouting quite a lot in the process. When I got home I still had to write [my journal]. I had just begun when a native arrived quite out of breath, bringing the news that the sick woman had died. He ran out of

3. Seal oil or fat for food, dog-food or fuel for cooking and heating in tents and *iglus*.
4. Most likely the card game called Old Maid.

the house again; then a second man came, followed by a third, and then two women arrived; that made five people who arrived with an announcement within the space of ten minutes. This afternoon I had brought Herr Dr some more [medication], but the people do not do as he says.

[Franz Boas visited and treated the sick woman on October 23, 1883: *In the afternoon they asked me to go and see a sick woman. She had pneumonia and was very sick, with a high fever. I wanted to put warm, wet poultices on her chest, but realized that it was impossible, because she was continually sitting with her chest and abdomen bare, catching the full draught from the door. So I could do nothing but give her some opium for her cough and quinine for her fever.*]

*Friday, 26 October.*
It is becoming quite winter-like here already; a quarter of the harbour has already frozen. At 7 this morning it was just -11°. This morning Mi Mo made a coffin for the Eskimo woman; he simply knocked some slats together, and it was done. Once it was finished they laid some shavings in it, and placed it on a sledge and then two men pulled it to the *tupik* where the woman lay. It was shortly before noon. I had to look after the meal and couldn't watch what they did any longer. That afternoon it began to snow again. Today the Eskimos had to build a wall of snow blocks around our house; there were two men sawing snow blocks and some hauling them away on stretchers. The blocks were a good 1½ feet thick, 2 feet wide and 2½ feet high. The blocks looked as if they had been planed. They had finished the job in no time. This evening the temperature was -13°.

[Franz Boas commented on this harmonious life at the station for his parents and sisters as follows: *I wish you could see how congenially I am sitting here now. My table is installed and now I am sitting on one side, Jimmy Mutch on the other side of the room, reading, while Wilhelm sits on another chair when he is not cooking or visiting Capt. Roach's cooper.*[5] *I think we will get on well together this winter.*]

---

5. The reference is to the Dane, Rasmussen, the handyman at the American whaling station, of which Captain John Roach was in charge.

*Saturday, 27 October.*

It was very cold again. The harbour was already full of ice as far as the American station. When one of the natives who had been on the look-out came back, his first and only comment was: "Ziko, ziko!"[6] For ice had already formed out in the Sound too. After my coffee I tried my luck at baking, and was quite successful. Herr Dr went out to make observations; I couldn't go, since I was busy with baking and cooking and he had to take Singnar with him. Mi Mo wanted to go out with the boats, but could not get away and came back. Then I was busy grinding coffee again; then one can't understand one's own words; its [grinding] has now lasted a couple of weeks. For lunch I had put some of my *Dreierbrötchen*[7] on the table. When we had eaten Mist. Mo said that the house had to be washed out, and I was to scrub out our room. This took quite a long time; I had to wash the pantry, living room, and the hallway, while three Eskimos tackled the porch and the workshop. Once I had finished this cleaning I began splitting some wood and in so doing cut my left hand, so that Herr Dr had to bandage it; I still wanted to do some baking, but it was too late. M. Mo went out with the boats again this afternoon; they first had to work for a couple of hours to get clear of the ice; they didn't get very far and they soon came back again; when we spotted them we immediately made tea, and had supper. Once I had washed up Herr Dr made some more observations and I had to help him. He placed the instruments in the lee of a dog-kennel, to get some shelter; I wasn't proud and crawled into the kennel to take notes. I had several feet of snow beneath me. It was a lot of fun, lying there for half an hour with a fair old north wind blowing; we were both glad when we were finished and could go back to the house. Once inside we first had a cognac. Cooper was there too; they laughed about the fact that I had crawled into the dog kennel. We had a musical evening's entertainment; a mixture of German, American and Danish songs were sung. The cooper left at 10:30 and then we thought of bed.

---

6. I. *siku*: ice.

7. A round or longish roll with a cross or long slit on the top that cost three *Reichspfennige* in Germany during most of the nineteenth century.

*Sunday, 28 October.*

When I went outside this morning I could see that the entire harbour was frozen over. One of the Eskimos came into the house, remarking: "Iki;[8] it's cold!" Then they crawled in front of the stove and warmed themselves. Today I made a pudding; once I had it on the stove I went outside again and could see that the Eskimos were already walking across the ice to the other island that lay a good half-hour away from the island we were on. Now there is work for the dogs. We had an excellent lunch today: first asparagus, chicken stew, pudding, and plum sauce. It was all a great success. Once we'd eaten and I was finished inside, I went out; I wanted to visit the cooper at the American station. But he had locked the door, and hence I went to see the Eskimos. At the same time the men came back from hunting. One of them brought a seal. Once the Eskimos had warmed up, they set about skinning the seal. Once it had been skinned and dressed, they began eating choice pieces. I got a piece of the liver and also a chunk of blubber. There were five men enjoying this meal; when they had finished they had eaten half of it! I got back to the house at 4:30; and then I had to think about supper. I made hot chocolate for supper. Herr Dr also brought some cheese out; it was quite a spread!

*Monday, 29 October.*

The cold is persisting; the ice is growing steadily thicker. The Eskimos quickly went out to hunt seals. This morning Herr Dr also went out on the ice to survey the harbour, since it was now solidly frozen over and he could go anywhere on the ice. For lunch I made roast caribou, potatoes, and Brussels sprouts. Mis. Mo also went out for the morning to look for whales. Now I had the place to myself; I first had to tidy up our dark little bedroom and then make shelves above our beds, so that we could leave more things near our bunks. When Si Mo[9] came back he asked that Herr Dr come back with him, and that Seniges'[10] child was sick. At 2 o'clock Herr Dr also came back to the house, and we ate right away. In the afternoon the Eskimos came back from hunting;

---

8. I. *ikii*: cold.
9. Jimmy Mutch.
10. Jenissy, Seniges or Senigus according to Weike.

almost all of them brought seals with them; this was good for the natives. For their provisions were getting scarce; they all brought us some meat till we had a large bowl full. I had to check the guns again and had to polish the revolvers until it got dark. Then I looked over the seal meat and prepared a large pan-full; at table they began laughing since I had selected the largest ribs, since they had more meat on them. Mi M. had already noted this; and when Herr Dr asked me whether there were no small ribs I said yes, but there was more meat on these ones. They both started laughing.

### Tuesday, 30 October.

This morning Senigus arrived to say that his child was dead. He was very sad. Mi Mo gave him a box that he could lay the child in. There was no longer any water to be seen; it was all covered with ice. Once we'd drunk our coffee, we saw Senigus carrying his child away. Two women walked behind him; one of them was carrying the child's things; the other just walked behind. The dogs also went with them; this comprised the entire procession. They are very superstitious here. The man whose wife died, still has to stay in his *tupik* for three days; the others who had lived with them there moved out immediately and left everything behind. M. M. [Mister Mutch] told us that the man had sat quite calmly to one side; he hadn't made a sound, and once the three days were up, he had rushed out of the *tupik* and left all its contents behind; he then built himself a snow house, and let the dogs demolish the skin *tupik*. Today everyone was out hunting again; there was even a woman with them. They came back as it was getting dark. This afternoon I had to bake bread again and make hot chocolate for supper. This evening we had a pleasant conversation. We had two Eskimos[11] with us, and we asked them to show us on the map[12] where everything was; after they had gone all around [the map], they didn't know where they had begun.

---

11. Jimmy and Pakkak.

12. Franz Boas asked Inuit to come to see him at the station at specific times, draw maps for him, and provide and explain place-names (cf. Müller-Wille and Weber Müller-Wille 2006:219-245).

*Wednesday, 31 October.*

It is still so dark here in the mornings that we have to have a lamp until 8:30. After we had drunk our coffee, I prepared two ptarmigan for soup; once I had everything on the stove, I had to do laundry. But I didn't have much room to hang it up, and had to dry everything by the stove. Shortly before noon I had finished with all the whites; I stuck all the woolens in and left them. In the afternoon I had to bake again; our fresh bread had all gone again. Today the ice outside the harbour had all moved off somewhat. There were some women here in the house, sewing a cover for Ito's *tupik*; in the meantime a man came in with an *Akjuch*.[13] Now the women could no longer work; they abandoned their sewing and Ito had to do his own sewing.[14] In the evening I visited Cooper and stayed with him until 9:30, and when I came home Herr Dr said that he needed more [things] for his outfit.

[Franz Boas reflected: *I wish you knew how comfortably we live here. My room is so pleasantly warm. Jimmy Mutch is as peaceful and obliging as possible, and since we are pooling our supplies we can prepare excellent meals. Wilhelm is improving as a cook day by day!*]

# November 1883

*Thursday, 1 November.*

In this dark weather I really overslept; I got up only at 7:30; it was snowing outside. Naturally we had our coffee later too; once I had washed up I had to get my pots in order quickly again; I didn't get around to washing my clothes this morning either. We had green beans and roast seal meat. I began doing laundry this afternoon, but when I thought I had just begun, there were other jobs to be tackled. I was glad when I had stowed my stuff away. As I came into the room Herr Dr said he couldn't see, and I had not got the lamp ready yet. Then I had to get

---

13. I. *ujjuk:* bearded seal *(Erignathus barbatus).*
14. A taboo among the Inuit: women could not work at one location with skins of land and sea mammals at the same time.

the lamps ready; in the meantime Singar arrived, bringing us some seal meat. He went into the room to see Herr Dr; the latter showed him books by ?Herl,[15] who also travelled in the north polar regions. Singar knew him too, and also recognized his companions. He saw a woman who was carrying a child in her hood; he said that is Kanakerh.[16] He was right here in the house; he lives here in Kikkerton and belongs to Mo's Eskimos; he no longer has any siblings; they are all dead. He [Boas] was quite amazed when Singar said that it was he; he stared at the picture all evening.

*Friday, 2 November.*
I had been given my time [by Herr Dr] for getting up, and had to roll out at 5:30; it was no longer quite dark. After we'd drunk our coffee I had to sew our *tupik;* I cooked my meal at the same time. After the meal I wanted to start sewing again, but Herr Dr came and wanted to pack boxes, and I had to assist him. But the box was so heavy that we had to enlist the help of natives to lift it off the ground; it wasn't long before we had filled every corner of the house. Outside the harbour the waves had broken the ice up again and one of the natives had drifted away with it. In the evening they came to say that they could hear him shouting; a boat was launched to rescue him. I didn't quite know whether it was Janki or his brother, until he came back. In the evening we played chess; there was again a strong wind and snow.

*Saturday, 3 November.*
Yesterday evening I asked Ito to wake me; he came at 5:30 and poked me in the ribs, so I knew I had to get up. Water for the coffee was already on the stove; while it was brewing I mixed some chocolate and brewed it for our morning coffee. We now have chocolate in the morning every other day. Today the harbour had broken up again, but there was only a narrow area of open water so that the ice could not move out. Mi Mo went out with the boats today. I baked bread again, but Herr Dr had

---

15. The copier appears to have been unsure as to how this name should be written; it is that of the American polar traveller, Charles Francis Hall (1821-1871) who stayed in Frobisher Bay and Cumberland Sound from 1860-1862 (Hall 1865).
16. Kanaka, born around 1860, is pictured riding in his mother's hood (Hall 1865:61).

given me the wrong baking powder[17] and the bread came to nothing; we couldn't eat it so I gave it to the Eskimos, who ate it with relish. In the afternoon we scrubbed out the house, since there was such a blizzard outside that nobody could venture outside. There was no water left in the barrel; some natives had gone out to fetch some, but they came back to say that there was no longer any water. We now had to melt ice. I had to make chocolate for the sick woman; there are constantly some sick people here. Every day Herr Dr has a new patient. It gives the natives the greatest pleasure to see Kanaker[18] as a baby; there is constantly somebody coming to see it.

### Sunday, 4 November.

The wind had slackened somewhat, but it was still not very clear. In the forenoon Herr Dr made observations in order to check our clocks.[19] I had not been out of the house for fourteen days; I was really sad that I could not get out. Today I cooked green beans; I had to cut them out of the can, they were so solidly frozen. When the meal was ready I set the table. Herr Dr told me we would be going out, at which I was really happy; Kiker[20] helped me to wash up, which we finished in a flash. I was all set to go, when a native, Bob, came and wanted to make a map; so Herr Dr could not go with me. I put on my *kolitan*, took my gun and then went up the hill, to do some thinking. In places the snow was so deep that I couldn't get through it. I had to turn back several times, but I kept going forward; I didn't plan to return to the house until it got dark. I had to run to get back home; the snow blinded me so that I couldn't see whether there was a level surface or a hill. I happened to tumble over a hump and landed with my head in the snow; I got back to the house at 4:30, sweating profusely. Then I had to think about supper again; after supper we played chess.

---

17. Franz Boas mentioned that he had given Wilhelm Weike cream of tartar by mistake.

18. What is meant is the picture of Kanaka with his mother in Hall's book (1865:61).

19. The time is determined from the sun's zenith position, i.e., the zenith is always reached at 12 noon at all locations.

20. Kikker.

*Monday, 5 November.*

We got up early today, at 7:45; as I emerged Ito said that he had slept so much. I quickly made the coffee, and then I already had to think about lunch, because now cooking is a tedious business here since the large kettle has to sit on the stove the whole time in order to melt ice for water. Over the course of the morning the weather improved and Herr Dr and Singnar went out on the ice to find a spot for our *tupik* since we want to sleep on the ice. I got the meal ready with great difficulty. The natives brought ice from the harbour and stacked it up near the house; they kept on coming in, each with a block of ice, in order to warm their hands. Kiker is the funniest of them; the two of us are always chatting away; I don't worry as to whether I am speaking correctly or not. In the afternoon I had to start baking again; the sun sets here again at 1 o'clock. When it grew dark all the natives belonging to the house came in; a crowd of them stood around in the workshop to get their evening schnapps. Thereafter Kanaker played some music and Kiker danced.

*Tuesday 6 November.*

Simmi[21] continued to get the *tupik* ready while Singar was piling snow on the ice where the *tupik* is to go. I was really glad that we would be getting out again, since I've had enough of being in the house. The *tupik* was all finished then this afternoon we organized our boat lines[22] and got everything ready for our departure. In the evening we played chess to pass the time and thereafter I read a comedy.

*Wednesday, 7 November.*

Today we had progressed sufficiently that we could move out onto the ice; this morning we took the *tupik* out. This was the first northern sledge trip in which I had been involved; we erected the *tupik* immediately; we laid boards beneath the floor on the ice and snow. We stayed still up here [at the house] for lunch. In the meantime Herr Dr and Si[ngar] were below, making a hole in the ice. When Herr Dr came up here again, we had to brew coffee again so that we could take it down with us after the meal. After the meal we travelled down there with a

---

21. Jimmy Mutch.
22. Franz Boas used these lines to measure the tidal fluctuations.

second sledge fully loaded; once we had stowed it in the *tupik* we had to head back again to fetch the rest. Once we'd got it all together we loaded the sledge and headed off again. But once back at the *tupik* we had no nails to nail the tide-gauge post together; I had to head back to the house to fetch a hammer and nails, as well as a bucket of fresh water, so that we could brew coffee tonight. When I came back we continued with the tidal measurements. Herr Dr had the first watch. I went with him at first, to see how things were done, until I had grasped it. We brewed coffee on the kerosene stove. The temperature inside the *tupik* was -10° and outside -12°. Herr Dr went to bed at 8 o'clock and my watch began then; initially the sky was overcast, but thereafter there was some aurora. It had become a little warmer; outside it was now -11°; the sky did not clear completely. By 12 o'clock I was still not tired; at midnight I woke Herr Dr since his watch was beginning then. My ink froze solidly to my pen; I constantly had to hold the pen over the lamp to thaw it out.

### Thursday, 8 November.

Last night I slept from 12 until 4; when Herr Dr, woke me at 4 o'clock the temperature was -14°. During my watch I froze as never before; when the coffee brewed I drank it; it remained cold throughout my watch; at times I could hear the ice cracking. In the dawn twilight Singnar came past the *tupik*; he said he was going to "Sial Keschen,"[23] but they soon came back again, since the ice off the harbour had broken away and they could not go far out. At 8 o'clock I went to bed up at the station; down here [at the *tupik*] we were two men to one sleeping bag; when one rolled out the other crawled in. I couldn't sleep at all from the commotion in the house; I also heard that Herr Dr returned once during the morning. I got up at 1 o'clock, washed and ate lunch. Then I heard from Herr Dr that we had to set up our tide-gauge differently; it was too irregular with the cord. Mi Mo gave us a boat's mast; the tide-gauge was reconfigured using it. When everything was ready we hauled a sledge-load of rocks down that were for buttressing the mast. Once everything was ready the mast was sunk; then the observations began anew; after the second observation I had to spend an hour when I had

---

23. Seal catching.

to check it every 10 minutes; I stayed outside the whole time. Herr Dr told me that I should keep an eye on the ice, since in this wind it could easily drift out. Things went well on my watch; I went to bed at 8 o'clock, when it was Herr Dr's watch; it was quite a while before I could get to sleep, since the wind was blowing terribly. All went well until 11:15 when Herr Dr came to wake me; we had to get off the ice, since it was starting to move. You wouldn't believe how fast I got into my clothes. While I was dressing Herr Dr gathered all the essential things together; we grabbed what we could carry in our arms, then rushed out of the *tupik* toward the land. It was almost high tide; travel across the fast ice was difficult, there were great cracks in it all over the place; we were constantly almost running into them. As we reached the land Herr Dr climbed onto a block of ice, but tumbled down the other side. On shore there was a driving snowstorm, so that one could scarcely face into it. We reached the house at 11:30, and went to bed. In a couple of minutes the ice had driven forward a foot.

*Friday, 9 November.*
After a good sleep we had recovered from our frightening experience; today the wind was even stronger and hence we remained indoors today. I had to cook again while Herr Dr had a really good lie-in. In the afternoon, after I had finished my work I had to go to the *tupik* to fetch the remaining things from there. But when I got to the ice, it was not safe to venture out, since the floes were still [heaving]; I went to Sinar's *tupik* but he was not home; I saw another native and took him with me; he had to walk ahead. I first went to the hole and shovelled the ice out of it, and then to the *tupik* where I packed up the remaining things. Once I'd gotten everything together, I tied up the *tupik* and we went back. Back at the house I unpacked the wet things and hung them by the stove to dry, and then I had to think about supper again. Once I had washed up I sewed buttons on Herr Dr's jacket; then I went into the workshop where I found Kiker; I took one of Herr Dr's book for him, in which there were pictures. He listed off his names; he knew only fifteen of them, but he said he had even more.[24]

---

24. Naming among the Inuit is a complex system, which indicates and perpetuates the relationships to dead or living relatives, and thus leads to a large number of names

*Saturday, 10 November.*

Today we were making arrangements for going back to the tide-hole. This morning I first had to do some baking, and hence I could not go. Herr Dr went with Aschuk[25] and [set] the mast straight again, but it would not stay down. Once I had finished the meal and had washed up, I went down there with a full load; it was my watch. Once I was there, I immediately realized that I had forgotten something. Herr Dr also came back and I fetched the forgotten item. It was not very cold, nor was there a strong wind. Singnar visited us again and taught Herr Dr a song. I was happy when it was 7:30, when we had coffee. We had some cheese there, and when one cut into it, it creaked exactly like when one walks around in snow when it is really cold. I was glad when I could crawl into my sleeping bag for a few hours.

*Sunday, 11 November.*

I had to get up at 12 o'clock, when my watch began; it was very cold. I managed to stand my watch; when the coffee was ready I drank it; when my time was up I was able to crawl straight into my sleeping bag. Herr Dr was on watch from 4 till 8 o'clock. The Eskimos had a celebration today[26] and Herr Dr went ashore to see what they were doing. They had gathered in one spot, and every time that somebody arrived, they were greeted with shouts. Once they were all together, they ran in a circle around the spot where the *tupiks* stood, one behind the other. Thereafter they went from one *tupik* to the next, and began shouting, and when something was thrown out of a *tupik*, they went on to the next one. Herr Dr was over there the whole time. At noon it was -12°. I cooked Brussels sprouts over here [at the tent]. Herr Dr came back here for the meal, but he had still not finished eating properly when the Eskimos began their games again. Now the devil had arrived; I had to stay out on the ice all day, looking after the tide-gauge, where I had to take a reading every ten minutes. My feet were like ice; if Herr Dr did

per individual. The first name is often that of a recently deceased person whose soul (character) is transferred to the newborn.

25. Akschudlo.

26. The "Sedna" ritual of the Inuit (see Boas 1888:583-591, also Boas in Müller-Wille 1998:137-138).

not come back out, I wanted to go back ashore to put on dry things. At 4 o'clock, -13°. Herr Dr came back out and I went ashore and put on dry things; I slept until 8 o'clock then I had to go out again. At 8 o'clock, -14°. When Herr Dr had made the coffee he woke me; he had cooked beef-steaks[27] that made an excellent supper. I was on watch again from 8 until 12. The natives were still engaged in their game; it might have been 11 o'clock when I still heard them shouting. At 12 last night it was -12°. I was really happy when I was able to crawl into my sleeping bag; Herr Dr had the watch from 12 until 4.

*Monday, 12 November.*

At 4 o'clock I had to go out again; at first I wasn't freezing too badly; as the day began to dawn I emerged from the *tupik* onto the ice, to check how it looked, since it had been cracking so much during the night; fresh cracks had developed everywhere. In the morning (...)[28] came to ask Herr Dr whether he had something for him to do, otherwise he wanted to go seal hunting. The water had risen so high today that our mast was under water. At 8 o'clock I woke Herr Dr and went back ashore; it was -13°. I wanted to sleep, but couldn't, since I had to cook; it wasn't long before Herr Dr came to tell me that the tide-gauge operations were finished: the mast had disappeared under the ice. After our meal Herr Dr went down with Singnar to sound the harbour; once I had washed up I followed them; our route was such that from the *tupik* we could head straight across the harbour. We wanted to continue across to the other side, but it was getting late and we had to go back ashore. When Herr Dr arrived, he hadn't thought about the keys [presumably for the station], that were still lying in the *tupik*, and I had to go back across to get them; after that I prepared supper.

*Tuesday, 13 November.*

Last night I again had quite a tolerably good night's sleep; once I'd lit the fire I went outside, but it didn't look pleasant in the slightest (-17°). I set about putting the room in order; while I was laying the table Mi Mo got up. Herr Dr arrived only as I was serving the chocolate; once

---

27. Here actually seal steaks.
28. Probably Singnar.

we had finished the meal Herr Dr went out; I was to cook. First I washed out some dishtowels and then I had to set about tackling my seal roast. We had so much that we had to give away about 20 lbs for the dogs. During the day quite a lot of seal meat arrived, so that by evening we again had a large dish full. Once Herr Dr came back we ate right away; once I had washed up, I had to get dressed, and then we surveyed the harbour from west to east, for 300 metres between the reefs; and then we paced it off at 445 paces. Once we'd finished this we went back home; I still had to prepare the beans, and then I had to think of supper. I had to fry some cod. Once we had eaten, another sick person was reported. Now constantly someone or another has something wrong with their throat. Once I had washed up I cleaned myself thoroughly. In the evening Schangu[29] and Kiker were here again; it was -18° this evening.

*Wednesday, 14 November.*
This morning after we had had our coffee I had to go to see Singnar; we wanted to go out but he had already gone out to hunt seals, so now we stayed at home. It was -19° today. I made a pudding today, but I had no luck with it since my pudding mould broke and I had to tie it up with string, so that it did not turn out too well. I'm having the damnedest time with the canned vegetables; they are so solidly frozen in the cans that one can't get them out. I placed the can in the oven for two hours and when I took it out they were still so solidly frozen that I could barely get them out; I cooked them for a further good half hour before they were thawed. In the afternoon I first soldered, and then washed stockings. Before supper Kiker was here again; he was persuaded to sing so that Herr Dr could learn the songs.

*Thursday, 15 November.*
This morning I jumped abruptly out of bed. Ito had lit the fire and had set the box of matches on the stove; it had caught fire, burning with a bright flame; I was wide awake fast. Once we had had coffee Herr Dr went out on the ice with Singnar. I had to stay home to cook, and at the same time I had to wash glass, since double windowpanes had been installed in the workshop. At lunch we had a fine seal roast with pota-

---

29. Shanguja, also called Qeqerten-Shanguja.

toes, and once I had washed up, I had to get ready to go out. Today Herr Dr had already frozen his nose by noon.[30] Once the sledge was loaded we harnessed ourselves to it and headed out onto the ice. When we had reached the spot where they had made the holes, Herr Dr sounded and Singnar coiled the line on the sledge and I hauled the sledge from one hole to another; when we had finished sounding, we started back. When we are outside we are quite a sight; when one breathes out one's breath settles on the fur of one's *kolitan* and it starts to freeze, and then one has a white rim of ice around one's face. From the time he had spent sounding, Herr Dr's entire *kolitan* was encased in ice, so that it had to be scraped off with an iron scraper. When we got back they were building up snow blocks behind the windows. After I had washed up, I spent a bit of time with the Eskimos, and came back at 9 o'clock. Herr Dr asked me if it was cold outside; it was -21°.

### Friday, 16 November.

Last night I was freezing in bed as never before. When I got up Mi Mo had already gone out to the *puschimut.*[31] I made the coffee then woke Herr Dr; he too had frozen badly; once I got organized I set out the ingredients for baking, but found that the flour was finished. Therefore I had first to go to Kakuscho[32] and ask him where the flour was kept, since neither the Herr Dr nor I knew. As I had bread in the oven, I had to get my meat on the stove, since it was already 10:30. Also two women came into the house to sew a *kolitan,* since it was warmer here than in a *tupik.* At 11:30 M.M.[33] came back and then I had to get busy so that we could eat. In the afternoon I made a small stand for an instrument. In the meantime it was also boat day,[34] when all the women came and picked up their bread, coffee and molasses. When they are here one can't

---

30. What is involved here is first-degree frostbite, that occurs on bare skin due to prolonged exposure to cold (e.g., with a wind); it leads to reddening of the skin, lack of feeling, and to reduced blood flow through the tissue; once it is warmed again, the skin may continue to be painful and itchy (von der Eltz and Schick 2007).

31. Word unclear in English or Inuktitut. From the context it is the lookout point 1 km south of the station, which, at 108 m is the highest point on the island called Qeqerten.

32. Kakodscha.

33. M. M.: Mister Mutch.

34. What is probably meant is the day on which James Mutch paid his boats' crews, i.e., gave the women provisions to feed their families.

even turn around. After they had left we brought in our caribou skins and each spread one on his bed, so that it would be warmer. After we had eaten Natukali's wife was here; she had to list names for Herr Dr In the evening I had plenty ... as today I got from Malli two ... seals and a walrus carved from walrus tusk. (?)[35]

*Saturday, 17 November.*
Today the weather was foul so that the Eskimos could not go seal hunting; hence they had to build snow blocks around the house; the result was a thick wall, over 3 feet thick, so that it would not be so cold in the house. It was -22° today. Herr Dr went out on the ice with Singar today and brought the *tupik* back ashore. In the afternoon I helped wash the house. In the evening Kakascha[36] came to say that a child was sick.

*Sunday, 18 November.*
This morning when we got up, Herr Dr went immediately to see the sick child. I had to heat water twice; we didn't get any coffee until after 9 o'clock. During the course of the afternoon the child died, and around noon he was already buried. The weather was better, like yesterday; the wind was not so strong.

[On the same day Franz Boas wrote: *In the morning I was called from bed to see the sick boy, who is dying. I tried to get him a little air by means of hot poultices; he regained some colour, but died under my hands at noon. The mother, weeping, shouted "Nuvukulu, nuvukulu"[37] and refused to be comforted. The boy was buried immediately. They had built a small snow house for him yesterday to allow him to die there.*]

*Monday, 19 November.*
Yesterday evening Herr Dr had to give me a nightcap, since I could not sleep because I had toothache. Sim Mo[38] was pulling my leg all evening,

---

35. The copier had included a question mark; two words in this sentence could not be deciphered, thus its meaning is not quite clear.
36. Kakodscha.
37. I. *nuvukulu*: the lovable one; term of endearment for children, in this case for the little boy.
38. Jim (James) Mutch.

because I had visited (…) and the Yuk Hare.[39] I twice had to take one before I fell asleep. This morning when Ito came to wake me, I fell asleep again, and he had to come back again to wake me. I made my hot chocolate and then woke Herr Dr Singnar was already here, too; we wanted to go out on the ice once we had had our drink. While I was washing up Herr Dr and Singnar got the sledge ready and then we harnessed ourselves to it and headed out across the harbour, to where Herr Dr made observations. Singnar and I had to set up flags, while Herr Dr remained at the first location. We did not go back for a meal, but then at 2:30 we had to go back because it was already dark. As we were travelling back Mitto[40] arrived with his dogs; we tied our sledge behind his and let the dogs haul it back to the house. It was -20°, but there was no strong wind, and hence it felt very warm, and we couldn't believe at all that it was so cold. We were back at the house by 3:45, and then we had lunch.

*Tuesday, 20 November.*

We went out again this morning. Singnar did not go with us; when we were out on the harbour we could see where the sun was almost rising, but we could not see the sun itself; we began surveying near the reef that lies on the east side. And then around Akuliruk.[41] We had three flags; we always had to walk from one flag to the next three or four times. In Junigen Haber[42] the really painful progress began, since the ice was very uneven there. The sun set at 3 o'clock; the sky was magnificent. We knew that it was now time to go home, since as soon as the sun has gone it starts to get dark. We still had a good distance back to the station. When we reached home Mi. Mo. had lunch ready; after we had been eating for some time, the feeling in our legs returned.

---

39. It is not clear as to what Weike was alluding to with regard to James Mutch. Mutch seems to have been "pulling his leg" because he had visited a male or female Inuk in the camp. The words "Yuk Hare" (a person?) are unintelligible (it could be "joker"). The copier wrote "pulling my leg" and "Yuk Hare" in Roman script, and probably could not decipher Weike's handwriting.
40. Mitu.
41. Akugdliruq.
42. Union Harbour.

*Wednesday, 21 November.*

We went out again today, but Singnar came with us; it was -23°. We went back to where we stopped yesterday; we started here in the harbour and then through Junigen Paschis[43] to Adams Island,[44] and then to the side in Junigen Paschis Anchorage; then we wanted to come back between two islands[45] but there was so much grounded ice there that we could not get through, and had to come back right around the island. When we got there, we went along the northern side of another island[46] from where we had a fine view of the countryside. It was just as the sun was setting—just the last rays, that we could see to the N East. It was time for us to go home, since we still had to cover a fair distance back. We reached the station at 4 o'clock; on the way we were really pleased at our progress: we began walking slowly, but our pace steadily increased, until we were running flat out.

*Thursday, 22 November.*

Today we again had a pretty good lie-in; it was already 8:30 when we got up; after we had had our coffee Herr Dr went to the lookout with J. M.,[47] while I stayed at home. They were back down by lunchtime and after lunch we unpacked things. While doing so Herr Dr remarked that here one thinks nothing of -24°; it is as if it were nothing at all; it is not even remarked upon. Once the things were put away, I had a thorough wash, and then I had to melt ice so that we had some water.

*Friday, 23 November.*

This morning when I got up and went outside, there was a superb starry sky; Kakascha came and told M.M. that they had never seen anything like it. The moon was still up, as well as the stars, and blue and red clouds extended from east to south, but in such a wide range of colours. Once it was daylight we again went out to survey around the eastern tip of Kikkerton. We started in the harbour. Around noon we passed

---

43. Union Passage.
44. Mitiluarbing.
45. Akugdliruq and Mitiluarbing.
46. Angiuq / Union Island.
47. James Mutch.

places where there was water among the ice, steaming as if it was warm. We passed the cemetery[48] and then we went home.

*Saturday 24 November.*
This morning we went back to the place where we had stopped yesterday. We had a good distance to walk before reaching the ice. Initially we had good ice to walk on, but as we came around the south end, it became a matter of jumping from one ice floe to another. I was in the lead and had to select my own route; then Herr Dr came behind me; Singnar came last, and had to stick there. Once we were around the south end, we got steadily closer to our harbour; from a distance we could see the water smoking in the Sound, where there was still no ice. At 1:30 we came around the north end into the harbour. Once we had finished our surveying, we needed only to clamber over the grounded ice again, and we were back home. Once we had finished our meal and I had washed up, I lay down on the work bench and fell gently asleep, until I was disturbed by a native whose gun had split.

*Sunday, 25 November.*
We celebrated a typical Sunday; we slept late; I was at the [sewing] machine all morning. In the morning Cooper was here too. In the afternoon I went out for a while, but now one can't go far, since it is already dark by 3:45. The best thing is that, because we get up later in the morning, we have tea an hour earlier in the evening; and hence I am finished an hour earlier in the evening. I find it quite tedious when we are stuck inside; I prefer to be outside.

*Monday, 26 November.*
Last night there was a strong wind, but it had slackened somewhat by morning. Once we had had our coffee, we got dressed to go out. The weather was dismal; when we were out on the harbour Herr Dr looked to see whether he could spot the flag through his instrument[49] but it was so dull that we had to turn back. Today the natives were not out either; they were banking snow around the house; the snow was piled

---

48. The whalers' cemetery on Qeqerten about 1500 m east of the Scottish station.
49. A theodolite (surveying instrument with a telescope).

only one foot deep on the roof, while around the sides it was three feet thick. I was washing and baking.

*Tuesday, 27 November.*
Last night there was a strong wind that had still not abated by the morning, and the snow was drifting so that one could not even open one's eyes when one went outside. We slept away the early morning, and got up only at 8:30. Last night the *iglu* of one of the Eskimos was blown away. Since nothing else in particular had to be tackled, I washed the house, and we ate lunch later than usual. We had to have a lamp burning all day; we couldn't see anything just with the daylight. Kiker was here in the evening and was singing for Herr Dr.

*Wednesday, 28 November.*
This morning as I came out of my room Ito came in from outside at the same time. Once I had lit the fire, Herr Dr was also awake and he congratulated me.[50] Then I went out again; when I came in with the water, there were letters lying at my place, at which I was really delighted. After our coffee I opened them, but didn't read them immediately. The weather was very fine, but we did not go out, for Herr Dr had said that it should be a rest-day. In the afternoon I was … [outside], but our enjoyment did not last long, because it became dark again. The women were here today too; they fetched the caribou skins, to make our clothing.

[Franz Boas noted: *I have letters from home for him* (Weike), *which also enclosed some notes for me. I gave him the* Don Quixote.[51]]

*Thursday, 29 November.*
Temperature -25°. Today we again went out to Akulsruk;[52] we initially had to run for a good distance. Herr Dr first went down to the harbour, in front of us [lies] Ukuliruk, in order to establish the high-water mark; Singnar and I went straight to Akulliruk. Once we arrived there

---

50. Weike turned 24.
51. "The Ingenious Hidalgo Don Quixote of La Mancha" was published by Miguel de Cervantes in two parts in Spain in 1605 and 1615.
52. Akugdliruq; Weike spells it also Ukulirik or Akulliruk.

I wanted to light my pipe, but it would not light since the tobacco was frozen. I first had to stick the pipe somewhere else, to let it thaw out again. When Herr Dr arrived we began running vigorously and were soon round the side to where it leads out to the Sound. The ice had broken up there and, because I was in the lead, I was afraid to travel across the broken ice and clambered over the grounded ice to the shore; this turned out to be a problem, since I could not get down again. Meanwhile Herr Dr had made his last observations and shouted to me to come; I shouted back that I was coming. I chucked my flag away, and slid down on my backside since I could not get down any other way, then continued on my way until I came to a track, whereby I got back out onto the ice. Then I saw a *Jeuk*[53] and wanted to chase after it, but since the ice was so broken I went round to the other side; but I could not find Herr Dr and Singnar, until I finally spotted them on shore. I ran as hard as I could; Herr Dr saw me and came towards me. He told me that they had heard the flagpoles falling and thought that I had dropped between the grounded ice masses, and had then gone ashore. But I had been looking around for them too; I had been constantly running west but Herr Dr and Singnar had walked east following the track until we spotted each other again and fortunately got together again. We still had to run a fair distance; once we reached the reef from where we could see the harbour, Paka[54] was coming after us. One person got off and Herr Dr and I sat on [the sledge] and thus drove home.

*Friday, 30 November.*

We went out again this morning; the temperature was -28°. Singnak did not come with us. We went across Union Island, but then onto the land and then down again; we could not go far on shore and had to go back out onto the ice until we had got through between the two islands. Then Herr Dr took his observations, and then we travelled across the broken-up ice, which had been all rafted over itself, to another island that lay 2000 paces from our position. Once we had reached it we clambered back on shore again. Once we had finished there and had gone back down again, I detected a strange feeling in my nose. I asked Herr Dr

---

53. I. *ujjuq*: bearded seal.
54. Pakkak.

what this might be; he told me my nose was frozen. I had to thaw it out, and thereafter we were constantly getting frostbite, first one of us, then the other, so that we constantly had to thaw the affected spots. And so it went, from one island to the other, until we had to go back to the house.[55] We saw the sledge coming back from [place name not recorded]. Once we had passed Alabachet[56] we saw that one of the sledges had stopped until we got to it, and then we had to sit on it. Once we had reached the harbour we got off and continued walking, letting the Eskimos sit on the sledge again. We reached the house just as it was getting dark.

# December 1883

### Saturday, 1 December.

We did not yet have any sledge with dogs and hence we had to stay at home today. Also we had plenty to do in the house. In the afternoon I prepared our alcohol stove so that it had five flames. Once I was finished with this, we lit it; this will be for when we and also some Eskimo women are here. There are constantly some of them here conjuring; scarcely an evening goes by, that nobody is conjuring here in the house.

### Sunday, 2 December.

Today we slept for an hour longer, since it was Sunday. After we had had our coffee, Herr Dr went out to Akuliruk; but he was back by noon, and once we had finished lunch, it was getting dark again already. We had supper at 5 o'clock. Then I had a good long evening to read.

### Monday, 3 December.

Today we drove out on a sledge, with twelve dogs harnessed to it. It was very warm weather; only -8°. We set off at 8:45; once we were out on the

---

55. See the explanation of these incidences of frostbite in the footnote for the entry of 15 November.
56. Probably Aqbirsiabing.

ice three of us[57] sat on the sledge, and then we raced off as never before. Last night there was quite a strong wind, it must have been blowing more strongly on the mainland than at Kikkerton, since there the snow had blown away as if it had been swept off. In some places there was still snow lying from last winter[58] but it too had been swept away, and out beyond the harbour to the west, there was also quite a lot of open water. We made our first stop at a small island; once we had finished there we went on to a larger island[59] that we swung around. It was already getting dark, although it was only 2:15. Once we were past the second island, we drove on to another one that we had paced halfway around last time. Now we paced off the rest of it. The wind was almost in our faces, so that one could scarcely breathe. This was the last bit of walking for today, but it was also the worst. Once we had finished we sat on our sledge and headed for home. The dogs didn't need to watch where they were going at all.

### Tuesday, 4 December.

Last night there was quite a wind; when I went outside the snow was drifting. We wanted to head out again. Singnak was here already and was harnessing the dogs. But when Herr Dr came out he said we could not go, since the air was so thick with snow, and hence we could not distinguish the islands. But later he still went out; I first had to clean the stoves and then wash the house. It cleared towards evening; to the extent that we could see the large island. A lot more snow had fallen again; it was still so soft that when one went outside one sank knee-deep in it.

### Wednesday, 5 December.

We set out again today; it was very cold with a strong wind. We left Kikkerton at 9 o'clock and had to travel a good ninety minutes to reach our destination.[60] We wore our caribou-skin *kolitans*[61] for the first time.

---

57. Franz Boas, Wilhelm Weike and Singnar.
58. Persistent snow patches that survive the summer are one of the cold-environment features of the Arctic (permafrost, snow and ice).
59. Manitung and Tuapain.
60. Manitung.
61. I. q*ullitaq*: caribou fur overcoat.

We arranged things so that we did not need to walk into the wind since otherwise one could expect that one's face would be constantly frozen; as indeed our noses had already been frozen a few times before. When we got going, we soon sweated because we ran as hard as we could. Once we had passed the spot where we once had breakfast, we travelled with the sledge to Cauttak[62], and from there we headed back to where we had stopped. We were back at the spot by 1:45; there we made ourselves comfortable on the sledge, and then we headed home as fast as the dogs would run. It was very cold and the snow was flying as never before. We had calculated how long it would take to get home. The [dogs] were running well, but we were still travelling for two hours. We were very happy when we were back home. In the evening it began to blow even more strongly and the snow was drifting more heavily.

### Thursday, 6 December.
Due to the blizzard we had to stay at home today, and went outside as little as possible. I got things ready to do laundry, and because the natives had not gone seal hunting, Kiker was here, and was doing laundry for J. M.; the two of us sat beside each other doing our laundry.

### Friday, 7 December.
Today we stayed at home again; since we had to unpack things it was 8:30 before we had our coffee. After I had washed up Herr Dr and I went out to the store and unpacked boxes; in doing so we froze quite badly; we were glad when we had finished. Then I had to make a start on our lunch. Dinner was at 2:30. We had to use a lamp for the meal. Today the temperature was -30 degrees.

### Saturday, 8 December.
The weather was nothing special today. Herr Dr went out later; in the morning I first had to bake and melt ice for water all day. When I saw Herr Dr coming back, I got the meal ready. In the afternoon I washed woolen clothes. In the evening Cooper came over and we played cards; this was the first time on land.

---

62. Kautaq.

*Sunday, 9 December.*

It was 8.40 when I got up—our usual Sunday lie-in. As I was making coffee Kakuscha arrived and told me that two sledges were coming from the other side of the Sound. When I told Herr Dr this he got quite excited! Kakuscha had to come in and tell us who it was; it wasn't long before they were in the house. In the afternoon the wind began to blow more strongly and the snow to drift. This evening I had to make tea for the strangers.

*Monday, 10 December.*

Today we were making preparations for starting out; initially I wasn't to be going along, until in the evening when it was decided that I would be going. I was given pants and stockings by J. M.[63] since I hadn't a caribou skin outfit ready, and since two children had died the Eskimos have not been working for three days.[64]

[On 13 December Franz Boas wrote: *I had almost gone alone with Ssigna because Wilhelm's suit was not finished, but Mr. Mutch took pity on me and lent him his outfit.*]

---

63. During the trip on the ice it was soon revealed that the pants were far too large for Weike and the skin boots too narrow and therefore could not keep him warm.
64. A taboo among the Inuit: for a certain period, the family was forbidden to work after the death of a relative.

# On the ice and in *iglus*
# in Cumberland Sound
# (11 December 1883 to 7 January 1884)

*Tuesday, 11 December.*

At 5 o'clock this morning Ito came and woke me; it wasn't long before the coffee was ready; when we had drunk it we got ready to set off. Ito and Tom had already gone ahead with their sledges. It was -36° this morning. Initially the going was very good and all three of us could ride on the sledge,[1] but once we had reached Cauttan the ice was bad; we had to take turns running. When we reached Panirtu[2] the moon had risen. When one had to run a little from time to time, the cold was not so bad. When we reached Aufpaluktun[3] Ito and Tom had already built an *iglu*.[4] It was on the same island where we had come with the two boats together in the fall. This appears to be a real landing place for the natives, and we were here again with four sledges, two from the other side[5] and two from Kikkerton. It was already 9:30 by the time the coffee was ready. We had a fully occupied *iglu*; there were eight people in it—six men, a woman and a child; we were all lying almost on top of each other.

*Wednesday, 12 December.*

This morning when I peered out of my sleeping bag, I could see that the natives were sitting in the *iglu* in their clothes. I did not see any sleeping bags, I therefore asked Herr Dr whether they hadn't brought sleeping bags with them; he said that they probably did not need to. At 9 o'clock we all dispersed; the natives went seal hunting, and we went

---

1. Boas, Weike and Singnar.
2. Pangnirtung.
3. Augpalugtung.
4. *Iglu* No. 1 at Niurtung. On this trip Weike numbered their *iglus*, but not always continuously.
5. The settlement of Anarnitung.

to the other side. We came back again at 3 o'clock; we had been walking steadily and the snow on the ice was so soft that one became more tired walking half an hour than in two hours at home on the street. After some time the natives also came back; Singnar and Tom had each shot a seal. Ito came back empty-handed. It is said that it is bad sleeping in a snow-house, but it offers many advantages; if one wants to cook one hacks off some snow from the walls, where it is ready when you need it.

## Thursday, 13 December.

Today we went over to the other side. Ito, Tom, and Singnar went hunting. When one steps out of the *iglu* it is very cold, but once one has been outside for a while, one doesn't feel the cold so much. At one point we had to turn back since there was open water that was smoking more than a factory chimney. Over these water holes[6] there is such dense fog that one can see nothing there. We headed more and more northerly and when we checked the time it was 1:30. When we got closer to the *iglu* we saw Singnar coming from it; he had cut up food for the dogs; he went back again to get water. When we reached the *iglu* Herr Dr checked the thermometer; it was -40°. We lit a fire to get some water, since thirst is the most terrible thing that tortures one here. After some time Singnak also came back; he had three seals; when they came back the soup was soon ready; the greatest pleasure that one can experience is to get something warm when one has frozen during the day. Ito said that next day he wanted to go back to Kikkerton. Herr Dr wrote a letter to J. M. that he should send the things after us as soon as possible. The main problem was that we had forgotten our cooking apparatus; till now we could cook only on the blubber lamp.

## Friday, 14 December.

This morning we packed the sledge to continue travelling. Ito and Tom were heading back to Kikkerton; they took all the dogs except Singnak's two; they remained here, but they could not help us in front of the

---

6. A polynya – an enclosed permanently open water area in the pack ice with the arctic frost-smoke rising from it; the latter develops from the contact between the warmer water surface and the cold air above the polynya.

sledge. They held us up more than helped us forward. We therefore had to let them run loose and we three pulled the sledge on our own. I led, in harness, and Singnar and Herr Dr were behind me closer to the sledge; it was strenuous work moving the sledge ahead in the deep snow. When we stopped we checked our rum bottle that Signak had hung around his neck under his clothes so that the rum (*Schnaps*) didn't freeze, for as soon as it hits the air it freezes. It was already so late that we had to look for a site for our night's camp. Singnak went ashore to check out the snow where we could build an *iglu*. We hauled the sledge up as far as possible and then Singnak sawed out snow blocks and we unloaded the sledge. When we had hauled everything up to the site Singnak had finished sawing blocks and then we built *Iglu* No. 2.[7] Herr Dr and I assisted so that it was soon finished. When we had got as far as moving things in, two of us organized the interior and the third man looked after the fire. From the time that we arrived, four and a half hours had passed before the coffee was ready. After we had drunk it we sought our sleeping bags, but they were not very pleasant since they were frozen inside.

*Saturday, 15 December.*

I did not sleep well last night; my feet were so cold that I could not get to sleep. I looked at the clock once; it was 4 o'clock. Singnar was snoring so much that I really envied him that he could sleep. At 9:45 we were ready to head outside. Singnak went hunting; we first went some distance along the island on which we had camped. But then it began to blow more strongly and the snow to drift, so that we didn't dare to go further in that direction, for if it continued to blow and drift like this we might have a problem getting back. We first headed to a small island and from there northwards into a bay, and then we climbed up onto the land. When we'd finished there, we pushed on. I was wearing a pair of J. M.'s pants that were a little long for me; this made walking even more difficult because the snow was so deep. We were again tormented by thirst, and since it wasn't so cold we took handfuls of snow, warmed it somewhat and then ate it, since our mouths were so dry that we could barely survive. We detected almost no wind outside, but when we

---

7. Near Sednirun.

reached the spot where it was blowing this morning, it was still as bad. Our tracks were totally drifted-in, so that we often didn't know which way to go. When we got closer to the *iglu* we could see that Singnak had a seal, since we could see the tracks where he had hauled it up. He was not long back; he had just lit the fire. The first thing we asked him was whether he had any water, but he had not got that far. When we had knocked the snow off our clothes we crawled into the *iglu*. I looked after the lamp, and we first brewed coffee then cooked seal meat. We looked out our rum bottle for the night, but it was all gone. We then had to brew schnapps. We took water with sugar and added alcohol; this made a fine punch. Singnak was of the opinion that it was better than nothing.[8]

### Sunday, 16 December.

At 6 o'clock was wake-up call to drink coffee since we wanted to get away early, but when we emerged from the *iglu* we could not leave; it was exactly high tide, and also really foul weather: snow and wind. Herr Dr and Singnark were the first to emerge and were checking to see if we could depart, as we had arranged with J. M. to be at a certain location by Sunday; we could not get there in one day however, since there was a good foot of snow on the ice. This morning I made another makeshift burner: I made three holes in a butter can, into which the wick was inserted; to another can I attached two strings to make a kettle.[9] The trunk was packed and left in *Iglu* No. 2. We were able to get away around 10 o'clock; we had to haul and could scarcely breathe; the sledge progressed no better than at a snail's pace. Herr Dr had the misfortune to stick his foot in a crack. At 12 o'clock we had to look around for a spot where we could build an *iglu*. But the entire coast consisted of a glacier, and thus we had to keep hauling for a while longer to reach a spot where we could get ashore. Once we had reached the grounded ice Singnar went ashore and looked for suitable snow; he found good snow where we could build the *iglu*. He immediately began sawing snow blocks and we carried our things ashore; once everything was ashore

---

8. Boas did not mention this home-brew in his journal.
9. Diverging somewhat from Weike, Boas wrote the same day: "*Together Wilhelm and I devised an alcohol lamp—this being the item we need most.*"

the *iglu* building went with a swing. It was already quite dark by the time we had finished our *Iglu* No. 3.[10] After we had drunk some water Singnark produced some frozen seal meat that we all got stuck into; he took his big knife and hacked a piece off it; it sounded as if he was chopping bones in two. Once we had had enough meat, we next tackled our soup, which thoroughly warmed our stomachs.

[In his letter-book intended for his fiancée, Franz Boas was philosophizing at a completely different level: *Do you know how I am passing the long evening? I have my Kant* (the German philosopher Immanuel Kant, 1724-1804) *with me and am studying him so that I shall not be too uneducated when I come home. Life here truly transforms people (but only temporarily; when I get to Kikkerton, I am quite sociable). When I think that this evening I,* your *Franz, was contemplating how good a pudding with plum sauce would taste, I almost have to blush. You have no concept of the effect of deprivation and hunger on a person. Perhaps Herr Kant is a good antidote! And when I think, on the other hand, of how a year ago I was among Berlin society and was following all the fine rules of "bon ton," and tonight am sitting in a snow house with Wilhelm and an Eskimo, eating a piece of raw, frozen seal meat, which first has been cut—into pieces with an axe, and in addition am drinking coffee almost greedily, one can scarcely conceive of greater contrasts.*]

*Monday, 17 December.*
The sun's altitude on December 17: 0°.[11] We emerged again at 8:45, when it was still completely dark. Singnak went hunting; when we first set off it was in the totally wrong direction, and we had to retrace our steps for a good distance; we had travelled a good distance when we found that there was grounded ice lying between an island [and the mainland]; we climbed up onto it, but once up there realized that there was no possibility of getting through it, and had to turn back. We made progress thereafter; today, for a short time, we saw the sun appearing on the horizon.

---

10. North of Pamiujang.
11. On that date, and just south of the Arctic Circle the sun barely skims the ice surface on the horizon to the south, i.e., at an angle of 0°. It reaches its lowest height on the winter solstice on 22 December.

We had to turn back at 1 o'clock to get back to our *iglu* before it got dark. When we got back Singnak had still not returned; using my makeshift burner I melted some snow for water; this was a faster operation than with the blubber lamp. Once I had enough water, I lit the blubber lamp too, and the result was that we were able to eat sooner. Singnak returned after we had eaten, but he had no seals; after he had finished eating, we cooked another potful of seal meat; this was our supper.

*Tuesday, 18 December.*

Today we slept late; it was too late for Singnak to go hunting, and we could not go far either. Herr Dr said we should go to *iglu* No. 2 to fetch some supplies. It was -35°. Just as we went down onto the ice, the sun was rising. When we got further out onto the ice, we experienced a breeze, which quickly grew in strength. We constantly felt our faces freezing and had to stop to thaw the affected spot. Fetching the supplies was not essential; we still had enough to live on. Since the sun was visible and it was fairly clear, Herr Dr first measured the sun's altitude and then made observations from on land until around 1 o'clock. Then we went back out on the ice and checked to see when the sun set. It disappeared at 1:30. We then returned to our *iglu*; it was -40°. Singnak's rifle was broken; the spring was where the problem lay and as a result it was inoperable; he had only one shell for his other gun. Herr Dr and I had not brought a gun. In the evening we had a consultation as to what we should do; if the sledge from Kikkerton had not arrived in two days; we decided to set off on foot with some provisions to a camp[12] that lay fifteen miles away, and have ourselves brought back from there. One hopes that this will not be necessary.

*Wednesday, 19 December.*

Today we emerged early; it was still not even 8 o'clock; Singnak went off hunting with his solitary shell. The moon was shining beautifully and there were many stars. At 9:30 we reached the spot where we had turned back; a little before 11 o'clock we saw the last star in the sky. We walked as far as American Harbour;[13] by then it was noon and we had to turn

12. Anarnitung.
13. Ussualung.

back. We got back to our *iglu*[14] at 8 o'clock, but to our regret discovered that no sledge had arrived. It was -45° in the evening. As Singnak came back he shouted: "*Piterhanlia!*"[15] This was all we needed; we now made preparations for setting off. We would start out at 3 o'clock next morning. Today Singnak had brought some things from the chest,[16] that we wanted to take with us. We still had enough blubber for the lamp to last the night, but that was all we had; once it was gone we could not cook any longer, and this was the main reason that we had to set off.

*Thursday, 20 December.*

We got up at 3:30 and dressed ready for travelling, and in preparation for our trip cooked some Carne pura soup. It was 5 o'clock by the time we had consumed it; then we set off, each putting his best foot forward. We had left all our belongings, apart from some food, which was transported in a bear skin, hauled by Sing[n]ak's dogs; this meant we experienced frequent stops. As we reached American Harbour, we had to endure a north wind so that our faces were constantly freezing, and because we were tramping through deep snow our feet were constantly cold; I was still wearing *kamiks*[17] that were too small. But the situation improved for us when we left the land on this side, and were no longer travelling west; but now we were repeatedly clambering over floes that had been rafted over each other. I can't remember how many times I tumbled head first. I felt some pain in my feet and told Herr Dr about it, but this was no help; I still had to keep running. Moreover Singnak's dogs now refused to pull and stayed lying in the ice; now we had to leave the bear skin there and Signak left his lance there too. Now our entire remaining food supply was placed in a small bag that I slung over my shoulder. Towards evening we heard the howling of dogs several times, but we couldn't spot any tracks. As we wandered around searching in vain for tracks, every few minutes we stood still and listened for

---

14. *Iglu* No. 3.

15. I. *pitaqanngilaq*: I didn't get any!, i.e., seals. Identification and translation of this sentence was provided by Kenn Harper (Letter to Ludger Müller-Wille, 4 December 2007).

16. At *Iglu* No. 2.

17. Knee-high boots made from ringed seal and bearded sealskins.

the cracking of the fast ice, in order to locate the land, for in the fog we could not go any further. But since we could hear the fast ice cracking all around us, we finally chose a specific direction; by navigating by the stars; by this method we reached a small island, but Singnak did not recognize it. We wandered around to look for other landmarks but we spotted nothing more, and then pushed on to another island which Singnak did not recognize either. Repeatedly, as we proceeded, Singnak kept shouting in Eskimo towards the land, in the hope that some native might hear him and could tell us where we were. But we got no answer so that we could not discover where we were. At the second location where we reached land, we looked for an area where there was no snow on the ice and we could wander around; here we partook of our meagre supper. We took a few pieces of bread; hacked off some chunks of butter with a knife, and shook them onto our gloves and ate the butter in chunks along with the bread; we stuck some sugar in the snow and then licked it up as our source of water. This is how we consumed our supper as we walked about. Singnak headed off in both directions from where we stood, but reported that he could not find anything. Then we pushed on again, until we again found a spot where we could wander around again. Singnak again went off to search for landmarks. Herr Dr and I wandered around the area; at this point we were fighting drowsiness, but we dared not sit or lie down. In this way, every few moments we crashed into each other like train buffers, so that one of us flew to one side and the other to the other side; this gave us a fright each time. Singnak had already been gone for almost three hours; the moon had risen when he got back and then we started off again, sometimes over fast ice, sometimes in deep snow. Finally we came across sledge tracks, but now Singnak led us in the opposite direction. Nobody can imagine how energetically we ran along the sledge track; but then we reached a point where we could see the frost-smoke from water holes.[18] Now we had to turn around and cover that entire distance again; we had run a good four miles along the sledge track. Finally we reached Anernatu[19] at 7 a.m. on the 21st and crawled into Ocheito's *iglu*.[20]

---

18. Sarbuqdjuaq.

19. Anarnitung.

20. Ocheitu or Oqaitung, who resided at the German Polar Station in 1882–83; *Iglu* No. 4.

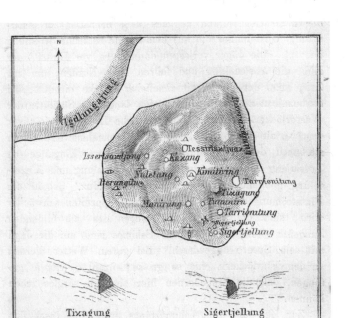

Anarnitung Island with Inuit *iglus* (*Schneehäuser*), boats (*Boote*), prehistoric houses (*Alte Hütten*), and ponds (*Teiche*), Cumberland Sound, 1883-1884 (Boas 1885a:77).

*Friday, 21 December.*

As we entered Ocheitu's *iglu* the [Inuit] moved out from under their covers and we crawled under them. A young woman (*Fräulein*) even pulled the covers up over me. Ocheitu and his wife took care that we received dry clothes, and in due course his wife prepared our supper, so that we could first rest somewhat. After I had slept a little, I checked my feet and to my dismay saw that two toes on my right foot and one on my left foot had developed frost blisters. Ocheitu lanced the two on my right foot immediately and bandaged them; those on the left foot were still quite hard.[21] The woman occupied herself with drying our

---

21. Franz Boas reported briefly: "*Wilhelm has frozen two toes on his right foot slightly, but has frozen the big toe on his left foot seriously.*" What is involved here is third-degree frostbite, which leads to the dying-off of the skin layers down to the bone and ultimately to gangrene, which at that time was cauterized with *Höllenstein*; the wounds heal

clothes all day. Ocheito went out to fetch our bearskin, and in so doing met Kanaker who had come from Kikkerton with our things; when he reached our *Iglu* No. 3 and saw that we had departed, he had loaded all our stuff on his sledge and had caught up with us; now we had everything here, except for adequate amounts of tea and coffee.

*Saturday, 22 December.*
Today we travelled with Ocheito to Scharbutu[22] where the water holes are; as I walked out onto the ice from shore I discovered that I had difficulty walking, my feet were so painful; we sat on the sledge for a good two hours, until we arrived there and I again had to get off the sledge. I discovered that it was impossible for me to walk due to the pain; I had to walk around until the *iglu*[23] was finished and I was able to creep in and crawl into my sleeping bag. Ocheito helped me inside.

[Franz Boas wrote: *Wilhelm, who has frozen both his big toes, insisted at Anarnitung that he was able to walk; but here he is so ill that I can undertake nothing with him, and sent him straight into the iglu that Ssigna and Ocheito built. … If only Wilhelm does not get sick; the last few days have been really trying.*]

*Sunday, 23 December.*
This morning Ocheito and Singnak went hunting. Herr Dr went with them. I had to stay in my sleeping bag with my blessed feet. During the night one of them had swollen so much that I had to cut the bandage away with my knife; everything inside my sleeping bag was covered with pus. When Ocheito bandaged me up again, he said that that foot was still frozen inside; on the other the frostbite was on the outside. Herr Dr did not stay away for long since he had broken his pencil and hence could not do anything. The sledge that had brought our *kolitangs*

---

slowly and leave scars, and result in pain and long-term problems when walking (cf. von der Eltz and Schick 2007). *Höllenstein* (*Lapsis infernalis*) or lunar caustic (silver nitrate) was then used as a disinfectant and a cauterizer (nowadays antibiotics are administered to remove dead flesh in wounds or gangrene). Inexplicably, Boas called this medicine *Bitterstein* or nephritis, a crystal compound, said to have a healing effect.
22. Sarbuqdjuaq.
23. *Iglu* No. 5 at the Sarbuqdjuaq water holes.

remained nearby. Ocheito and Singnak soon came back also; first we cooked supper then travelled back to Anarnitung. I rode on the second sledge since its load was lighter, and hence would soon be back again. I was put in my sleeping bag and then lashed on the sledge. The Eskimos derived great pleasure from tying up a "gentleman."[24] I was tied up so tightly that I couldn't make the slightest movement; and this is how I was transported. When I reached Anarnitung three men grabbed my sleeping bag and carried me to the entrance to the *iglu* and then I was pulled inside.

[Franz Boas noted in addition: *Unfortunately, Wilhelm's left foot is still very badly frozen, so I probably can't take him to Kikkerton. We stuck him in his sleeping bag, lashed it on Nuvukdjua's sledge, and travelled home together.*]

*Monday, 24 December.*

We were wakened at 2 o'clock since Herr Dr and Ocheito were travelling to Kikkerton. Kanaker and Singnak were setting off in a different direction to pick up the trunk from *Iglu* No. 2, and since my feet were so bad I remained in Ocheito's *tupik*[25] until Herr Dr came back from Kikkerton. First I made a list of everything Herr Dr was to bring back. Before he left I brewed up the last of the coffee; now all I had left was a little tea. Kanaker set off quite a long time later than the others because one of his dogs had run away, and could not be found. I didn't hear what time they left. At noon Ocheito's wife made tea for me, and when I checked the bread bag, I discovered what the situation was there. In it were two large chunks of bacon and very little bread. On Christmas Eve I had a mug of water and bread. I couldn't have any tea if I wanted to have any for Christmas. I went to bed early since I hadn't slept much the night before since six of us were packed in, in a row. We were arranged as one packs herrings—head-to-toe alternately. Kanaker was constantly sticking his feet in my face.

---

24. In this connection, meaning a European. It is obvious that Weike got a kick out of this title.

25. Wilhelm Weike meant *iglu* and not *tupik* (tent); *Iglu* No. 4.

*Tuesday, 25 December.*

My two sleeping companions scarcely made a move towards getting up, and hence I too had to stay in bed, since the lamps were not in a good condition and hence it was cold. We got up at 9 o'clock; my breakfast was raw seal meat; at noon the woman made tea for me; with which I ate some bread; in the afternoon she cooked seal meat. When it was ready I got two pieces of ribs and a pannikin (*Panenk*) full of soup, which did my stomach a world of good. In the evening three men provided great entertainment, seeing who could produce the best music; they sang and danced here in the little entrance passageway. They were here until 10 o'clock and when they left we again had some cooked seal meat with soup and then we headed for our sleeping bags.

*Wednesday, 26 December.*

Ocheito's wife has arranged things so that I get tea once per day, but every time I drink some of it, she adds more water and boils it up, so that there is always tea available. Otherwise the refrain is: Where are you, seal? I am really enjoying the seal meat; I'll soon be able to walk on my bad foot again.

*Thursday, 27 December.*

Here I think that God nourishes him who sleeps for a long time, for when I am awake Ocheito's wife seems to think that I must always eat. First there is raw seal meat; next hour cooked seal meat; and finally frozen; this goes on all day long. I don't care so much about food; if only my feet were in good shape again. I've already had to cut away a good chunk of skin away from the big toe of my left foot, and the nail is still waggling to and fro; it will probably drop off some time. Since Herr Dr and Ocheito left we constantly have visitors here, from morning to night. There were three men and two women here this evening; first they were singing, and one of them played the *Killaute*,[26] which was made of a tin plate. When this finished they practiced some conjuring, so that it was 10:30 by the time they left and I crawled into my sleeping bag.

---

26. I. *qilaut*: a shaman's drum, a round wooden frame with a handle, over which de-haired sealskin is stretched; here, since there was no proper *qilaut* available, a tin plate took its place.

*Friday, 28 December.*

This morning when the so-called tea-soup was ready, I got out my tin box in which I had been keeping my breadcrumbs; I consumed this last little remnant and then I had nothing left. I had no inkling that Herr Dr was so close to Anarnitung. It was 1:45 when the sledges were spotted, to my great delight; it wasn't long at all before they arrived. Soup was prepared immediately, and we couldn't wait for it to be ready. After we had eaten we put up our Christmas tree[27] and celebrated Christmas, which made us very happy. Once the candles had burned out, the tree was packed up and stowed away again, and then we concentrated on my feet. The skin was cut away completely from my left big toe; the nail had to come off too, but it was still connected at one side; in the case of the right foot the skin was simply removed completely underneath, and then the foot was bandaged.

[Franz Boas reported: *Wilhelm's toe does not look as bad as I had feared. The nail and part of the ball have dropped off.*]

*Saturday, 29 December.*

This morning Ocheito went hunting and Herr Dr went out too. I was left alone with the women; I would have preferred to go out too, but for the moment this is not possible; I have all I can do to trundle out of the *iglu*, because of my feet. At 12 o'clock I prepared the soup, so that when Herr Dr came back, it would be waiting for him. It wasn't too late when he arrived and he was really pleased that everything was ready and that we could eat. In the evening when Herr Dr checked my feet, the right one was better, but when we looked at the left one I thought I would burst. The nail was still firmly attached on one side, and was terribly painful; when it was being cleaned on the side where it was attached, it pushed into the flesh on the other side, so that, in the end, I even experienced a minor fainting attack, but not too serious.

*Sunday, 30 December.*

Herr Dr went out again today, and since it was Sunday I wanted to cook something special; I made a cooking pot from a tin can and cooked

---

27. Apparently, Boas and Weike had brought an artificial Christmas tree, decorations and candles from Minden.

plums for dessert, since we happened to have some here. In the evening I treated my feet myself; I cut everything away and then washed them and Herr Dr bandaged them.

*Monday, 31 December.*
Today we got up at 6 o'clock and after we had had our coffee, and as day was breaking, Herr Dr set off with Ocheito' sledge. I had the meal ready early, but today they stayed out for a long time, for it was already quite dark when they came back. Ocheito had been lucky today; he had shot two seals. And it was high time too, since today we had had to get some blubber from others for our lamp. Once Herr Dr had undressed, we had our meal. As soon as this meal was out of the pot, we refilled it for the evening meal. After eating Herr Dr first had a short sleep, but it did not last long; thereafter several natives came in and one of them sat down on Herr Dr's feet. That was the end of his snooze. By then the chocolate was ready, with which we wanted to close out the old year; when we were ready we organized things for our New Year's Eve celebration. Herr Dr gave Ocheito a bottle of cognac, while we had a bottle of Swedish punch. But now we were short of a glass. But we did have a can that had contained smoked sausage spread; I cut it down and made a drinking cup out of it. Then Herr Dr set a plate of cookies on our table, and we played a game of 66. And so we enjoyed a pleasant evening. But our bottle of punch ran out, and then the cognac met the same fate. At precisely midnight Herr Dr went outside and fired three shots from Ocheito's gun, to greet the New Year of 1884.

# January 1884

*Tuesday, 1 January 1884.*
*The New Year has begun,*
*God has given it to us.*

Today Herr Dr set off with Ocheito for a few days to a fiord[28] located nearby. Ocheito's wife was sick too, so now we were good company for

---

28. Kangertlukdjuaq.

each other; one of us lay on one side of the *iglu* and the other on the other side in front of the lamp. This afternoon another woman and a man were here conjuring. This was the first time that I was in the *iglu* when they were conjuring. The weather is very consistent—still very cold.

[Franz Boas reported: *Ocheito was uncommonly amused by the fact that in our first iglu at Ssednirun Wilhelm had frozen his nose in his sleeping bag.*]

*Wednesday, 2 January.*
We have a bad situation here: if one of the natives is sick, rather than take medicine they prefer to practice *ankuten* [conjuring]. Herr Dr had told the woman that she ought to gargle; she placed the medicine beside her, crawled under her skins and fell asleep and would not be roused. Yesterday evening I had given her some linen to make a cold compress; she had laid it aside and that was that. This morning I prepared another panful of gargling mixture, and demonstrated it for her; but that did not help much either. At 2 o'clock Herr Dr came back; coffee had just been prepared for me, then more water was added to it, and then there was enough for the entire group. We enjoyed a very good appetite. In the evening Herr Dr made more observations.

*Thursday, 3 January.*
This morning, when we got up, Herr Dr first took another observation, and then we had our coffee. They did not go out today, but had a rest day instead. Over the course of the afternoon Herr Dr was taking photos again,[29] and then we had lunch. By then it was already dark again. We had a good amount of *Karjak*[30] after which we had a good afternoon snooze. Ocheito's wife moved to another *iglu*, and here one of us was snoring louder than the other. In the evening Ocheito was telling Herr Dr stories, which made him laugh a lot, and then we had a leisure evening playing 66.

---

29. These photos did not survive, because Franz Boas was not successful in developing the glass plates.
30. I. *qajuk*: seal fat soup or broth.

*Friday, 4 January.*

We got up at 6:30, and then things were made ready for a three-day trip. Herr Dr had already gone outside, but came back in again to write a letter to J. M., since somebody was to travel to Kikkerton, and bring back things for us. One of my toes is fortunately healed again, but there is still a deep hole in the other one; so I still have to be patient. Towards evening we had a change of weather; it became warmer, and we had a south wind with snow. In the evening two men again came in to *anku-ten*. While this was going on I fell asleep; I woke up again after 11 o'clock.

*Sunday, 5 January.*

The weather was still the same: snow and a warm wind. But Ocheito's wife showed no signs of improvement, since she refused to gargle; she was constantly making an effort to bring up phlegm from her throat, and thereby made the situation even worse. The man Padlukulu, who wanted to go to Kikkerton, had not set off because of the snow. Herr Dr and Ocheito came back at 1:30; they had been unable to do anything outside due to the snow; now Ocheito wanted us to move to another *iglu* because his wife was sick, and so that they could conjure better. The sledge had not set off for Kikkerton because of the driving snow, and since it was quite warm, we got our things ready to travel back, since, as long as the woman was sick Herr Dr could not do anything here.

*Sunday, 6 January.*

We had quite a night last night. His wife was coughing constantly, and Ocheito was singing at the same time, so that we could not sleep; I was happy to see the morning coming, but at that point I fell asleep. We got up at 6 o'clock and got dressed ready to travel. Once the coffee was ready we drank it, then they got the sledges ready, so that we were able to get away around 9 o'clock; as we drove off from Anarnitung I was sitting astride a sledge, as one sits a horse, holding on firmly with both hands. When we reached the ice we found the snow there was deep, so that our progress was slow. We were travelling with Kalakalu;[31] he kept whipping his dogs, but the snow was so soft that we still were not making any speed. It was not long before another sledge caught up with us, since it

---

31. Padlukulu.

was travelling faster, and passed us, since it was not so heavily laden. We were travelling over chaotic pressure ice. Around 4 o'clock we reached Imigen where we planned to spend the night. As we travelled across the pressure ice the sledge at times stood almost vertically. On our arrival I went into an *iglu* and undressed; just as I was undressed Herr Dr shouted that we would be staying somewhere else. I had to dress again and move to another *iglu*. We stayed with Teisen.[32]

[Franz Boas noted: *A good day for Wilhelm's feet.*]

*Monday, 7 January.*
Last night we had lain down for the night at 9 o'clock, but at 12:30 Teisen got up again; he was bound for Kikkerton too, and wanted to get away. But we snuggled down again until around 3 o'clock, but we got no peace thereafter, and we had to get up. The coffee had been brewed before 12:30; we set off at 3:30. We had four sledges, so that it was quite a convoy of sledges. At first the going was very bad, and by the time we reached some good ice it was getting dark and once again we had to navigate by the stars to see where to go. We travelled all day; it was not particularly cold. We reached Kikkerton around 4 o'clock; the first thing we did was have a meal, since we had had nothing all day.

---

32. Tyson, also Napigang, at Imigen, *Iglu* No. 6. He was probably named after captain Tyson of the *Georgina* who was in Cumberland Sound in 1860 (cf. Hall 1865:135).

# Frostbite and recovery at Qeqerten (January 8 to April 10)

*Tuesday, 8 January.*
It feels great to be in a house again, when one has been out in the open for so long. My left foot was cauterized with *Höllenstein* today, which was quite a feeling! I was glad when Herr Dr set it aside. In the evening it began to blow out of the north again.

*Wednesday, 9 January.*
Last night the *Höllenstein* gave me a lot of pain, and the north wind was blowing so strongly that I awoke from sleep quite often. We got up at 9 o'clock. Herr Dr did not feel well and stayed in bed almost all day. But towards evening he felt better; the wind dropped too; it was a really beautiful, moonlit evening and most of the visiting natives got ready to head back.[1] Towards evening all of J. M.'s dogs ran off across the ice.

*Thursday, 10 January.*
As I was getting up this morning Uschuk[2] came in and said that the molasses had overflowed. The workroom was almost half full of molasses; it took us all morning to clean it all up. Once I had finished my work, I tackled my feet; I pulled off one nail almost completely. Herr Dr arrived with the *Höllenstein,* but I had already covered the foot up. The dogs had all returned except for two.

*Friday, 11 January.*
There was quite a strong Kingnait wind[3] today, so that the land was largely cleared of snow. Today J. M. sent a native off with a sledge to look for the two dogs, but when he came back the dogs that had run

---

1. To Anarnitung.
2. Ursuk.
3. A northeast wind blowing over the Qeqerten archipelago coming out of Kingnait Fiord.

off were not with him. I had quite a lot to do with my feet since yesterday evening I had forcibly removed the nail from my right foot, and now, this evening, Herr Dr came and cauterized them both with the *Höllenstein*, which was far from pleasant for me. He said that with each cauterization my feet would be better two weeks sooner.

*Saturday, 12 January.*
We now get up so early, so that we might finish our coffee by 8 o'clock, at which J. M. is far from happy. Jenises[4] had to go off again this morning to look for the two dogs; it was not very cold. J. M. was not too pleased about it, but still the entire floor had to be washed. Kakuschar[5] had made a large slipper for one of my feet. Herr Dr was packing up things that we no longer need here. My foot was cauterized and the two dogs came back.

*Sunday, 13 January.*
Yesterday evening the cooper was here, and so we brewed a small pot of coffee; hence it was after 11 o'clock before we headed for bed, and we got up at 9 o'clock this morning. After we had had our coffee I had to look after my feet because one of them is so painful. Herr Dr came and checked on it and cauterized it again, in order to remove the dead flesh. It is a real pain when one can't use one's feet.

[Franz Boas showed his concern: *Wilhelm has a lot of pain in his feet, which I am now burning with a jade stone.*[6]]

*Monday, 14 January.*
I slept badly last night; one of my feet felt as if it was on fire, to the point that I renewed the bandage. J. M. was making a coffin for a child that had died. Herr Dr was packing things up, and I was getting things ready to do laundry. It was moderately cold and fairly clear weather. In the evening Herr Dr had a man from Saumia here,[7] drawing maps, and at 10 o'clock he took observations.

---

4. Jenissy.
5. Kakodscha.
6. Actually *Höllenstein;* see footnote under 22 December 1883.
7. Anarsin from Saumia, a large peninsula of Baffin Island, southeast of Qeqerten.

*Tuesday, 15 January.*

Today the Saumia Eskimos[8] left again; there was a light wind but it was colder than it has been this year so far. Our thermometers are broken— two of them were blown away during the last Kingnait wind. And I can make nothing of the English thermometre [with scale in Fahrenheit]. In the forenoon my left toe was cauterized, so that it was almost completely white from the *Höllenstein*. I placed a board under my foot so that it was not in contact with the ground.

*Wednesday, 16 January.*

Today the temperature had dropped again to -38°, with a fairly steady west wind. J. M. went off to check how his dogs run in harness. He equipped himself as an Eskimo does for a long trip, with rifle, lamp, and a large knife on the sledge. During our winter trips we had travelled around without any means of protection.[9] In the evening it was 41°.

*Thursday, 17 January.*

Today Herr Dr went to the lookout to take observations. Today it was decided that the travels would begin again. Simi (J. M.) wanted to set off with a sledge and Herr Dr wanted to go with him. Now we had plenty to do, to get everything ready. Herr Dr went to the storehouse and unpacked things; I had to bake pancakes for their departure. In the evening a sledge arrived from Anarnitung, bringing news of Ocheito.

*Friday, 18 January.*

The man from Anarnitung[10] wanted to go back today; he had reported that Tyson was no more willing to have J. M. in his *iglu* than Herr Dr; J. M. was worried and didn't want to travel with Herr Dr.[11] Herr Dr

---

8. Anarsin and Tom.

9. They had both been lucky that during these trips they did not encounter any polar bears (*Ursus maritimus*).

10. Nuvukdjua.

11. The issue here concerns Tyson who had his *iglu* at Imigen. Franz Boas did not mention the connection with James Mutch, only that he himself was not welcome at Tyson's! Tyson, along with other Inuit was convinced at this point that Franz Boas, who was trying to help the sick Inuit, was actually the cause of the epidemic and thus was blamed for the numerous deaths (diary entry for 17 January 1884, Boas in Müller-Wille 1998:168-169).

could not go with this sledge, since he was not yet ready; J. M. wanted to lend Herr Dr his dogs, and then he [Franz Boas] wanted to travel there with Singnar on the 19th. The temperature is hovering between -38 and -40°; moderate wind.

### Saturday, 20 January.
Herr Dr wanted to set off at 6 o'clock this morning, but we overslept; so now he could not leave today. At 9 o'clock he went out with Singnar to survey the island[12] further, since we had not finished it. In the meantime I had to clean the stove and to clean up our room. I did not need to do any cooking at noon, but was supposed to have a meal ready by 5 o'clock. Suddenly Herr Dr came back at 2 o'clock. Now I had to rush to get something ready.

### Sunday, 20 January.
We got up early today. All of a sudden Herr Dr began shouting; it was already 9:30. This was not such a disaster; one can sleep here better than anywhere else. When I rolled out my mate[13] already had the water boiling; I made coffee and sliced some ham to fry it; it was ready by the time I had laid the table. At 3 p.m. we had rabbit soup; it was so solidly frozen inside the house that I first had to chop it up.

### Monday, 21 January.
Ito came at 4:30 and lit the fire; we got up at 5 o'clock. Herr Dr wanted to set off again today. Singnar was here too, and harnessed the dogs. It was around 6 o'clock when they departed;[14] so now I was here alone again, and wouldn't be able to utter a word of German, except when I was cursing; and then nobody could understand me. I made tea for J. M. and took it to him in bed. At lunchtime I ate alone. In the afternoon he brought some schnapps from the storehouse; its temperature was -37°, yet still not frozen. Rather than the Eskimos getting some of it to drink, a bucket of rum was diluted with a bucket of water; this was the Eskimos' "schnapps."

---

12. Manitung.
13. His assistant, one of the Inuit employed by Mutch; Weike writes *"Matt"* (mate).
14. For Anarnitung.

[Franz Boas explained Weike's situation as follows: *Wilhelm must still stay at home, since his foot is still not better. The right one is sound again, but there is still a substantial hole in the left one… It is really good that this has not happened to me; what would I have done if I had lost all this valuable time.*]

*Tuesday, 22 January.*
Today the sky was far from clear; sunshine was visible on the mainland to the northeast, but the Kikkertons lay in fog. We had country food at lunchtime. In the afternoon J. M. went out on the ice again. In the evening Herr Dr's sledge already came back again and Mutch's dogs along with it. The Eskimo Captain Kischu[15] had been off looking for a wife. Poor man! At 10 p.m., -42°.

*Wednesday, 23 January.*
My foot is well on the mend, I am now cauterizing it daily with *Höllenstein*. It is the greatest thing when I am chatting with Mosch,[16] half in English, half Eskimo; I string together the words that I know, so that he can understand; then he says it correctly in English. I can understand well enough, but can't compose a reply. In the evening Palakalu and Hanebaldjsek[17] arrived from Anarnitung and reported that Ocheito's wife had died. Captain Rosch also arrived. -40° when it got dark in the evening.

*Thursday, 24 January.*
Palukalu and Hanebaldjsek started back this morning. Captain Rosch was here in the morning. In the afternoon J. M. went out again with young dogs harnessed to his sledge, since they have to learn to pull. We are now eating country food every day. It was clear over the Kikkertons today; every day we check the sun, to see how much higher it is. -40° when it got dark.

---

15. Keiju, captain of one of the Scottish whaleboats run by Inuit.
16. Mutch.
17. Padlukulu and Hannibal Jack.

*Friday, 25 January.*
Today the temperature was -47°. One wouldn't believe how one pays attention to subtle changes here, particularly how much higher the sun rises each day. Today it lit up our chimney for the first time, but not the roof, since it is still not high enough. Then we again focused attention on when it set: 10 past three o'clock. As it got dark J. M. came to me in the workshop and said: "Weicke, make up a really good fire."[18] But I didn't at first know why; the temperature was -48°.

*Saturday, 26 January.*
This morning the thermometer still read -48°; in the house we had a hotter fire than ever before, but we still could not get the temperature inside up to 15°. In the morning I washed the dishes; in the workshop when they mopped the floor it froze; in the afternoon the temperature rose to -44°. Today the sun did not reach the roof; I didn't notice when it rose.

*Sunday, 27 January.*
It was a dismal day, but not very cold. The temperature was only -39½° throughout the day. The sun almost appeared; for the first time it shone on the roof. Now we nurture a hope again that each day it will rise higher. In the evening it was still -39½°.

*Monday, 28 January.*
It was fairly clear, but there was fog over Kinneid; not very cold, -38° in the morning. Today J. M. took a walk to Hepeland and inspected our cairn.[19] Country food for lunch. In the afternoon we had a general gun-cleaning session since they really needed it. In the evening we had a great choice of food, to the point that we didn't know where to begin. Very warm: -30°.

---

18. This is the only time that Wilhelm Weike wrote his surname, namely "Weicke," as it does appear in some early historical records and documents. The copier rendered his name in Roman script.
19. What is meant is the island that the whalers called "Happy Land" (Akugdliruq), north of Qeqerten Harbour, on which Weike had built a cairn.

*Tuesday, 29 January.*

It was very dull today, but not cold. At noon it was only -21°. J. M. went out to fetch ice. I was washing. In the afternoon the wind got up, with drifting snow; in the evening it was -23°. In the evening Captain Rosch and his wife[20] came visiting.

*Wednesday, 30 January.*

This morning it was overcast; this morning I made up Herr Dr's bed with fresh sheets so that everything would be in good order when he arrived. In the evening two sledges arrived from Imigen with furs; they said that Herr Dr was on his way to Aniartun. I made coffee for these strangers and Mosch settled things with them as to their furs. I had just sat down to write when Herr Dr came in the door.

*Thursday, 31 January.*

We got to bed late last night, and at 4:30 this morning Uschuk arrived to go to [work]. When I got up later he was lying asleep in the workshop. In the morning we had all sorts of things to do, to get things in order. Captain Rosch was here a few times. In the evening we made things ready for Singnar, since he wanted to get off again[21] with the dogs.

# February 1884

*Friday, 1 February.*

Today was not as gloomy as yesterday; as Uschuk was lighting the fire J. M. enquired about the wind strength. It was also quite cold: -31½° in the morning and it stayed there all day. Today the Eskimos built a large *iglu* for furs because J. M.'s fur store was full. In the evening it was -35°.

*Saturday, 2 February.*

Nothing happened here all day. There was a lot of discussion as to how we could most easily get back here [home]. This morning Captain Rosch

---

20. A local Inuit woman.
21. To Anarnitung.

had gone back to Nenantulik.[22] From here the Eskimos wanted to go to Palli[23] and Herr Dr did not know what he should do; whether he should go there with them or not. In the evening they came to say that they did not want to leave yet, since a child had died.

### Sunday, 3 February.

This morning the child was alive again, and therefore they wanted to depart. We had just finished our coffee when they arrived. Now there was a mad rush, to get Herr Dr's things in order; he wanted to go with them and to buy dogs. It was already noon by the time we got everything ready. I got a meal ready for Herr Dr and then he set off; it was 1 o'clock when they drove off. In the evening the child died after all.[24] This morning it was -30°.

### Monday, 4 February.

I did not feel well today, but said nothing about it. In the evening the cooper was here; but I couldn't stand it any longer and had to confess to not feeling well; my face was quite blue.

### Tuesday, 5 February.

Yesterday evening I took a good slug of warm cognac and wrapped myself securely in my bed sheets so that I wouldn't be cold. I felt better today, but I had to be careful as to what I ate. There was a strong wind and blizzard all day; Herr Dr came back in the evening, since he had been unable to go any further. When we went to bed the wind was even stronger. Herr Dr was glad that he was back home.

### Wednesday, 6 February.

The wind blew strongly all night, and continued to do so today, with heavy drifting snow; when I got up this morning it was -4° in the room; the heat was going up the chimney.

### Thursday, 7 February.

Overcast and blizzard.

---

22. Naujateling.
23. Padli on Davis Strait, at the east side of Kingnait Pass.
24. A boy, who died of diphtheria.

*Friday, 8 February.*

It was a gloomy day with a strong wind. In the afternoon I wanted to do some baking but did not have enough flour in the house. In the meantime three sledges arrived from Annanitu; Ocheito came with them. He is quite up-beat again; he told us that he wanted to take another wife.

*Saturday, 9 February.*

Today I was quite busy, cleaning and constantly making coffee. In the evening there was discussion about seal hunting; the natives at Annanitu had no bullets left, so Seniges and I had to spend the evening pouring bullets; we had finished by 10 o'clock. Today I was wearing *komings* for the first time.[25]

*Sunday, 10 February.*

Today was an early start because Ocheito and Kiker were to go to Somen Fiord[26] to fetch walrus meat. Sledges arrived in the afternoon; I was at the cooper's at the time, and found strangers in the house when I got back.

*Monday, 11 February.*

Today we got things ready again for Herr Dr's departure; he wanted to go to Anarnitung to hunt seals. It was very fine weather, although just a little cool: -40°. This afternoon there was a black fox out on the harbour ice. J. M. and Ocheito went off to shoot it, but it ran off.

*Tuesday, 12 February.*

I had to get up early, at 5 o'clock to make coffee. Herr Dr got up and woke Ocheito. They set off at 6:30. Today I made a new lid for my chest. Schalm[27] wanted to go hunting today without a lance. Jeniges and Ronodi[28] had forgotten their sledges along with the lance.

---

25. I. *kamik*: skin boots that Wilhelm Weike was wearing for the first time since he got frostbitten.
26. Salmon Fiord / Eqaluaqdjuin.
27. Salmon, the name of an Inuk translated from the Inuktitut (I. *iqaluk*).
28. This name does not occur in Franz Boas' writings.

*Wednesday, 13 February.*
This morning when J. M. shouted, "Wili,"[29] it was 8 o'clock. It was a very fine day; when I got out I said: "It is warm today." When J. M. checked the thermometer it was only -36½°. In the afternoon I was engaged in carpentry work again. The sledge that arrived yesterday evening went back today. In the evening Ateina[30] was here, and listed her names; she has just 30 names.

*Thursday, 14 February.*
The weather today was beautiful, -38°. The sun felt really warm. In the morning I was preparing our travel box again. Another strange sledge arrived in the evening. Lira.[31]

*Friday, 15 February.*
It was overcast today, accompanied by cold. We had a northwest wind. In the evening it strengthened, snowing at the same time.

*Saturday, 16 February.*
Today we had a strong wind and blowing snow. All day long the temperature was -29°. The heat always escaped up the chimney. Lira, and also Tyson, went back today.[32]

*Sunday, 17 February.*
The northerly gale persisted today; one couldn't see even three paces because of the blizzard. We went outside as little as possible, so that the door did not need to be opened.

*Monday, 18 February.*
Last night the storm was as bad as ever; when I got up the temperature in the room was -5°. I watched the barometer over the course of the morning, as it began to rise; in the afternoon the wind dropped and the sky cleared.

---

29. Willi = Wilhelm; Weike was called "Willy" by the whalers and Inuit. Franz Boas addressed him as "*Wilhelm*" and called him with the formal "*Sie*" (You).
30. Atteina.
31. This name is not mentioned by Franz Boas.
32. Lira to Anarnitung and Tyson to Imigen.

*Tuesday, 19 February.*
Today the weather was somewhat better; -32° in the morning. It was very fine all day, and in the evening -33°.

*Wednesday, 20 February.*
Today was absolutely fine weather. I had to get up at 5:30, since a sledge was to go to Salmon Fiord for seal "beef."[33] At noon we had a southerly wind. In the evening Herr Dr came back from the other side [of the Sound].

*Thursday, 21 February.*
During the night there was quite a strong south wind blowing; it was still the same this morning. Until noon the snow was drifting so that one could not open one's eyes. Then the barometer suddenly dropped sharply; the wind first swung round to the west and then it blew quite terrifyingly out of the North. Today a walrus[34] was chopped up inside the house; the stench was terrible!

*Friday, 22 February.*
Today there was still quite a wind blowing, but with very fine weather. In the afternoon Herr Dr and J. M. were discussing going to Salmon Fiord on the 23ʳᵈ; this will involve quite some preparation.

[Franz Boas revealed himself to be more optimistic as to Weike's health: *Wilhelm's foot is now almost better again; only at the tip, where the wound has extended to the bone, is it still refusing to close.*]

*Saturday, 23 February.*
Today people were out and about early; there was quite a strong south wind. Herr Dr did not go with them, since the sky looked so ominous. They[35] drove off with two sledges. They had not long gone when it began to blow more strongly, with drifting snow. Herr Dr was glad that he

---

33. Seal meat; the Inuit and the whalers had cached meat (seal, walrus and whale) under rocks at various hunting locations and brought it to the station in winter.
34. Weike writes "*See Hors*" *(sea horse)*, a term that the Scottish whalers used for walrus at that time.
35. Mutch and the Inuit whom he employed were fetching walrus meat from a cache.

had stayed here; they came back at 5:30. What they brought back was a delicacy [walrus meat] for them. I went to the provisions house in the afternoon; on my way back to the house my eyes were stuck shut with snow.

*Sunday, 24 February.*
There was still quite a strong wind today; at noon we were experiencing a north wind with heavy drifting snow. Two more sledges arrived in the afternoon. This was the first time that we could eat supper by daylight. I was at the cooper's in the evening.

*Monday, 25 February.*
The two sledges headed back again today. Herr Dr made preparations to travel to Warhams Island; he is to leave tomorrow. J. M. got his bread back up until the end of February. In the evening I was chatting to Eischiworn.[36]

*Tuesday, 26 February.*
This morning I had to get up at 4 o'clock to prepare coffee; Herr Dr left at 6 o'clock; the weather was very fine. In the afternoon two sledges arrived from Annanitu. Wilhelm from Nau Antalik[37] also arrived this evening; he spent a couple of hours with us in the evening.

*Wednesday, 27 February.*
Herr Dr has hit upon very fine weather this time; I would have liked to go outside today too, but I just didn't have the time during the day. J. M. went out in the afternoon. Herr Dr came back at 6 o'clock; bears had emptied three casks of oil;[38] they saw quite fresh tracks.

*Thursday, 28 February.*
Today I again got things ready for Herr Dr's departure; he was heading to Nau Antalik. The weather was fair. Bill[39] was here in the afternoon; another sledge came in the evening.

---

36. Eisik.
37. Wilhelm Scherden from Naujateling on the west shore of Cumberland Sound where the *Lizzie P. Simmons* was frozen in.
38. Whale oil.
39. Wilhelm Scherden.

*Friday, 29 February.*
I had to get up at 4 o'clock this morning; I lit the fire and then went and woke Kanaker, who was travelling with Herr Dr. The weather was again really beautiful today. In the afternoon I visited Wilhelm and the cooper. In due course J. M. came looking for me. In the evening J. M. invited them here. Bill wanted to head back tomorrow. Herr Dr had left at 6:30.

[Franz Boas wrote: *Yesterday morning* [28 February] ... *I went to the American station to visit Wilhelm* [Scherden], *the mate. It feels quite wonderful to be able to speak German to some person other than my Wilhelm once again!*].

# March 1884

*Saturday, 1 March.*
The weather was not very pleasant here today. In the afternoon it began to snow again. We had a south wind. A general clean-up.

*Sunday, 2 March.*
Today it was very dismal; the visibility was very poor. In the morning I was was treating my gums first; in the afternoon I dressed warmly and went for a walk on the ice. It was the first time since freezing my feet that I was outside for any length of time.

*Monday, 3 March.*
Today the weather was beautiful. I had to stay in the house in the morning. But at noon, once I had "cleared the decks," I got ready to go out; I went out on the ice to beyond the reef. I walked over Akuliruk and came back to the harbour from the west. After I got home I had to make supper; after the meal *1 Gef. E. Kaetz.*[40]

---

40. This abbreviation (*Gefäß* – jar?) and the name (a firm?) could not be clarified – a drink or medicine?

*Tuesday, 4 March.*

This morning when I stepped outside I felt that it was cold, -36°. North wind. Kanaker came back in the evening. Herr Dr had remained at New Antelik.[41] Later Ikira[42] arrived too.

*Wednesday, 5 March.*

This morning the temperature was only -26°, but even so nobody went out hunting: they came into the house saying: "Too much *ikki*!"[43] The wind was northerly which is not good. In the morning it was foggy; it cleared up over the course of the day. Ikira went back today;[44] Ito and Tom travelled to Salmon Fiord to chop out walrus meat. In the evening another sledge arrived from Biro's camp.[45]

*Thursday, 6 March.*

J. M. travelled to Salmon Fiord today; the weather was foggy, with a northwest wind. Herr Dr was planning to come back today; I was expecting him at 6 o'clock, but it was a little before three when he arrived. We had to wait a long time for J. M.; it was just 9 o'clock when he arrived and supper was burned to a crisp.

*Friday, 7 March.*

It was still foggy today. J. M. headed off for Salmon Fiord again. Here at home they had walrus meat. But he got back home earlier. In the evening another two sledges arrived from Annarnitu.

*Saturday, 8 March.*

It was a really beautiful day today. Fret[46] headed back again. I had plenty to do in the house and could not go out. In the afternoon I was clearing up in the provisions store.

---

41. At Naujateling on board *Lizzie P. Simmons.*
42. Ikera.
43. Too much cold!
44. To Naujateling.
45. Piera at Imigen.
46. Fred Grobschmidt from Naujateling.

*Sunday, 9 March.*

It was very warm today; it was above freezing in the sun. Herr Dr was getting his things ready for a trip to the other side[47] to buy dogs, if the sledge does not arrive from Palli today. It was somewhat above freezing in the sun at noon; half an hour later we checked again; by then it was -18° again.

*Monday, 10 March.*

The weather today was nothing special. A south wind with some snow falling. Herr Dr bought our first dogs, two from Arne, which was all he had. Major sledge repairs.

*Tuesday, 11 March.*

Herr Dr could not leave today due to foul weather, with a very low barometer. In the morning there was a south wind; but towards noon it was northerly. The sledge repairs continued today, first the runners, then … [the sled itself.]

*Wednesday, 12 March.*

This morning the weather was favourable so that Herr Dr could set off. I woke Mukelmann and Arne and the two others who were to go with Herr Dr so that they could have coffee.[48] It took a long time, but at 10 o'clock they drove off with sixteen dogs harnessed to the sledge. It was a beautiful day. A north wind and -26° in the evening.

*Thursday, 13 March.*

Today J. M. set off for Newogen at seven.[49] I had the station all to myself, with Uschuk. We bolted the doors, and then we began cleaning. In the

---

47. To Saumia in the southeast.

48. Muckelmann, actual Inuit name Mummiachia, the only Inuk on whom Franz Boas and Wilhelm Weike bestowed a German nickname. "*Muckelmann*" is a name of endearment for a nice, lovable person, animal or even car, etc.; also "*Muckel*" or "*muckelig*". Muckelmann, Arne and two others, whose names were not given, accompanied Boas on this trip. Another origin could be "muckle man" (Scottish "muckle" = large, giant) by which perhaps Mutch named this Inuk who was taller than others (communication by William Barr, 2010); this could have been derived from the person's Inuit name.

49. Nuvujen.

morning somebody knocked at the door. Uschuk asked who was there, a Kattluna?[50] It was Bill, who had arrived last night. During the day we had some fun with the women. They were not allowed inside the house, so they closed the shutters over the windows. In the evening Tyson came with furs. Hallo Captain. -29° in the evening.

### Friday, 14 March.
The weather was very fine today; it was 30 below zero this morning. Several more strangers arrived today, Ikira. Bill was here in the afternoon. J. M. arrived back at 6 p.m.; another sledge (Keiju's) came with him, and another one. Bill and Cooper were here in the evening.

### Saturday, 15 March.
This morning more sledges arrived. Today J. M. hired his new sealers;[51] the weather was very fine. The large coffee pot was on the stove all day because people were coming in the whole time. Bill started back again this morning. In the evening Ocheito and Palukt also arrived. The sky is always magnificent here, after the sun has set.

### Sunday, 16 March.
The weather was very fine today: -22° with a light northwest wind. In the afternoon I walked out to the west, out of the harbour, and then through Junigen Paschit[52] and back into the harbour past the reef. I was walking on the ice for three hours. There was a very fine aurora in the evening.

### Monday, 17 March.
Today I made two lances and a harpoon. We had a temperature of -23° this morning. Tyson set off for Palie[53] this morning. Ito and Tom went off to hunt caribou. Towards evening we had a sea wind and the sky became overcast; it was no longer so cold, -12°.

50. I. *qallunaq*: a non-Inuit person (plural: *qallunaat*), root *qallu* whose etymological origin is not fully ascertained (Kenn Harper, pers. com., August 13, 2011).
51. Inuit who hunted seal and walrus in the employment of J. M.; Weike wrote the word "*Sielers*" (*sealers*).
52. Union Passage.
53. Padli.

*Tuesday, 18 March.*

-18° this morning; it was very fine weather. J. M. and Jeniges went off to hunt caribou this morning. In the afternoon four sledges arrived from Padli; the party included Schongu and Palalu;[54] they had plenty of freshly killed caribou meat. They came in and drank coffee. Kakusch[55] brought me two caribou legs and told me if I wanted to eat, I should begin right away; then both of them felt ill.

*Wednesday, 19 March.*

The weather was not good today: foggy; one could see no further than the reef. J. M. told me today that I should give Sonnen[56] coffee and bread since we would need him when we went to Padli. He has three wives, and two sisters. Freht[57] went back today; in the evening another sledge arrived from Neu ang.[58] It cleared up in the evening and the wind increased. Temperature -28° in the evening.

*Thursday, 20 March.*

Ito came back late last night; they had seen plenty of caribou but did not get any. It was after 8 o'clock when Si[mi][59] wanted to borrow dogs from J. M. and harness them to go hunting. The temperature this morning was -33°. In the evening Hamla Jek came with furs. -33° outside.

*Friday, 21 March.*

J. M. came back at 20 past midnight last night. It was still -33° in the morning; very fine weather, with little wind. Hannibald Jek went back again today. The natives from Padli were also talking about heading back. Throughout the day I frequently looked out towards the reef to see whether Herr Dr was coming. J. M. said he wished Herr Dr would be home this coming night. -37° at 8 p.m. this evening and -38° at 10.

---

54. Shanguja from Padli, also known as Padli-Shanguja and Padlualu.
55. Kakodscha.
56. Salmon.
57. Fred Grobschmidt.
58. Naujateling.
59. Jimmy.

*Saturday, 22 March.*

Some snow fell today; -24°. Visibility was poor. Cöninak[60] was talking today about wanting to go back. We were doing the best we could. They got a good meal today. A sledge arrived in the afternoon; we thought it was Herr Dr, but when it came ashore we saw that it was Paknat.[61] I had already laid the table for Herr Dr. In the evening we bought a further three dogs from Kenningna. -20°.

[This day's entry is followed by a list of payments for the five dogs bought from the Inuit *Cöninak* and *Schangu* written on an unnumbered sheet inserted into the journal.]

| | |
|---|---|
| *3 dogs from Cöninak.* | 2 handkerchiefs. |
| 2 cans of powder. | 8 lbs lead. |
| 1 packet of matches. | 60 plugs of tobacco. |
| 2 cans syrup. | *Schangu* [2 dogs]. |
| 1 can coffee. | Lead, 4½ lbs. |
| 10 lbs bread. | Biscuit, 200. |
| 2 knives. | Tobacco, 40 plugs. |

*Sunday, 23 March.*

This morning I had nothing more urgent to do than to harness my three dogs[62] and to tie them up. Coginak went back this morning; Schangu was also making preparations today and will be leaving tomorrow. The weather was not very pleasant today; -22° in the morning with some drifting snow and a strong wind; -25° in the evening.

*Monday, 24 March.*

Schangu came with the two dogs this morning. J. M. paid him. They left in the forenoon. -26°. Nakojaschi, Schlerapin, Sammen[63] with his wife and children, and a fellow from Padli. In the morning we had to chop up food for the dogs. I also freed up boxes in the forenoon. Herr Dr came back this afternoon.

---

60. Kenningna who travelled to Qeqerten from Padli.
61. Pakkak.
62. The three dogs acquired from Kenningna.
63. Nakojaschi, Ssegdloaping and Salmon.

*Tuesday, 25 March.*
Easter.[64] We now had a good team of fifteen dogs. Today we discussed what all we had to take along. This morning the temperature was -28°. It was beautiful weather. In the evening Palikulu[65] arrived. Our dogs got a good feed today. J. M. gave us some bread.

*Wednesday, 26 March.*
J. M. was already out of bed by 5 a.m.; he wanted to set off,[66] but the weather did not appear to be very good, and hence he decided not to leave till later. In the morning we gave the dogs a big feed. In the afternoon I brought bread into the house, and then I still tallied the things that we were to take along.

*Thursday, 27 March.*
-14°. There was quite a strong wind with drifting snow today. This morning we first tended to the dogs; thereafter we brought our things into the house and packed up what was to go to Padli, as well as the large chest that had to go home.[67] This was the first day that I no longer had a bandage on my left big toe. The wind was blowing all day. In the evening Herr Dr packed his things up. A sledge arrived from Annaneitu.

*Friday, 28 March.*
I went outside at 5:30 this morning. The weather was quite fair, -24°. Simi and Uschuk were getting the sledge ready; this took a long time this morning. The sledge was still not ... [ready]. It was after 8 o'clock before Herr Dr drove off; at 1 o'clock I received a note from Herr Dr, via Rolti[68] whom Herr Dr had encountered out in the Sound. J. M. arrived at 2:30. In the evening the temperature was -20° and the wind swung into the south.

64. Weike was mistaken; Easter was on April 13 in 1884.
65. Padlukulu.
66. For Warham Island.
67. The chest was to be transported by one of the Crawford Noble Company's ships via Scotland to Germany, where it arrived at Minden in the fall of 1885.
68. One of the Qeqerten Inuit; name not mentioned by Boas.

*Saturday, 29 March.*

We had a strong wind last night; when I went outside this morning there was heavy drifting snow, so that one could not even face into it. None of the natives was outside. J. M. started making a sledge for Herr Dr; I was clearing things up in the attic and sorted out the things belonging to Herr Dr. I sharpened and repaired all the hand-tools, so that we would not have to do so much outside.

*Sunday, 30 March.*

Today the weather was very fine; a great deal of snow had fallen during the night; it was warm and windless. This was the first day that the snow started to melt on the roof. In the afternoon I went for a sledge ride with Ocheito.

*Monday, 31 March.*

More snow had fallen last night; the weather was overcast. Northwest wind, and it snowed all day. Today I was pouring bullets. J. M. was again working on the new sledge, but he had no good bone[69] for it, and could not complete it. Today the natives were building snow blocks around the skins [of their tents], to prevent them from starting to thaw out. Today was the first day that the ice largely melted off the windows in the work-shop. Snow-blindness is now becoming a constant problem.

# April 1884

*Tuesday, 1 April.*

The weather was really foul, although it was not cold; there was heavy snow falling, but it was so warm that the snow felt like rain. In the morning we were checking our guns, and in the afternoon I was pouring bullets for the summer. When I get up at 5:30 in the morning the natives have already gone hunting.

---

69. Whale rib bones that were used as sledge runners; Weike uses "*bone*" in the original text.

*Wednesday, 2 April.*
Today it was still overcast and snowing. In the morning I did laundry; this was the first laundry that I was able to hang outside. In the afternoon we were doing blacksmith's work. Making hooks and lance shafts. We did not see the sun today.

*Thursday, 3 April.*
There was not much wind today and it was fairly clear. J. M. was preparing to travel down to Warham Island; it was twenty minutes before nine when he set off. Along with Uschuk I was digging out boxes that were buried deep in the snow. The sun was showing through occasionally, and hence it was very warm outside. Towards evening we had dense fog and some snow, but one could still see the fast ice.

*Friday, 4 April.*
The weather was foul today with fog and snow throughout the day. A lot of snow had fallen last night and it was very warm. In the afternoon I took care of bread-day,[70] since J. M. was still not back. In the evening Iwi arrived from Neu Antulik.

*Saturday, 5 April.*
Today the weather was somewhat better; the snow had stopped and it was even fairly clear so that one could see the big island.[71] J. M. came back at 9:30. It was very warm throughout the day. When one is outside and it is somewhat above 0°, one finds oneself thinking how amazingly hot it is! Towards evening the fog rolled in again. Iwi did not leave for Palli today.

*Sunday, 6 April.*
The weather was better today. Iwi set off for Palli today, taking a box with him. J. M. told him that two sledges should be sent across to fetch Herr Dr.[72] In the afternoon I was at the lookout, scanning the area; from here one has a fine view of the ice and the high land.

---

70. Weekly distribution of bread to the Inuit employed by Mutch.
71. Qeqertuqdjuaq, northeast of Qeqerten.
72. To take Boas and Weike and their boxes over Kingnait Pass.

*Monday, 7 April.*

Today the weather was quite pleasant. Fred arrived from Neu Antelik today. Simi also came back; in two weeks he had shot two caribou and the other hunter one.[73] At 12 o'clock Herr Dr also came back from Leke Kuddie.[74] Singnar had shot one caribou and Lira three.

*Tuesday, 8 April.*

Today we were working on the sledge that Herr Dr was to have, but it needed a lot of work since we had removed the entire bed; now we had to dig out planks from under the snow and make lashings; this meant we had plenty of work.[75] I was out in the fresh air in the evening.

*Wednesday, 9 April.*

Today we were again packing the boxes that were to go to Palli, and three men were working on the sledge to get it ready. J. M. wanted to lend Herr Dr his dogs so that he could travel with two sledges. Today we were working like never before. It was 7 o'clock when J. M. said the sledge would not be ready. The weather was quite pleasant; I had got my sleeping bag and everything else more-or-less ready.

*Thursday, 10 April.*

The weather today was beautiful, and both our sledges were also ready; hence towards evening we were in a position that we could take our boxes down onto the ice. We took three sledge-loads down, and then we went back to the house to continue working; it was 9:30 before I was about finished.

---

73. Simi, a second Jimmy and a further companion had been hunting.
74. Lake Kennedy / Nettilling.
75. The Inuit sledges were built of whale bones and driftwood, i.e. of individual pieces of wood for the runners and cross pieces which, to provide the essential flexibility, were lashed together with thongs, usually of bearded seal skin.

# By dog team over Kingnait Pass
# and along Davis Strait
# (April 11 to July 18)

*Friday, 11 April.*
At 5 o'clock it was -27°; once I had the fire going I went and woke the Eskimos who were to go with us. At 7:30 the sledges were taken down from Kikkerton onto the ice to load them. We had a total of 33 dogs, and there were five men with the two sledges.[1] In the process one of Herr Dr's dogs became sick, but it was not long before it recovered. We did not harness it with the rest. The weather was beautiful, and we made quite rapid progress. We made a stop at Sabungenut[2] and ate some bread and bacon. Then we pushed on into Kingnait Fiord. I was glad when I was able to take off my snow goggles at 5 o'clock; there were quite a lot of black spots on the land, so that they were no longer necessary. At 6 o'clock we made a halt to build an *iglu*[3]; it was quarter past 12 when we ate supper.

*Saturday, 12 April.*
We got under way again at 5:30; we had a bit of a Kingnait wind, which made it a little cold. We had high mountains on every side where there wasn't a bit of snow. In places the ice was as smooth as a mirror, which was very tough for the dogs. As we got further up the fiord the wind grew even stronger; we unloaded the things that we would need for the night, since this was a good spot for an *iglu*. In fact, we had to unload boxes from the second sledge so that they could get through the rough ice. I had to remain with the boxes. Thereafter I walked behind the sledge, but could not face into the wind; I had to tack. As I reached the sledges we came to two bad spots where the sledges had to be unloaded.

---

1. Franz Boas, Wilhelm Weike, Ssigna, Kikker and Pudlaujang.
2. This place name is not mentioned by Franz Boas.
3. At Niutang.

Sled dog with harness, Baffin Island, 1884 (line drawing by Franz Boas; Boas 1888:532, Fig. 487)

Then we came to a narrow strait between high hills that was not very long, however. When we emerged from it we had reached the head of the fiord. The first sledge was left here; Herr Dr and Ssignar started back while I stayed until Kiker arrived with the second sledge, and then we drove back. We built our *iglu* at the narrow strait.[4] Herr Dr and Palauga brought up the things from the first site where we had thought of building the *iglu*. When they arrived we discovered that the bread bag had been torn open on the rough ice,[5] and hence we had to search for the bread until it got dark. Today we saw a smashed raven's egg and also a second nest. It was 12 o'clock when we ate supper.

[Franz Boas noted dryly: *As he was fetching it in the evening Wilhelm ripped the bread bag and everything was scattered along the trail. We will have to go to retrieve the bread tomorrow morning.*]

---

4. At Kitingujang.
5. The ice near the shore is constantly being raised and lowered by the tide and thereby is broken up and rafted.

*Sunday, 13 April.*

Easter Sunday. The weather today was foul so that we could not go far. A strong wind with drifting snow. The natives had to feed the dogs. Herr Dr and I went out to reconnoitre the route ahead, but we went much further to where the sledges were standing. It was impossible to walk into the wind; the way back was faster because we walked with the wind. The two boxes were brought up, although the dogs could barely pull against the wind.

*Monday, 14 April.*

Today there was still a fair wind blowing; Kiker headed back. We pushed on in order to complete our station; there were places where we were travelling over rocks; at first we would spread a bear skin over the rocks, but at two places we had to unload the sledge and carry the boxes across. At the last of these places we loaded the boxes on the second sledge and drove it across the rocks. Then we had to haul our things across a pond. We occupied a station at the end of the pond; from there to the terraces we had to travel across several ponds. There the sledge was constantly being blown along by the wind with the dogs being dragged behind. We made faster progress with the second load than with the first one since the dogs already knew the way. It was not very late when we reached the *iglu*.[6] Singnar and I had to feed the dogs; when they had finished eating we crawled into the *iglu*.

*Tuesday, 15 April.*

This morning we drove back again; there was still a fair wind blowing with some snow. As we emerged from the rough ice, on one side I had to watch out for the sledge. Before the narrows it was travelling so fast, that I could not jump aside quickly enough and landed between the sledge and the ice, and was dragged along with the sledge; after we'd emerged from the narrows, the sledge was again blown along by the wind. In the course of the morning we saw Robi[7] and Iwi, who had still gotten no further than this.[8] As we emerged from Kinneit we

---

6. At Kitingujang.

7. Robby.

8. They had both left Qeqerten a week earlier.

Wilhelm Weike in Inuit skin clothing holding a dog-whip, Minden, 1885. (Photo: Studio M. Sweers, Minden; *American Philosophical Society*)

Franz Boas in Inuit skin clothing holding a harpoon and imitating seal hunting, Minden, 1885 (Photo: Studio Hülsenbeck, Minden; *American Philosophical Society*)

encountered a south wind with drifting snow, which ultimately became so thick that we could no longer see anything. Near Sa[b]ungenut Iwi had left their *iglu* standing, and we were planning to stay there. But as we started unloading the weather cleared and we drove on further. The snow was very soft and deep, so that we had not gone much further when it grew dark. We stopped near an iceberg and built an *iglu* for the lamp. For sleeping we used the large house alongside the sledge; this is the best house on shore.[9]

*Wednesday, 16 April.*
We got up this morning at 3:30, and after we'd had our coffee we pushed on. Singnar went hunting, while we three drove on to Kikkerton. When we reached the southern tip of Kikertaluk[10] we encountered a north wind with drifting snow. Between Kikertaschuk[11] and Kikkerton the snow lay so deep and was so soft that we could make only slow progress, but when the dogs picked up the Kikkerton trail, we picked up speed. We reached Kikkerton at 12:30. There, for the afternoon, we did nothing but eat. After Kiker had returned, Ink[12] had gone mad and J. M. had had to shoot it.

*Thursday, 17 April.*
Today I was making bullets, both shotgun shells and slugs; I was working at this all day. It was quite clear today. In the evening I had to get things ready for Herr Dr, since he wanted to set off for the west side again. Out on the sound there had been quite a strong wind blowing, with drifting snow, but we had detected nothing here at Kikerton.

*Friday, 18 April.*
We got up at 5:15 this morning, and Herr Dr and Sim[13] set off after coffee. It was very warm today. I spent the entire day getting things together and packing them, and also made an ammunition box, and in the evening traded two knives, a saw, steel, and pipes for ammunition and oilskins with Iiwi. Around eleven it started blowing strongly out of the south.

---

9. Near Qarsaq; they probably erected a "*house*" of snow blocks alongside the sledge.
10. Qeqertalung.
11. Qeqertuqdjuaq.
12. The name of a dog.
13. Jim also known as Ssigna.

*Saturday, 19 April.*

We still had a strong wind out of the south with drifting snow; it was very warm at the same time. Yesterday evening I could not see anything on paper; my eyes could not stand it. And today it was no better. One could do nothing outside today; I was again looking things over and packing them inside the house. In the afternoon I did a thorough clean-up; towards evening it started snowing again. We had a musical evening and some liquor; this did not involve working with papers and my eyes remained all right.

*Sunday, 20 April.*

There was still quite a strong wind from the south today, but very warm. Over the past few days the first birds have been seen here; they always arrive with a south wind. The sky did not clear. In the evening I was at a conjuring session; this was followed by singing and dancing, involving Kiker and Schalewali.[14]

*Monday, 21 April.*

Today we had a strong south wind with drifting snow; over the course of the forenoon the wind swung into the north; the driving snow was so heavy that one could not even see ten paces. Later it became some-what clearer; but towards evening it became thicker again. After 8 o'clock we went down below and dug out the small boat[15] and brought it to the harbour.

*Tuesday, 22 April.*

Today the wind was the same as yesterday's, south wind, force 8[16] with drifting snow; in the afternoon it swung into the north again, equally strong. At noon I was dumping a bucket of water and could not find the house again. Around 6 p.m. it became clearer, -20°. The wind was no longer so strong.

---

14. Charlie; proper name Kakodscha.
15. Boas' boat *Marie* that could be rowed or sailed.
16. Force 8: gale-force, 75 kph.

*Wednesday, 23 April.*
The weather was foul; a south wind with some drifting snow. This morning we were getting the sledge ready. In the afternoon a sledge arrived from Neuwugen with furs. At 9 p.m. Herr Dr came back; later another sledge arrived with furs.

*Thursday, 24 April.*
This morning the wind was southerly at first; over the course of the morning the wind swung to Kinneit and began to blow seriously, with drifting snow. Today we were packing things again and looking over everything that was to go with us. In the afternoon another sledge arrived from Palli, Konignan.[17] In the afternoon I opened the last box of bread, and the things for me very … to Pira.[18]

*Friday, 25 April.*
This morning Herr Dr travelled to Tinitschua[19] for dog food and furs. The weather was nothing special; it became somewhat clearer, but immediately afterwards it was snowing again, and the wind swung from one side to the other. Today I finished packing the large box and nailed up other boxes, so that they can be put out of the way; I also packed the photographic things; in the evening I was at the cooper's.

*Saturday, 26 April.*
This morning the wind was westerly with some snow; it did not become properly clear. One sledge arrived during the morning. In the afternoon I had a thorough clean-up. The wind swung into the south. Kaningna set off for Neu antelik; today the captain's women … weather.[20]

*Sunday, 27 April.*
The weather this morning was beautiful: a very light south wind and clear; in the afternoon I walked out of the harbour to the west. When

---

17. Kenningna.
18. Some words illegible. Pira = Piera.
19. Tiniqdjuarbing. Boas actually started his trip on 26 April and returned on the 29th.
20. It is not clear which Inuit captain and women are meant; the reference to "weather" could not be deciphered.

I was among the rough ice it started to snow so that I had to turn back. Thereafter I was in U's[21] *iglu* until 4:30, but then I had to come back to make tea.

*Monday, 28 April.*
This morning we were out and about early, since at J. M.'s they started work in preparation for going to Warham's Island; they were getting the boats ready; he had fifteen Eskimos working. In the afternoon I was out on the harbour getting the [small] boat ready. In the evening Herr Dr returned. Three sledges were made ready for the trip; they were to be taken down [onto the ice].

*Tuesday, 29 April.*
This morning three sledges started for Warham's Island. The others were here working again. We were packing things again; in the afternoon it started snowing again. After finishing work the men were outside playing ball. At 8 p.m. the temperature was only -11°. A minor detail: the end of April.

*Friday, 30 April.*
It was not very clear today. Herr Dr sent two Eskimos with a sledge and dog food to Kinneit.[22] In the morning I finished packing the large box; thereafter I had to polish the steel runners.[23] Towards evening I soldered up the large box.

[In a summary letter to his parents, that reached Minden via Aberdeen in the fall of 1884, Franz Boas wrote: *I am longing so much for news! I shall leave this letter here to let you know that if I miss the ships, which is very probable, and if a ship should call here, that I am well and happy. The same applies to Wilhelm. On our very first trip in December he froze his big toes, and has had to sit in the house all winter, while I have been constantly on the move.*]

---

21. Possibly Ursuk.
22. This involved a total of seven seal carcasses that were cached as dog food.
23. The steel runner was fastened to the wooden runner to enhance the glide of the sledge especially on melting snow and ice on which water was lying.

# May 1884

*Thursday, 1 May.*

May began very pleasantly; the weather was quite fair and even warm. J. M.'s sledges came back in the morning. We were continuously packing things so that we can get our boxes in order. In the evening the cooper was here, and we had a small farewell celebration.

*Friday, 2 May.*

The weather was beautiful again. Today the natives had to prepare the things for cleaning skins. In the evening the boats were loaded on sledges. Captain Rosch also arrived.

*Saturday, 3 May.*

Ascension.[24] The weather today was really beautiful, and very warm. We managed to make such progress with our things that we'd packed all the boxes except one. In the afternoon I did a clean-up. Towards evening the sledge came back from Kinneit; the dogs looked quite terrible; they had not been getting enough food. It was 10 o'clock when we came inside; by then the dogs had been fed.

*Sunday, 4 May.*

Captain Rosch came at 5 o'clock this morning to say goodbye, since he wanted to return to Neu Antelik; we had a Kinneit wind but it was not very strong. Towards noon it became a south wind with heavy snow, which lasted all afternoon. The water was pouring off the house, it was so warm.

*Monday, 5 May.*

Today we still had a lot to do to get all our things together, since we wanted to get away on May 6 if the weather permits. Herr Dr had invited the cooper for the evening; all day long the natives came running with all kinds of things to sell to Herr Dr.[25] Towards evening we hauled the boxes across to the storehouse.

---

24. Weike was again mistaken; in 1884 Ascension was on Thursday, May 22, and Whit on Sunday, June 1.

25. Boas bought "ethnographica" from the Inuit on behalf of Adolf Bastian (1826-1905) for the Berlin Museum of Ethnology; these items have survived in Berlin to the present. Bastian was then Professor of Ethnology and Director of the Museum.

*Tuesday, 6 May.*

We got up at 4:30 this morning. The natives were all wakened immediately. Today J. M.'s natives went down to the water with their boats to go whaling.[26] It was around 9 o'clock when we left the station. J. M. and the cooper accompanied us as far as the harbour; we were travelling with a flag-bedecked sledge.[27] The snow was soft and hence we made slow progress. We were travelling with two sledges, one driven by little Appak; the other by Singnar accompanied by his wife Batti;[28] Herr Dr and I completed the party. We had a total of 25 dogs. It cleared up towards noon and then it became very hot, so that we shed our *kolitans* and sat on the sledge in just our shirts. At the southern tip of the large island[29] I first had to search for *cumans*[30] in Herr Dr's shirt. There were quite a large number of seals on the ice but the dogs were raising such a ruckus, that we couldn't get close to them. At Salungemut we stopped at the same iceberg where we slept last time. This was the first time since last fall that we used our *tupik,* since one could no longer build an *iglu.*

*Wednesday, 7 May.*

Today we stopped to hunt seals. When we saw that there were none in the vicinity Singnar travelled west with one sledge, since he had left a seal lying on the ice and wanted to get it. Apak and I drove straight on, taking some boxes with us; when he started hunting I drove the sledge. It was very warm, with a fair wind; we had no luck at hunting. The seals dove into the water so fast.[31] At 3:15 we stopped and turned back and got back to the iceberg at 6 o'clock. Simi had already started cooking, and prepared our supper.

---

26. To the southern floe-edge at the entrance to Cumberland Sound.

27. Boas and Weike did not mention which flags they were flying, apart from the fact that Boas had with him the boat's flag with Marie's name.

28. Appak, also known as Shorty; Batt = Betty, the wife of Singnar who was also known as Simi or Jimmy.

29. Talirua.

30. I. *kumak:* louse (human lice: *Pediculidae*).

31. What is involved here is hunting at the seals' breathing holes that the seals keep open from when the ice starts forming by constantly surfacing and climbing out onto the ice. The seals maintain several breathing holes and thereby have to visit every hole frequently, since on average the length of their dives is only up to twenty minutes.

*Thursday, 8 May.*

We pushed on today; we were seal hunting all day, but again with no luck. It was very warm today. Finally we tried waiting at a breathing hole,[32] but still got nothing. We saw plenty of seals lying on the ice, but could not get within gun range. We stopped for the night near where the singing house stands.[33] First, Herr Dr and I inspected this singing house at Kinneit. Appak had caught two young seals; we ate one and the dogs hauling Appak's sledge got the other.

*Friday, 9 May.*

Appak and Batty stayed behind to hunt. Singnar, Herr Dr, and I went on ahead with the large sledge. There were again quite a lot of seals lying on the ice. Singnar shot one. As we got close to the head of the fiord, there was a lot of water on the ice, and it was worst among the rough ice; there occasionally the entire sledge was under water. We again met Tyson with his wife and son in Kinneit; they had come back to fetch their things from the land. They helped us as far as our depot of boxes; we had intended heading back to the *iglu* since there was dog food there, but once we had unloaded the sledge, Appak arrived and we pitched our *tupik*. Tyson (and his family) ate with us, and thereafter they went back to their dogs.

*Saturday, 10 May.*

Today I had to go back with Singnar and feed the dogs. Herr Dr and Apak went ahead with one sledge; after we had fed the dogs, we took the other seal with us up to the *tupik*, took on a load of boxes, and drove on, following Herr Dr. Once we were across the first ponds we had to unload the boxes and carry them over a small hill. Then we were driving along a hill-slope so that the sledge was higher on one side than on the other. Herr Dr met us; then we had to hand over our team and our load, and head back with the other team to feed the dogs. Thereafter

---

32. To kill a seal at its breathing hole the Inuit would stand motionless and patiently at the hole, to harpoon a seal at lightning speed as it surfaced, and to haul it up onto the ice.

33. I. *qaqi*: the Inuit singing house or community house, where singing sessions, dances and shamanistic rites were held; this house, built of rocks, whalebones and turf, stood near Niutang.

I had to nail a bearskin beneath the large sledge; we wanted to protect it somewhat, since we had to travel over so many rocks.

*Sunday, 11 May.*
Today we pushed on with all our things. The sledge with the bearskin travelled so badly that we had to unload some things. Herr Dr came back with his sledge and picked up these things, and then we pushed on, and hauled everything over the rocks; by evening we had got everything across the rocks. Then I drove ahead with Appak and one load. This involved almost entirely things we needed for the night. Herr Dr also came up and we pitched the tents.

*Monday, 12 May.*
This morning we went back again to bring all the boxes together; we brought them almost to our campsite. Then I with Singnar and Apak had to go ahead with a small sledge fully loaded; the going initially was bad, but then it became even worse. Simi did not want to go ahead; I pushed on with Apak and reconnoitred the route. On seeing that it was too bad, I went back and reported to Herr Dr; he then checked the route and when he saw that it was impassable we looked for another route over a couple of hills. But all this time our two Eskimos had not stirred from the spot; I brought them back and we fed the dogs.

*Tuesday, 13 May.*
This morning we set about carrying our things over the hills. Herr Dr had packed things so that a substantial portion of our things was left behind; we didn't know if we'd be able to fetch them later. This was arduous work, and we could scarcely see that we were making any progress. As compared to the distance we would have travelled by sledge, now we had to carry everything three times as far. Except for a few boxes we hauled the things to Kikerteluk,[34] where we stopped and cooked supper. When I called him to come and eat, Herr Dr asked what time it was; it was 1:15. Since there is no longer any night one never knows what time it is, and we just kept on travelling; two boxes were finished off here; they were to be left behind.

---

34. Qeqertelling.

*Wednesday, 11 May.*
Nothing.

*Thursday, 15 May.*
Caribou hunting.

*Friday, 16 May.*
Caribou hunting.

*Saturday, 17 May.*
Rest day.

*Sunday, 18 May.*
We continue travelling.

*Monday, 19 May.*
Rest day on Iwi's island.[35]

*Tuesday, 20 May.*
Today we split into two parties. Herr Dr went ahead with two sledges and I headed back with one sledge to Kinneit to fetch things. Singnar and Apak travelled back with me to Kinneit and two sledges set off from the island to hunt caribou. It was very hot today. When we got back to the end of the salt water we encountered a strong wind; the land was all covered with water and the snow had all melted, so that we had great difficulty travelling further. I went to the spot where we had last spent the night;[36] in the meantime the natives had cut up Appak's caribou and had harnessed all the dogs to Singnar's sledge. When I saw that they did not want to take their sledge, I told them I wanted to go back. Then the dogs were harnessed and our things were again taken back. When we had everything loaded, we headed back. The two sledges that were hunting caribou also headed back with us. Towards evening it was freezing again, and the snow hardened. It was 10:45 when I reached the camp [Oqilegung] from which I had started; I wanted to travel through the night to join Herr Dr the next morning, but the natives refused

---

35. Oqilegung at Padli.
36. Simiutang, the night of 17 to 18 May.

because they had not slept the night before since they had been hunting. I pitched my *tupik* and brewed coffee; it was after midnight by the time it was ready.

*Wednesday, 21 May.*
I got up again a little after 4 o'clock and got ready to push on but I could not rouse the natives out; I had already drunk my coffee but they still did not want to come out; they got up at seven and took the *tupik* and everything with them. They reached the island[37] only shortly before we did. They lived at the camp[38] where Herr Dr is now. The natives said it was close, but although we drove hard all morning, it was still three in the afternoon before we reached the camp. Fortunately Herr Dr had not left for Ekzeter.[39] This camp lay on Döver Island[40] at 67° 3' [N].

*Thursday, 22 May.*
This morning Herr Dr drove off with his sledge to survey some of the island;[41] I was left to guard the *tupik*. During the night there had been a strong wind with drifting snow. In the course of the morning a herd of reindeer came across the ice. In an instant the sledge was down on the ice in pursuit of them, but the caribou smelled it too soon and galloped off, so that they [Inuit] did not get any. When Herr Dr came back we had supper. All the women and children had been out picking berries today, and brought us some.[42] Towards evening the men came to draw maps for Herr Dr, I went hunting and came back at 11 o'clock.

*Friday, 23 May.*
I wanted to travel on today at first, but I did not like the weather. Herr Dr was snow-blind today; my eyes were also sore, and this is why I did not want to head out. I went with Samen[43] to feed the dogs, and afterwards I stayed at home. The natives came running with berries the whole

---

37. On 18 May.
38. Padloping.
39. Exeter Sound / Qarmaqdjuin.
40. Durban Island / Aggidjen.
41. Padloping.
42. Frozen berries from last year; probably blueberries (*Vaccinium uliginosum*) (see footnote under 17 October 1883).
43. Salmon.

day, so that we were eating continually. Towards evening it began snowing again. Zieringa[44] was here again cracking jokes.

### Saturday, 24 May.

Herr Dr's eyes were somewhat better today, and he headed out; mine, on the other hand, were so much more painful. I was sewing so that I did not once need to leave the *tupik*. When Herr Dr came back we had supper and then we had a pot full of berries. The weather was overcast, like all the past few days. [Padli-] Schangu and his wife were here to play dominoes.

### Sunday, 25 May.

First I had to repair boxes. Since we have to get into them every day, their lids had been knocked out of shape. Once I had finished this we had a thorough wash and hair-cutting session. After our meal I went hunting, and after I got back I had to cook again. We were waiting for the natives. When they returned from hunting we wanted to feed the dogs. It was already 10:30 when I drove off with the sledge, accompanied by one of the natives; we returned at 2 o'clock.

### Monday, 26 May.

Due to the foul weather we had to stay here today; the second *tupik* was pitched, and all our things were moved into it, so that we would have more room in the large one. Snow and thick fog. We cleaned the guns thoroughly and other than that we left the tent as little as possible.

### Tuesday, 27 May.

The weather was the same again today; the sun peeped through somewhat, but to no great effect. Last night I had forgotten to take my large knife inside with me, and when I came out this morning it was gone. The dogs had carried it off and since the snow had been drifting during the night, looking for it was hopeless. We were making some repairs to our sledge; the bone runners had suffered badly on the land; the heads of the screws were projecting quite markedly.

---

44. Sirinirn.

*Wednesday, 28 May.*

Due to the foul weather we had to stay here at Palag[45] again today. Schangu's child had died. There was a strong north wind with snow; the land is entirely white in the daylight. When I wanted to cook I had to go looking for firewood. Each time I went out the dogs came along. At one point Pilulak came running up with my big knife. Once I had recovered it, I gave him a thrashing and then let him go. In the evening we had a celebration with a bottle of punch.[46]

*Thursday, 29 May.*

The weather was somewhat better today, and therefore we prepared to set off. We were travelling with three sledges: [Padli-]Schangu and his wife, Ziringa, and Herr Dr and myself. It was around 10 o'clock when we drove off from Paloping. It was very warm. Two sledges were heading off in the same direction to go hunting. In the morning Herr Dr was driving the dogs and I sat on the second sledge. When we had reached Kakeluga[47] we had to unharness Pöbing[48] and place her on the sledge, since she was about to present us with pups. Herr Dr laid the whip on the sledge and took Pöbing with him on the second sledge. Now I had to drive. In due course we encountered *manila* and *maug* together.[49] The snow was again starting to freeze, making travelling difficult; once the sledge bogged down so badly that I could not haul it out on my own, and the dogs were starting to refuse to pull. I gave a couple of them a good working over, till the sweat was running off me. When we got closer to the land again, Herr Dr resumed driving and I had to look after Pöbing; then I began to freeze terribly. It was already after 10 o'clock when we made a halt and pitched camp for the night. By 12 o'clock supper was ready; by the time we had finished it, dawn was breaking. According to my watch the sun rose at 12.50 a.m.; my watch was somewhat slow. Ziringa went hunting. I went to bed at 1:15.

---

45. Padloping.
46. A year previously Franz Boas and Marie Krackowizer had secretly become engaged in Stuttgart.
47. Qaqodluin.
48. A pregnant bitch; her name was Pegbing according to Boas.
49. I. *manilaaq:* rough ice; *maujaq:* soft snow.

*Friday, 30 May.*

I had toothache all night long, so that I could not sleep. I got up again around 4 o'clock, got dressed, and then slept until 7 o'clock. Then I had to get up to brew coffee; by around nine we were ready to load up. This morning our problems with Taerlik began again. Herr Dr made his trace very short and worked him over with the whip handle. When it came my time to drive, I lengthened his trace, to give this a try, but it did not help. He was letting himself be dragged along by the other dogs. We met another sledge that was travelling to Palli to fish for salmon[50] and we stopped and [talked to] the family. Joto[51] looked just like a bandit; he was wearing a large hat along with his dirty skin clothing. The weather was not very agreeable; there was fog over the land. Since Taerlik[52] did not want to pull, we took him out of harness, and he ran along with the other dogs. Finally he became tangled in the traces and let himself be pulled along. Then I stopped and worked him over with the whip-handle until he lay motionless. We left him lying and drove on. When we reached a point that we could see the island[53] clearly, I thought we had another hour to go, but it was a very long hour. Dense fog rolled in, so that we could not see a thing. My nose froze horribly. It was 9 o'clock when the island emerged from the fog and the camp came in sight. The distance I had thought would take an hour to cover, had taken three and a half hours; everything is deceptive here like this. When we arrived we pitched the *tupik* and I began cooking; two rabbits went into the pot. It was again somewhat after twelve when we went to bed.

*Saturday, 31 May.*

The weather was really beautiful this morning. Schangu and Ziringa were paid off, since they wanted to head back.[54] By noon the sky was again completely overcast, and hence Herr Dr did not get any observa-

---

50. What is meant is arctic char (*Salvelinus alpinus*; I. *iqaluk* or *iqaluppik*), a freshwater fish that can also live in salt water. Later Weike also used the term "trout" (25 July 1884).

51. Tauto according to Boas.

52. Boas does not mention this dog's name.

53. Qeqertadjuin.

54. Boas paid the Inuit in kind with European consumer goods.

tions. In the afternoon another sledge arrived from Kiwitun.[55] After we had eaten lunch I became horribly snow-blind, so that I could no longer tackle anything. I took a handkerchief and tied it tightly over my eyes; I fell asleep but at 5 o'clock Herr Dr woke me; I was to make tea. By then the weather was quite foul, and it was snowing heavily. After the meal Herr Dr fed the dogs again, while I stayed in the *tupik*. Taerlik has come back; we plan to give him another chance.

# June 1884

*Sunday, 1 June.*
[Whit.] My eyes felt somewhat better today. Herr Dr went out, but as far as possible I stayed in the *tupik*, so that my eyes could recover properly. Since it is Whit, I skinned two rabbits and began cooking one and laid the other aside. Herr Dr came back very late so that my rabbit was thoroughly cooked. When we had finished our supper, we played cards until 12 o'clock and then went to bed. We are doing exactly like the natives: working at night and sleeping during the day.

*Monday, 2 June.*
Herr Dr was snow-blind today. After we had had our coffee I had to feed the dogs. I removed the fat from the hide and gave it away [to the Inuit] to dry it. It was very warm today. While I was away, feeding the dogs, the dogs ate half of the rabbit out of the pot. I took Taerlik's marrow bones away from him today.

*Tuesday, 3 June.*
The weather was very fine today. Herr Dr drove off to the big island.[56] Throughout the day we had wind squalls, which would blow at full force for an hour, and then it would fall calm again. Little Pöbing honoured us with pups today; I had put her house in order; when we went to bed

---

55. For years Qivitung had been a port-of-call for whaling ships and a gathering place for the Inuit.
56. Qeqertalukdjuak.

she produced her first [pup]. The natives got no seals today. Herr Dr is snow-blind.

*Wednesday, 4 June.*
By this morning Pöbing had nine pups. She had killed four by treading on them. We moved her house on shore. We had a south wind, Force 6,[57] but this changed over the course of the morning and it became very pleasant. Around noon I was washing myself down near the *tupik*, but because no bare ground had emerged there, after lunch I went up the hill to a pond and had a thorough wash.

*Thursday, 5 June.*
Yesterday evening both Schangus [Qeqerten-Schangu and Padli-Schangu] arrived. We had crawled into our sleeping bags around 10 o'clock. I could not sleep since I had quite a serious case of hives.[58] I got up again at 1 o'clock and went outside. After walking around the island, I lay down between two rocks, laid my gun under my head and slept until 4:30 when I returned to the *tupik* since my feet were cold. I awoke at 7 o'clock and made coffee. Thereafter we fed the dogs and loaded the sledge since we wanted to push on to Kikertukschuak[59] with our things. There were only poor tent-sites on the small island where we were then camped. Schangu said that there were better sites on the large island. We drove off at 12 o'clock, accompanied by Tyson. The weather was foul, with a strong wind and snow. It was 3 o'clock when we arrived; we pitched the *tupiks*. In the morning there had been nobody here, but by evening there were four tents pitched; two sledges went back again. In the evening the weather was really foul, with a fairly strong southerly gale. I prepared some dilute vinegar, to rub myself with it.

*Friday, 6 June.*
Today the weather was very fine, although with quite a wind. In the morning another sledge arrived here from the small island. We got ready,

---

57. A strong wind, 50 kph.
58. Hives, or *urticaria*, which is also associated with a fever, can be caused by a sudden cold spell or extreme solar radiation, which had been the case on the pack ice. A common remedy at the time was an external application of diluted vinegar to the hives; Boas and Weike had a supply of vinegar in their medical kit.
59. Qeqertukdjuaq.

since we wanted to travel to Makaktufennak[60] in the afternoon. Around noon we packed up our things, loaded the sledge and closed up the *tupik*. We drove off at 2 o'clock. There was some fog but it was very warm. Progress was often very difficult; it took us an hour and 40 minutes to travel from Kikertukschuak[61] to the other side on the mainland. After we had been travelling on the mainland some distance we ran into horrible *mauga*, so that we were constantly sinking knee-deep, and then we were standing waist-deep in water. And then it also began to snow; we had to shout at the dogs in order to make any progress. We didn't want to turn back, even though we were making very slow progress. We kept trying, until we saw rocks at the foot of the high mountain, and decided to stop there; when we reached the spot, we found that it was rocks that had fallen down; that was not a good sign. We could not stay there and we travelled some distance further and pitched our *tupik* on the sledge. Some of the rocks were lying on the ice fifty metres from the foot of the mountain. That evening we ate our food cold; we really enjoyed our bread and butter, and had a can of soup and bouillon with it.

*Saturday, 7 June.*

Last night we slept quite well on the sledge; when we awoke we had a good appetite, but we wanted to drive on to the shore before starting to cook. We reached an island, but it was so steep-sided that we could not get ashore; hence we drove on to another point, but it was also unsuitable. And so we drove on, from one corner to the next, until we reached the camp[62] where Köninan & Konera are; we stopped here and started cooking. It was 12 o'clock when we drank our morning coffee. After our meal we drove on to Maktatuschenak; after that, driving was also terrible. Today water was pouring down from the hills. As we got higher up, there was a strong wind, but here there was bare ice; it was time for us to turn back. We were terribly hungry; so we stopped and ate a little, and then started back. On the way back it began snowing again. We reached the station at 9 o'clock; the natives had already organized dog food and hence we needed only to bring the dogs to the spot.

---

60. Maktartudjennaq, later also rendered as Maktatuschenak.
61. Qeqertukdjuaq.
62. On Qeqerten on the Padli coast.

*Sunday, 8 June.*

When we woke this morning and stepped outside it was foggy; after coffee we got the sledge ready, since we wanted to travel to Panirtu.[63] We drove from one corner to another, to try to see if the weather might improve; the snow was very bad. Then we tried driving in the rough ice; it was somewhat better there, we only had to watch that we did not fall into the water. When we got further inland, it became somewhat clearer, and the snow improved. But ultimately we had had enough so we turned back Then the dogs' barking largely ceased, since on the return trip the dogs were running somewhat better. We were battling against wind and snow; today it was like a bad December day at home. Herr Dr and I were hoarse from so much shouting. We got back to our *tupik* at 6 o'clock. It was still snowing. The water was continually dripping from the *tupik*. We then played cards until 11:30. My hives were tormenting me night and day.

*Monday, 9 June.*

It was still foggy today. We got ready to travel back. It was around 9:30 when we set off from Kikerton.[64] It took a long time before we got the dogs going. Sonera's son caught up with us and we let him go ahead; then we let our dogs run freely. We were chatting companionably on the sledge, and later we began having a good feed on the sledge. We also met Nakojaschi who was hunting.

*Tuesday, 10 June.*

Today we stayed in camp; the weather was beautiful; we were at 67° N. Today we had plentiful water, and hence I was able to wash a couple of shirts for us. Thus far we have had such bad weather and no firewood that it was difficult even to wash a shirt. It became foggy again towards evening.

---

63. Pangnirtung Fiord on the Padli side, connected by a pass with Pangnirtung Fiord of the same name on the opposite, west side in Cumberland Sound.
64. Qeqerten on the Padli side.

*Wednesday, 11 June.*
[Padli-] Schangu and Tessiwan[65] drove on ahead today; they took some of our boxes with them. Today Herr Dr drove down to Kikertakschuak, to make an observation there. Around noon the weather was superb and hence Herr Dr got a good observation. He came back at 2:30. We ate right away. Two natives fed the dogs. After our meal Herr Dr took another time-observation. The natives had been playing cards all day. In the evening another two sledges departed. We closed up our *tupik* and climbed up onto the big island. We reached the top at 9:30, the sun was still high in the sky. From there we had a fine view over the entire region. On the way back down, on reaching some snow we lay down and glissaded. It was after midnight when we crawled into the *tupik*. Sitting in our sleeping-bags we ate two ptarmigan. We get up to eat and are still eating when we go to bed.

[Franz Boas mused: *Yesterday* [June 10] *Wilhelm and I were picturing how it will be when we arrive* [back home]; *we have no clothes, because they are on top in Kingnait* [in the boxes left behind]; *for better or for worse we will have to go ashore in Eskimo clothing. How warm will the welcome be?*].

*Thursday, 12 June.*
We packed up our sledge this morning, since we'll be pushing on. Tyson was also travelling on. It was a very warm day. All three of us[66] rode on the sledge. I had lain down and was trying to sleep, but without success. We negotiated the bad spot quite well; we didn't break through even once. We reached the campsite very early in the afternoon.

*Friday, 13 June.*
This morning seven sledges left this site to travel farther north. The weather was superb. We were the last to set off. The snow was very good. Over the course of the morning we experienced some wind, so that it became a little unpleasant. It was not long before we overtook Tyson; our dogs were running very well. We passed an iceberg, near which

65. Tessivang.
66. Weike, Boas and Schangu.

there were two large cracks, which we crossed only with difficulty. Once we were past this spot, it was not long before our sledge took the lead. We had reached a point where we could see the spot where the ships anchor. We did not continue to Kiwittun yet; the natives said that there was no good *tupik* site there yet. We pitched our tent on an island;[67] it was around 4:30 when we made a halt. After we had eaten I drove off with the dogs to fetch a seal from the ice. By the time I got back with it, Teisen had also arrived. Then we fed the dogs and thereafter we relaxed for the evening. In our sleeping bags by 12:15.

### Saturday, 14 June.

The weather was nasty. When I went out, it was snowing. While I was making coffee, a duck landed near the rough ice and I shot it. Around noon we had a strong north wind, Force 6, that persisted all day. Snow and strong wind.

### Sunday, 15 June.

Last night we experienced another gale to the point that we thought our *tupik* would collapse. We propped it up on the inside with poles and guns. The wind was still the same this morning; there could be no thought of cooking and hence we had to be satisfied with dry bread. Thus we stayed holed-up until noon, not even leaving our sleeping bags; it was horribly cold. Schangu visited us; otherwise we all dozed away the whole day. When it was time for supper, the weather was no better; we had not even drunk a little water for 24 hours.

### Monday, 16 June.

At 12:45 last night the wind had slackened a little, and we crawled out to cook; we drank a little pot-full of coffee, which was not bad. The sky was clear, with even some sunshine. Herr Dr drove off, while the natives lay down and slept; they emerged again at ten this morning and went hunting. Herr Dr had said that he would be back by noon to take an observation, and hence I prepared lunch. Herr Dr returned early enough to take the observation: 67° 53' N. After our meal we had a snooze and then we fed the dogs again. It became very cold again towards evening.

---

67. Tununirn.

*Tuesday, 17 June.*

Today Herr Dr went out again and Schangu drove to Pamiwian.[68] I made small shotgun shells because we had run out of them. It was very warm today. Two boxes and two seals were taken along to the next station because we want to get further tomorrow. In the evening at 8 o'clock fresh ice had already formed again. The sun was still very high, but the ground is too cold.[69]

*Wednesday, 18 June.*

Schangu came back this morning to fetch us. We wanted to travel further; the weather was beautiful. We did not have far to go; in only ninety minutes we were at the harbour. We pitched our *tupik* on the left side of the harbour; Kiwittun is on the right side. Our side is called Pamiwian.

*Thursday, 19 June.*

Herr Dr drove off this morning and I began packing since we planned to leave the large *tupik* standing and to travel to Cape Ketter[70] with a light sledge. Since we have to come back here, we can leave all our things here. Schangu will be going part-way with us but will then go caribou-hunting, while Sonnen[71] will come with us to Cape Ketter. In the evening I shot a tern.[72]

*Friday, 20 June.*

This morning we packed up everything in the *tupik* tidily, and then we closed it up securely, and packed the remaining things on the sledge. It was around noon when we set off.[73] We travelled across the harbour and from there across an isthmus; otherwise we would have had to make such a major detour if we had tried to go around the headland. The land was fairly low but the snow very deep, so that making any progress was dreadfully strenuous. We made better progress once we had reached the

---

68. Pamiujang, the next station or campsite.
69. Boas noted that day that Weike had climbed a nearby mountain in the evening to scan the coastal area.
70. Cape Kater.
71. Salmon.
72. Arctic tern (*Sterna paradisea*).
73. Boas recorded: *"Today we are leaving the harbour just as we did a year ago."* Here he is referring to their departure from Hamburg on June 20, 1883.

crest and started heading downhill. One of the Schangus fell off the sledge and couldn't catch up; the sledge had to stop until he caught up again. When we had reached the sea ice again we made faster progress; moreover we had a trail to follow since we were following in Ikeraping's track to the island[74] where his *tupik* was located and where we stopped. He had come here yesterday so that his mother Piukiga,[75] who had been left to die here, would not immediately be eaten by the dogs. In the afternoon we saw the first flowers in bloom. There was plenty of caribou meat here.

### Saturday, 21 June.

At 11 o'clock on Saturday we set off from this island, accompanied by both Schangus and their three wives; the other natives remained here. It was terribly hot; we ultimately ran into *mauga*, which meant dreadfully hard work; we had to travel around the end of one island, but here there was very good ice. The first time that we reached a crack, two of the dogs fell in and got a saltwater bath; we hauled the sledge across and pulled one dog out, while the other got out on its own. A little further on Schangu spotted two caribou on Manitu;[76] he stayed behind with his sledge and went hunting, while the other Schangu[77] transferred to our sledge. Now the terrible *manila* and *mauga* combined, which meant damnably strenuous work, which repeatedly brought the dogs to a halt. When we reached the island where we were to camp for the night, we had to search for a long time to find a site where we could pitch camp. As we reached the rough ice for the second time, the dogs began to race until they reached the rocks. When we went to check we found the fresh tracks of three caribou. It was 6:30 when we stopped. Schangu had not gotten anything; his gun had misfired, since water had gotten into it. Our campsite for June 21, 1884 was on Nellurliar;[78] 68° 7'.

---

74. Attereeling.
75. Piukkia. Weike is alluding to the Inuit custom of leaving behind dying people alone in a tent, under certain circumstances, so that they may die in peace.
76. Manitung.
77. Qeqerten-Schangu.
78. Nedluqseaq.

*Sunday, 22 June.*

We stayed here until noon since Herr Dr first wanted to record the sun's altitude. Q[eqerten] Schangu went ahead with the other sledge. It was 12:45 when we set off; initially we had bare ice with water lying on it so the dogs could run freely. When we left the island where we had slept, there was *mauga* and hence we soon caught up with Schangu. We trailed behind him for a while because we were having to stop constantly, but then we went ahead. I had taken over driving the dogs today; keeping the dogs pulling gave me great pleasure. Herr Dr said that there was no benefit to have [the other sledge] go ahead of ours since the dogs still would not run, but I got them really moving so that the other sledge was left far behind. We passed an island[79] where there were two *nauga*[80] but we could not get the dogs to stop. Schangu went back and shot one of them. It was 9 o'clock when we stopped and pitched camp for the night;[81] by the time I had washed up, it was 12:30. Herr Dr had toothache.

*Monday, 23 June.*

We could not continue today due to snow and fog. Schangu went off to hunt caribou. We heard a ptarmigan calling here and we went in pursuit. Schangu had set off before me; he saw it and fired twice but missed. I was on the other side of the island but saw nothing; we finally met up on the hill and headed north across the island back to camp. There I arranged half a caribou leg between two rocks, lit a fire under it, and roasted it; finally it was covered over with earth.

*Tuesday, 24 June.*

It was foggy today and hence we could not start early. While we were drinking our coffee the ptarmigan began calling again, close to our *tupik.* Herr Dr and I wanted to go after it, but before we got organized it had flown away. After our coffee I went up onto the island in pursuit of it; up there, I lit my pipe; in the meantime I heard it calling again. I headed in that direction and, since I could not see very far, I had to

---

79. Nannuqtuaqdjung.
80. I. *nauja*: gull.
81. At Tupirbikdjariaitung.

locate it by its calls. It was the basis of our midday soup. Tububick-bumgian,[82] 68° 19½'. We had lunch here. Herr Dr took another observation. The fog lifted somewhat. Since it was still not clear enough to push on, we went to bed. At 5 o'clock we were roused out; we set off around 5:30. Initially it was fairly clear, but later there was fog and snow. After we'd been travelling for probably two hours we reached a wide crack; two dogs fell into it and had to be hauled out again. We travelled along the crack since it was too wide to cross, until we reached a spot where it made a bend and where a piece of snow-ice lay in the middle of the crack. The dogs spotted a seal on the other side and charged enthusiastically across so that the sledge did not even touch the water. Subsequently we reached a second [crack], where we again had to make a major detour to get across it. Thus at 9 o'clock we reached Cape Hörl,[83] where we stopped since Schangu wanted to stay here. We crawled into our sleeping bags at 12 o'clock.

*Wednesday, 25 June.*
Last night the dogs were barking terribly so that we had trouble sleeping. Herr Dr got up once and thrashed them; thereafter I was dreaming and thought Herr Dr had called for me to get up. Herr Dr was lying awake and when he saw me getting dressed, he asked me where I was going. I said that he had awakened me; then he said it is 4 o'clock. I had checked the time half asleep, and thought it was 8 o'clock. I was relieved that it was not as late as that. Due to the bad weather we could not continue today. The fog lifted somewhat. Schangu went off to hunt caribou.

*Thursday, 26 June.*
Schangu came back with two caribou. We've stolen dear God's sweet time.

---

82. Tupirbikdjariaitung.
83. Weike was confusing Cape Hewell / Niaqonaujang, which lies further north and which they did not reach, with Cape Hooper / Nudlung.

*Friday 27 June.*

Schangu stayed at Nudelung[84] with his wives while the other Schangu[85] drove on with us with the sledge. The weather had now improved so that we could travel again. At first the going was quite good, and we could make rapid progress. We had started at 10:15. Meanwhile I ... was sitting on the sledge and a foot ... [of water lay on the ice]. Around 3:45 we had to make a detour around some rough ice, and thereafter the going was good again. Occasionally we would cross a wide crack, and at 8 o'clock we reached a crack where one could even have used a boat; we stopped here.[86]

*Saturday, 28 June.*

This morning we pushed on; we had quite fine weather. As we crossed the first crack the rear end of our sledge dropped into it, but we hauled it out again. After we'd been travelling for a couple of hours we ran into dense fog, so that we had to travel by compass. But in so doing we could not always maintain our course; we reached a crack, along which we drove until we reached a large island.[87] But we did not want to stop there since there was a small island nearby on which there was a camp.[88] We set a course to reach it, but between the islands there was so much water on the ice that occasionally the entire sledge was under water. As long as the dogs were walking, we kept moving but when they were forced to swim, the sledge stopped dead, with the young ice piling up in front of the sledge. Then we had to hop down off the sledge into the water. When we reached the second large island[89] there was no room for our *tupik* and, furthermore, it began to snow. We spotted a small island nearby,[90] where we could pitch the *tupik* and headed for it; it was snowing so heavily that after an hour everything was white. Herr Dr pitched the *tupik*, Schangu fed the dogs and I prepared supper; I was really happy when it was ready.

---

84. Nudlung / Cape Hooper.
85. Padli-Schangu.
86. At Idjortung.
87. Kingnitung.
88. Audnirn.
89. Naujateling.
90. Ivissaq.

*Sunday, 29 June.*

First thing this morning we got our things in order; our guns looked terrible. Herr Dr wanted to take an altitude here, but he could not discern a clear edge on the sun, so nothing came of this. We pushed on again at 12:20. We had first checked out from up above where the best route lay, but ultimately we ran into *mauga* in the water. The sun re-emerged and travelling became delightful. Our dogs were running quite well; after travelling for over two hours we reached the mainland. There we travelled along the rough ice, where the ice was quite good. We had probably been travelling along the rough ice for an hour when we saw a black spot on the ice. A large crack was full of teal[91] which we tried hunting. Herr Dr shot one and I shot two. We did not want to stop for long, and pushed on again. Since we could not travel across the land any more, we made a stop on this side at 8:30. After supper I went off to hunt ducks with Schangu again. I got two and Schangu one; hence we had seven birds in the *tupik*.[92] We got back at 12:30.

*Monday, 30 June.*

At 6:30 Herr Dr woke me to get up, but when I looked out of the *tupik* there was dense fog with snow falling. Then Herr Dr said: "Sleep as long as you like!" I went back to bed until 10:30 when I got up and brewed coffee. By noon the sun had broken through to the point that Herr Dr was able to get a sun-shot; then a fairly strong wind got up and the snow began to drift. In the afternoon I made another attempt to light the fire, but the wind was so strong that I did not succeed. I got it started twice with gunpowder, but before I knew it, it went out again. Then we had to open one of our cans of meat and have recourse to the bread bag, which had already become seriously reduced. Our campsite:[93] 69° 30', June 30, 1884.

---

91. *Anas crecca carolinensis.*
92. Weike had miscounted, but corrected himself on July 1. The bag was six ducks.
93. Kouktelling / Cape Kater.

# July 1884

*Tuesday, 1 July.*

The wind and snow were still the same so that we had to delay cooking. In the afternoon the situation was somewhat better, so we lit the stove[94] and prepared our six ducks. We made soup from the breasts and legs; for lack of dog food we fed the backs, a piece of caribou meat and two other birds to the dogs. Our blubber was again exhausted. We got our things together for pushing onwards. Here we had to cross an isthmus.[95] The weather was so thick that we could not see Schangu and his sledge, and we constantly had to travel through melt-ponds. In one of them the dogs fell through; they tried to swim, but they were pulled backwards [by the sledge] so they crawled up onto the sledge. There was no alternative; we had to manhandle the sledge out of there, and thus repeatedly landed waist-deep in water. Once we had hauled our sledge out of there, we pushed on again. Schangu had stopped; there we first untangled the traces, then we travelled on. But this was not for long; we had to stop since the wind had obliterated the tracks. Schangu came back, and we pitched our *tupik* on the sledge. Then we dug out the bread: half a piece of bread and two pounds of meat shared between three men; it was like a drop of water on a hot rock; and then only one hot meal every 24 hours.

*Wednesday, 2 July.*

The weather was still the same this morning, but we had to push on due to the lack of dog food, and so we got started. After we had been travelling for some time Schangu lost the trail and hence we were travelling blind until we picked it up again; then we stopped, pitched the *tupik* on the sledge, and made ourselves comfortable. Herr Dr wanted to shoot a dog and to feed it to the others, but Schangu was of the opinion that it was too good a sledge dog, and hence its life was spared until next day if it were no better. Herr Dr went out to get a drink of water; in the meantime Schangu told me that he was hungry and wanted to take

---

94. The kerosene stove.
95. Near Niaqonaujang.

some of the meat that he was supposed to be transporting for the natives. When Herr Dr came back, we told him this; he was happy with the suggestion and hence we tackled the meat. Schangu took some cross pieces from his sledge to use as fuel and we made soup.

*Thursday, 3 July.*
This morning we brewed coffee early, and then we pushed on. We'd already been travelling for quite some time when it cleared up, and we could finally see the ice. Which of us would get there first! By then we had travelled quite some time overland before we reached the ice. Schangu had gone out hunting from the shore. As we came down off the land we were passing over snowdrifts; I negotiated the first one successfully, but at the second one a dog broke its trace and ran ahead, but too far to the right, and the others followed it. So my sledge went racing down with break-neck speed and I was thrilled. Once I came through this, we came out onto the ice. Schangu was still off hunting; ultimately he shot a seal and hence our dog's life[96] was spared. We were planning to head for a small island and to spend the night there. As we approached closer we spotted human tracks, then on the island[97] we spotted a *tupik*. It was occupied by a man and his wife;[98] they were the entire community.

*Friday, 4 July.*
The weather was not particularly good today. At noon the sun broke through sufficiently that Herr Dr was able to get another latitude: 69° 32' N. This is our northernmost point and now we plan to head back to Kiwittun. Ships also drop anchor in the vicinity of this small island. We took to our sleeping bags early in the evening.

*Saturday, 5 July.*
After sleeping for thirteen hours I crawled out of my sleeping bag at 8 o'clock. The natives went hunting. The swelling in Herr Dr's cheek had gone down somewhat and hence he too went off to fetch firewood; he soon returned with four thick planks on the sledge. At noon, out of

---

96. Named Neinessuak by Boas.
97. Siorartijung.
98. According to Boas the man was Utoaluk; he did not provide the woman's name.

boredom, I made hot chocolate. When the two Eskimos[99] came back they had killed four seals; two of these were brought straight back and provided food for both the dogs and ourselves; now we'll have meat with our coffee in the morning since our bread is exhausted.

*Sunday, 6 July.*

This morning I woke Herr Dr at 6 o'clock since we're aiming to head back. After coffee we loaded our sledge and at 9:15 we set off southwards. We did not travel overland again, but aimed to stay on the ice and travel around the point.[100] The weather was quite good and the ice was not too bad either. Here we could see many icebergs, so we had quite a feast for our eyes. It was quite a long haul to the point; along the way we saw many footprints. We spotted a hare, and we would have shot it, but it ran off. We travelled for quite some time thereafter, and then it became so foggy that one could not see one's hand in front of one's face, and at the same time it was very cold. Since we could no longer see, we stopped and pitched our *tupik*. Around 11 o'clock it became cold again; we spotted seven caribou on the headland on which we were camped. We set off to hunt them; I went with Schangu, running as never before, and got quite close to the caribou. But ultimately we were in such a bad position that we had no cover and one of them spotted us and they raced off. We then tried an Eskimo trick[101] to lure them towards us, but they would not come within range. Schangu fired a few times and I tried my luck too, but all our shots fell short and hence we had to start back. On the hike back we each shot a duck; so at least we had something, and we enjoyed a very fine midnight sun; it was 2:30 when I went to bed.

*Monday, 7 July.*

At 7 o'clock I woke Herr Dr; the weather was again very fine. After coffee Herr Dr took another observation, and so we frittered away the time and it was 11 o'clock before we set off for Hannes Bay.[102] Once we were on the

---

99. Padli-Schangu and Utoaluk.

100. The headland of Cape Kater / Kouktelling.

101. A technique used by the Inuit whereby caribou are driven in specific directions, in order to get them within closer hunting range.

102. Home's Bay, now Home Bay.

other side, the going was good, but from where our *tupik* had stood to where we rounded the last headland, the ice was very bad. When we had been travelling for some time, we came across some teal, and shot a few. Along our entire route there were ducks sitting on the water. After our first attempt at shooting some, I fell into the water along with my gun and had to scramble out again. There was no possibility of changing out here on the ice, and hence I had to sit all day in wet clothes. In the afternoon I became snow-blind again. We were shooting ducks all day as we travelled, but even so still made good progress. Towards evening I was again trying to hunt, and fell into the water again. It was still not very late when we stopped,[103] but there were many ducks here.

*Tuesday, 8 July.*
This morning we drove on. We were travelling along the tide crack, but ultimately it disappeared and we had to head through the water to reach Apadeling,[104] but from there we again had a crack to follow. It was cold and rainy, but we were able to follow the crack steadily and made good progress. The weather was really foul, and hence we were really glad to reach the small island[105] where we could pitch our *tupik*. Schangu found an egg.[106]

*Wednesday, 9 July.*
The weather was still dismal as we continued on our way, but we were again able to travel along the crack. To celebrate Herr Dr's birthday[107] this morning we had bread, the last of the chocolate, and a can of meat. A sleeping walrus was lying by the crack and Schangu shot it, but the crack was too wide for us to cross it, and hence we had to leave it lying. We were still able to travel along the crack as far as the rough ice, but there it disappeared and hence we had to travel through the water as far as the first small island[108] where we stopped; it was raining again. That evening we had six ducks for supper.

---

103. At Niaqongnausim.
104. Avaudjelling.
105. Agdliroling.
106. According to Boas that was an arctic tern's egg (*Sterna paradisaea*).
107. Franz Boas turned 26.
108. Northwest of Saviksonitung.

*Thursday, 10 July.*

This morning our breakfast was quite meagre; we took three cans of soup and bouillon and made a breakfast of them. This was all right for half an hour, but then we were hungry again. We had to travel through water from this island to Sawik serrandlu,[109] and then travelled for some distance along the island and from there across to the mainland; there was not much water on this crossing. The weather was horribly cold. Thus we reached Nudelung in the evening. As we were travelling out of Home Bay we did not look around at all. For supper I cooked a nourishing pea soup, to which I had added meat from the caribou shot on June 26.[110] I [ate my fill] of it.

*Friday, 11 July.*

In light of the lack of meat and coffee I had to make pea soup this morning. After the soup Schangu shot a seal, and then we travelled on into the fiord[111] where [Qeqerten-] Schangu was already. At first the going was quite good as regards the water, but we had to cross over to a headland, but there was a small lake in our way; ultimately our dogs started trotting through the water. Once through it, we headed along the rough ice; off the headland we spotted a caribou on the ice, and Schangu drove his dogs towards it. Herr Dr had to take an observation here and hence we had to stop before our dogs spotted the caribou. As we pushed on again Herr Dr's briefcase fell off the sledge; we noticed this only at the next headland and hence we had to turn back to recover it. Schangu stopped at a small island in order to unload wood; as we reached it, he headed off to the other side of the fiord, while we continued along the rough ice. But there was such a pronounced bend in the fiord that we decided to cut across and in so doing had to travel through water. Initially all went well, but gradually the sledge lost contact with the ice and began to float, while the dogs were swimming. Only one of them turned back and sat on the sledge. It was followed by a second one, but it was chucked off. The lead dog stayed behind, and two others tried to climb onto it, but it began to push onwards again. Once we were past this stretch of water,

---

109. Saviksonitung.
110. Shot by Qeqerten-Schangu.
111. Nudlung.

we had to shake the water out of our sleeping bags. Then we travelled on along the rough ice; we had to cross some more water, but the depth was manageable. We saw another snow-covered glacier on the mountainside. In the evening we reached the end of the fiord, where Schangu had pitched his *tupik*. But there was nobody at the *tupik*; we went inside and we pounced on his caribou meat; it was already starting to have an interesting smell. Once we had satisfied our hunger somewhat we pitched our *tupik* and began cooking. Thereafter we went to bed. My sleeping bag was so wet, that I could not get into it.

*Saturday, 12 July.*

This morning [Padli-] Schangu arrived with two fish that he had caught during the night. So the onus was immediately on me to crawl out, light a fire, and make tea then cook the fish. By 9 o'clock we had already consumed them both. Today we had quite enough to do with drying our things. Throughout the day Schangu was bringing us fish; in the afternoon I cooked a third one. In the evening [Qeqerten-] Schangu also came back; he had plenty of caribou meat.

[Franz Boas wrote in his letter diary to his oldest sister Toni, on the occasion of her and their mother's birthday, and poured out his thoughts: *You once feared that when I came back I would again be as reserved as I once was; that my protracted solitary life would have made me more taciturn, but don't believe it. Send a person into the wilderness, such as I have been living in (for Wilhelm is scarcely company), and he will experience the need to communicate, the need to see people around him with whom he can live, and how I long for my work. You have no idea; and how I long (I'm almost ashamed to admit it) for vegetables and potatoes. The life we are now living (for a week we have had no bread) has a totally (unnerving) demoralizing effect on a person. I often catch myself noting that we are talking about good things such as savoy, peas, cabbage, fruits, things that ought to leave one quite indifferent! But when you live for two months on seal and caribou and very little bread, then you know what sort of effect it can have. We are already revelling in the thought that we will get some rice from the ship!*]

*Sunday, 13 July.*
Today we had to start drying our things again. Both Schangus went off hunting. Today we got the leg of a young caribou and sixteen tongues. The little dogs had gotten into the *tupik* during the night and had gotten into our fish, so that we had a meager breakfast. During the morning I cooked another fish and then I was given the caribou meat. The sky was clear initially, but over the course of the morning it clouded over. As long as we are here up the fiord, we have this horrible *Awananir* wind,[112] which makes it very cold.

*Monday, 14 July to Friday, 18 July.*[113]

---

112. I. *avagna'nirn*: north wind.
113. During this period Weike made no journal entries; see Boas' entries in Müller-Wille 1998:244-245.

# Waiting for the whaling ships at Qivitung (July 19 to August 24)

*Saturday, 19 July.*
Yesterday we had come right around the headland[1] in fog. After we had finished our morning soup we loaded the sledge and then pushed on. We were travelling along the rough ice. [Padli-] Schangu quickly caught up with us with his sledge then went on ahead. The fog was drifting rapidly; ultimately it became sufficiently clear that one could see Tununir[n]. We arrived shortly after noon. We found everything in good shape; I got my cooking pot going and Herr Dr made a sausage sandwich. Once the chocolate was ready we began eating; as much bread as anyone wanted, and in the evening tea again.

*Sunday, 20 July.*
Today was a holiday. Schangu went seal hunting with his entire family; when he came back he had eight seals. The ice here is drying quickly. The natives had seen Schangu on the ice from Tununirn and they all arrived in the evening to visit us.[2] I developed a tooth abscess. It had not cleared completely by this evening. The snow has largely melted.

*Monday, 21 July.*
It rained during the night and the dogs were making such a row that I could not sleep and had to get up several times to drive them away. Schangu again went off with his family. Schangu's mother and Kunurisian[3] arrived today. I did some laundry; it was a very fine day for it today. The ice in the harbour has become almost totally dry. Today I found some really beautiful flowers on the heather here; the flower

---

1. Kangeeaqdjung.
2. Boas wrote: *"Tyson, Bob, Tessigang and a couple of boys came to visit."*
3. According to Boas she was Bob's wife, but did not name her!

looks like that of lily-of-the-valley.[4] Each time I brought in some heather I brought a flower for Herr Dr. In the evening he went out to the ice edge.

*Tuesday, 22 July.*
It is already becoming perceptibly dark here at night; today was a beautiful day, very warm. I cleaned the guns; they looked very fine from the last trip. In the afternoon the natives from Tununirm came over again; Teisen brought some skins. In the evening the entire party went back again. Herr Dr bought a crane[5] chick from Bob.

*Wednesday, 23 July.*
The weather was quite good, but windy. Today Herr Dr gave the seal-skins to [Qeqerten-] Schangu to make into new clothes. Jek[6] stayed here over night; Herr Dr also bought four skins from him. All the men went hunting. Towards evening there was a change in the weather, and there was a new bank of fog every half hour. We thought of them as the acts in a play. Now when we want to cook meat we open a can of meat, take the fat from it, and fry the meat in it. After we had finished supper, we lay down in the *tupik* and began chatting; soon it was 12 o'clock, but the natives had still not come back. We hung up our empty bread bag.

*Thursday, 24 July.*
The natives came back at 3:30. In the morning Schangu and Teschiwan set off to go fishing in a nearby fiord.[7] It was very warm today, and we could see the ice-edge from the *tupik* for the first time. We had laid our sleeping bags out to dry; the pups were sitting on them, so I threw a rock at one and hit it on the head, and it went flying; it was still alive when we went to bed.

---

4. In the German version this plant was incorrectly termed a blueberry (*Vaccinium myrtillus*). William Barr identified it as arctic heather (*Cassiope tetragona*), which Weike was clearly gathering for fuel. Its flower is much more like the lily-of-the-valley than the blueberry flower (William Barr, 2008; see also footnote under 22 September 1883).
5. Sandhill crane (*Grus canadensis*).
6. Jack.
7. Koainilling.

[Franz Boas confirmed: *In the evening Wilhelm threw a stone at poor Waldmannn* [one of the named dogs] *and almost killed it; I'm afraid the poor animal will die.*]

*Friday, 25 July.*
It was a beautiful day today, with little wind; now what we are wishing for is a lot of wind. Every time one of us goes out of the *tupik*, he first looks out towards the ice-edge. There are now major changes in the water on the ice and the fast ice is becoming very bad. Towards evening Herr Dr went to Kiwittun to spy out the situation and Schangu went with him to fish in a pond on the headland. They came back at 11:30; Schangu had caught four trout, one of which had been devoured by Attelschuling [a dog]; he got a thrashing.

*Saturday, 26 July.*
After coffee I went out to fish at the pond; it was very warm and there were many flowers on the other side, with which I adorned my hat. I was there until noon and caught two trout. After we had had lunch we fried the two trout. Schangu and Teschiwan came back in the evening. Schangu had shot a caribou and the lad had shot a calf. Today Herr Dr was adding mountains and glaciers to the land.[8]

*Sunday, 27 July.*
The weather was very fine. Herr Dr wanted to go to Kiwittun to take observations, but as noon approached the sky clouded over. In the afternoon Herr Dr went to spy out the situation; Schangu brought his boat across; and in the meantime Tyson arrived with the boy who lives with Iwi. In the evening Ikeraping came back; after our meal I wanted to go out with the dogs, when I spotted two ptarmigan. I brought the dogs back and fetched my gun. Herr Dr had seen the smoke of a ship.

[Franz Boas stated: *Since Wilhelm was too lazy in the afternoon I climbed the (lookout) hill.*]

---

8. Boas was inserting mountains and glaciers that he had surveyed from the coast on his map.

*Monday, 28 July.*
This morning, after we had had our coffee we packed up our things, to move to the other campsite. The natives hauled everything across along with us; we have a fine campsite here. It was glorious weather. In the evening we got an *Awananir* wind; our only wish was that it would continue for 24 hours, and that the ice would move [out].

*Tuesday, 29 July.*
It was still quite windy this morning, but not strong enough for us. Schangu and Ikeraping went to visit the other Eskimos on the island;[9] Herr Dr went up to the lookout. Gradually the wind died. In the afternoon I was engaged in carpentry. When Herr Dr came back he reported that he had seen the ice edge quite close by. The ice is now very bad. [Qeqerten-] Schangu reported that he wanted to go back to Kikerton. When [Padli-] Schangu came back he brought some caribou meat.

*Wednesday, 30 July.*
Quite fair weather; an *Awananir* wind. The natives went off hunting; Bob and Teschiwan wanted to go to Pali; Schangu started back to Kikerton. Herr Dr gave him a letter for J. M. Nakojaschi arrived in the afternoon. After we had had our afternoon coffee, there will be no more tea, for our sugar was exhausted. I went up to the lookout. I took a flag with me to plant it up there. The ice edge was fairly close; there was a lot of water out there.

*Thursday, 31 July.*
I got up at 8:30; during the night the dogs were kicking up a real racket; at 5:30 one of the pups was yowling loudly outside the *tupik,* and when I looked out it had got hung-up. It had got a fish-hook embedded in its foot and since the rod was firmly fixed it could not get free and was howling terribly. I took it into the *tupik;* I could not get the hook out, so I cut the line away and let it run off. We were still experiencing an *Awananir* in the morning, but in the afternoon it swung round to become an *Ekschun.*[10] Bob and Teschiwan came back because they were

---

9. Tununirn.

10. I. *iki'rtsuq*: a southeasterly onshore wind.

worried that the ice might break up. In the afternoon we were turning somersaults and jumping with the natives. In the meantime thick fog descended and the weather became foul, and hence we stayed in the *tupik* after coffee. Toba[11]—that's all for this month.

# August 1884

*Friday, 1 August.*
Today it was foggy again but quite windy. In the afternoon Akschulu,[12] Jek and Teisen, his son-in-law, arrived. After we had had our coffee I played ball with the natives.

*Saturday, 2 August.*
[Padli-] Schangu, Teschiwan, Ikerapin, and Jack went to the headland today.[13] The fog was still as thick as ever and the wind the same. Schorti[14] was here in the morning, to borrow a sledge from Herr Dr and to move over here with his *tupik*. In the afternoon the camp was complete when Iwi, Teisen, and the second Jek arrived. After lunch we were playing cards, betting on when the fog cleared, and a ship arrived. In the evening we sang until the ... [sun set].

*Sunday, 3 August.*
Today we celebrated both Sunday and a birthday.[15] After our coffee in the morning, we counted our bread: 21 pieces of bread and a box full of crumbs. When the bread bag was empty we hung it from the top of the *tupik*. Then Herr Dr laid some paving stones in front of the door, while I cleaned up inside the *tupik*. At noon we opened a can of meat and in addition we had duck soup. I wanted to go out after our meal, but my stomach was so full that I turned back. Then Herr Dr went out to the lookout. We fed the dogs in the evening.

---

11. I. *taba*: that is all.
12. Akkudku.
13. Kangeeaqdjung.
14. Shorty, English nickname of an Inuk called Appak.
15. The birthday of Marie Krackowizer, Franz Boas' fiancée, who turned 23.

*Monday, 4 August.*
It was still foggy today, and it rained all day, so that one could not do much outside, and hence we stayed in the *tupik* all day; I went outside only when I had to go for the cooking pot. In the evening we first had a general delousing, since we had detected the first head-lice. And then we crawled into our sleeping bags at 7 o'clock and played some cards.

*Tuesday, 5 August.*
The weather was still the same, but without the rain. The natives went hunting. It cleared up somewhat towards noon and hence after our meal I went up to the lookout. I could not see much, however, since the fog returned, but I could see a lot of water. When I came back I prepared supper. After I had washed up, I crawled into my sleeping bag out of boredom. It started to rain again and a sledge came back.

*Wednesday, 6 August.*
Rain and fog all day, so that we could do nothing outside and just ate and slept.

*Thursday, 7 August.*
Schangu did not come back yesterday evening. It was still foggy this morning, but it gradually cleared up. The natives went to *Okaniwing*.[16] The two dogs[17] that had run away are still not back. After lunch I went out to look for flowers; when I came back Herr Dr went to the lookout. There is very little wind; the *Awananirn* that we are longing for refuses to come.

*Friday, 8 August.*
It was clear today and it was very warm in the sunshine. After coffee I went to Kiwittun to look for flowers; in so doing I was sweating profusely. When I came back Herr Dr pressed them immediately.[18] Then I had to think of cooking again, since Herr Dr said he was hungry. We are eating with great enjoyment as long as we can, since our bread will

---

16. Idjuniving.
17. Angutikan and Neinennak.
18. Boas preserved the specimens in a plant-press.

soon be exhausted. The bread bag is now hanging up high, but we do not starve because of that. We were smart to empty the bag and hang it up on the *tupik*. Toba—till it be full again. We picture for ourselves that it would be so nice if it would breed, and when we go and look at it again, it would be full. It will take a while before it will fill up by itself.

### Saturday, 9 August.

The *Awanarnin* we had been hoping for arrived during the night, but still not strong enough for us. All day there was dense fog and it snowed as if it was the end of November. During the course of the afternoon it stopped snowing. For lunch I made soup, into which I threw the last crumbs of bread; now we have just a few whole pieces [of bread] and then it is gone. This evening we were unable to get any freshly killed seals either, since nobody has gone hunting in the past few days, and hence we opened a can of meat, and I also made pea soup.

### Sunday, 10 August.

Schangu came back from Nalunguak[19] at 2 o'clock last night; while they were away, both Schangu and Jek had each killed a caribou. Here Herr Dr took the sun's altitude to get the time and our latitude, and in the afternoon he went up the hill with Schangu to take observations. The wind we had been longing for arrived today; some snow also fell at the same time; as the day wore on, the stronger the wind became. Herr Dr was constantly watching the barometer. Yesterday evening I had lain down to read, but at 10 o'clock my light went out; it became dark so that nothing could be seen in the *tupik*. This is really unpleasant for us, in that one can no longer do what one wants at night, since it is dark. Schangu, Teschiwan and Jek came back at 2 o'clock. Schangu paid us a visit immediately. In the morning we received a caribou leg, a liver, and a tongue. They had shot only two caribou while they were away. In the morning it was clear with some wind and hence Herr Dr prepared to go up the hill to take observations. He first took the time and the sun's altitude here. After the meal Herr Dr and Schangu set off; when they came back *Annora Akschalu*[20] started up which really delighted us.

---

19. Nedluqseaq.
20. I. *anu're oqu'qtsuaq*: there was a southeast wind blowing.

The barometer was still dropping, and towards evening it also started to snow a little. Teisen brought two *naug* and two divers.[21] *Toba*— enough for now.

### Monday, 11 August.

It had snowed so much during the night that the land was entirely white; the wind had blown all night; the barometer rose very rapidly this morning. Over the course of the day the snow largely disappeared from the land, but it still lay very deep on the ice. In the afternoon I went up the hill to the lookout; the ice had changed a great deal, since I last saw it. Some of the natives were out hunting. This evening it was still very windy, with the wind coming in gusts.

### Tuesday, 12 August.

This morning the natives went off hunting early; the weather was quite fine. In the afternoon Herr Dr went up the hill to the lookout; in the meantime Jek came back; he had shot an *Uguk*.[22] In the evening it started to blow a little; it was very unpleasant outside, and hence we had crawled into our sleeping bags by 8:30. Schangu came back late, bringing a caribou.

### Wednesday, 13 August.

Last night we had quite a lot of wind and it had again been snowing hard, so that the land was again quite white. The sun broke through however, so that today the snow melted considerably. The wind persisted all day today; in the evening it swung around, to become *Ikürzuk*.[23] For tomorrow morning we still have a piece of bread; the bag has become full again. The only thing that is really unpleasant for us is that it becomes dark, since we are not accustomed to this at all. We are constantly hoping for more wind. We pass most of our time by eating; this evening we were drinking coffee for two hours.

---

21. I. *nauja*: gull; diver: arctic loon (*Gavia immer*).
22. I. *ujjuq*: bearded seal (*Erignathus barbatus*).
23. I. *iki'rtsuq*: an onshore wind from the southeast.

*Thursday, 14 August.*
Today the wind we had been longing for arrived, but it also brought a lot of fog and snow with it, so that it was far from pleasant to be outside, and hence we stayed in the *tupik* most of the time. In the afternoon, we were so delighted that we didn't know what to do, because it was blowing so hard. Herr Dr played the concertina and I accompanied him by drumming, and finally we had to parade the guard; Herr Dr was drumming on a large tin can while I played on the botanizing drum.

[Franz Boas wrote: *In the afternoon Wilhelm and I made a disgusting row with tin drums and plates, tattoo etc. The Eskimos must certainly have thought we were* ankuting.]

*Friday, 15 August.*
In the evening the wind swung around again and all night long it blew very strongly from the other direction; it was snowing at the same time, so that one soon could not even see for fifty paces. In the morning we had a cold meal, since it was blowing so badly that we could not brew coffee. We stayed in our sleeping bags until the afternoon; then at 1:30 I turned out and made coffee. The wind had slackened somewhat, and the snow had also stopped. Towards evening it was calm; the snow had already frozen hard.

*Saturday, 16 August.*
The natives went hunting today; the weather was quite tolerable today. After lunch I took my gun and went for a stroll. Since Schangu had brought the two ptarmigan chicks, I thought I might still encounter others here on the land. It rained in the afternoon; and in the evening the rain became quite heavy. It was dark when Schangu came back

*Sunday, 17 August.*
Today it was raining heavily. In the morning, before we'd had our coffee, Schangu's mother arrived and sang some songs for Herr Dr. Over the course of the morning it was raining quite heavily; the natives went hunting but were already back by noon. All of a sudden a strong *Awananirn* began; and with it the rain ceased. Schangu visited Herr Dr and examined maps of different countries, and was amazed that everything looked

so close. In the afternoon the weather improved somewhat; we were repacking things, since we have no time during the week.

### Monday, 18 August.

The *Awananirn* was still blowing quite strongly, so that one had to believe that it was helping. Herr Dr went to Kiwittun to climb the hill, but due to the strong wind he did not get all the way up. After we had had our coffee I too went over to Kiwittun again. Down by the pond I discovered the graves in which four whites lay buried.[24] I scanned the water and then went back to camp. We saw the first stars again this evening.

### Tuesday, 19 August.

It froze quite hard last night; the ice on the water was at least as thick as one's finger. Initially we had wanted to go to Kiwittun to make observations, but since the sky was overcast, we stayed here. I spread our sleeping bags out so that the lice might crawl out. Teschiwan went to fish for salmon; while all the other natives went hunting. After lunch I headed up inland to check out the situation once more; when I came back we devoured our supper. Schangu was still here, giving Herr Dr vocabulary. At 9:30 in the evening Schangu came and reported that Nakojaschi had seen a ship offshore. Schorti made his sledge ready since he wanted to go out this evening; but we wanted to sleep over it first.

### Wednesday, 20 August.

I got up at 5 o'clock this morning so that I would be ready early, since we wanted to go to the floe edge to look for the ship. We had our coffee at 6 o'clock; and then we got ready. Schangu harnessed the dogs. Once we were all ready, we put our things into the large *tupik,* except for the two large boxes that stayed where they were. Once the *tupik* was secured[25] we set off with the sledge; Teisen and Jek had gone on ahead but it was not long before we caught up with them, since our dogs were moving at a trot. When we reached the headland,[26] we stopped since

---

24. Franz Boas did not mention these graves.
25. What is meant is that the tent was tied shut and secured with rocks all round, so that it could be determined if it had been opened.
26. Kangeeaqdjung.

there was water there. We could see the ship;[27] it was still a long way off. It became foggy and hence we turned back. Once we were back home we cooked ourselves a fine soup. It started snowing again, with an *Awananir* wind. In the afternoon Schorti also came back; he had not reached the ship.

*Thursday, 21 August.*
This morning Herr Dr went up to the cairn to check whether the ship was somewhere offshore. The natives went in a boat to Kangerschuk[28] to hunt walrus. It was close to noon when they set off. When Herr Dr came back he reported that there were many cracks offshore. In the afternoon I was up the hill on this side, but was back by 6:45. While I was up there, the ice had broken away, so that one could see the water from the *tupik*. The natives came back at 10 o'clock; Schangu had taken three walrus, the meat of which was put aside for our dogs.

*Friday, 22 August.*
In the morning the sky was initially overcast. After we had had our coffee it was clear. Herr Dr took a time observation and then went up the hill. The natives went back to Kangerschu; they took their things with them since they planned to sleep there. Herr Dr came back; he had not gone right up; the edge of the sun had not been discernible. In the afternoon I boiled our clothes so that they would be free of lice and would be clean again. At 9 o'clock Schorti came back from Kangerschu.[29]

*Saturday, 23 August.*
It was not very clear this morning [so that] Herr Dr could not take the observation. The main thing we did was to feed our faces, as they say here. My new pants were ready. Schorti went off again, but he came back again because he could not get across the crack. I went for a walk with the dogs around the headland. Herr Dr walked over the headland, to wake himself up.

---

27. The Scottish whaling ship *Arctic* under Captain Adams.
28. Kangeeaqdjung.
29. Boas wrote: *"He had shot two walrus and two seals."*

*Sunday, 24 August.*

An ordinary Sunday. The sun barely showed itself; at 9 o'clock Herr Dr took a time observation, and thereafter the *tupik* was secured; once this was done we went up to the cairn. Once up there, we had to take the observations as quickly as possible, since it was becoming foggy. Once we'd finished we packed the bag and headed home again. Once we had finished our lunch the natives also came back from their walrus hunt;[30] it was horribly cold in the evening. *Toba*—enough for now!

---

30. Boas wrote: *"Shangin had shot three walrus."*

# Homeward voyage on board the *Wolf* (August 25 to September 1)

*Monday, 25 August.*
After we had finished lunch Schangu's Itu came and reported that there were two ships offshore.[1] Then all that was left to do was to get the sledge ready and head off. We raced out, as fast as the dogs could run, and reached the ship[2] in the evening; we were given a very warm welcome and Herr Dr received several letters.

*Tuesday, 26 August.*
This morning the *Wolf* arrived, along with another ship.[3] Herr Dr went aboard [*Wolf*] and asked if he would take us with him. The captain replied that if we were back aboard in good time, he planned to sail the next morning. Then we headed ashore as fast as possible to fetch our things; I was on board by 1:30 and went to sleep.

*Wednesday, 27 August.*
This morning, Wednesday, *Wolf* put to sea at 9:30.

*Thursday, 28 August to Sunday, 30 August.*[4]

*Sunday, 31 August.*
We would have been here in the evening, just as the ship got to the harbour[5] and then back again. Last night the ship was hove-to due to ice.

---

1. These were the Scottish whaling ships *Jan Mayen*, Captain William Douchars, and *Nova Zembla*, Captain David Kilgour, both out of Dundee (Boas in Müller-Wille 1998:257 and ship list, p. 268-269).
2. *Nova Zembla*.
3. These were the whaling ships *Wolf*, Captain John Burnett, out of St. John's (Newfoundland) and *Cornwallis*, Captain McGregory, probably from Scotland (Müller-Wille 1998:268-269).
4. Wilhelm Weike made no journal entries from Thursday 28 to Sunday, August 30.
5. Exeter Bay / Karmaqdjuin.

# September 1884

*Monday, 1 September.*
It was quite windy in the morning, and a gale in the evening that lasted all night. Herr Dr and I were seasick.

[The continuation of the voyage via St. John's and Halifax to New York, as well as Wilhelm Weike's and Franz Boas' separate homeward journeys from New York to Minden are described and explained by the authors in their commentary following the journal and the letters.]

# Back in Germany— Correspondence with Franz Boas (1884-1889)

Minden, Monday, October 13, 1884.

Dear Herr Dr:

My sincere congratulations on Fräulein Hedwig's engagement.[1] I arrived safely on the 9th [October, Thursday]. The crossing was very fine. There were several young people on board, so that I had pleasant company. One family travelled with me to Minden. The greatest thing that happened was that L. Kloy, who was the last of my friends that I saw at the station in Hanover when I was leaving last year,[2] was the first person I saw on my return. He was on his way to see his bride. They were to be married next day. We had two hours together at the station in Wunstorf and hence he was able to tell me many things about what had been happening in Minden. Dear Herr Dr, on the 11th [October] a letter arrived from Mr. Much [Mutch] to the effect that our things are in Scotland.[3] He also asked about the barometer. If you are writing from there, be so kind as to greet Mr. Much for me. If you are writing to *Wolf*'s captain[4] please pass on my greetings to the captain and his cousin. There has been quite a lot of change here. Two new houses have been built on our street;[5] one of them is located on the parade ground, in the Leonardi's garden, and the other in the Staht's

---

1. Hedwig (Hete) Boas, Franz Boas' younger sister, who had become engaged to Rudolf Lehmann.
2. On 17 June 1883.
3. Boas had left many boxes at the Scottish whaling station; these were shipped via Aberdeen to Hamburg/Minden in late summer, 1884.
4. John Burnett.
5. Marienstraße.

garden.[6] The street in front of our house has also been fixed up. Trees have been planted on the street below. There is not much fruit here; the fruit harvest has turned out badly and hence it is very dear. But it is not as warm here as in New York. It is more comfortable here. I hope you will also be returning home too. With many greetings from your

Wilhelm Weike
Please give my regards to Herr Theo[dore] Meier.[7]

Dear Herr Dr:
Since Wilhelm is writing to you I want to take this opportunity to send you and your dear bride the heartiest congratulations for a double engagement.[8] Oh, Herr Dr, if only you could be here to ensure that you have good luck, this is the only thing. I hope that you will arrive soon, Herr Dr, please accept best wishes for yourself and for your dear bride, from your

Mathilde Nolting
[Wilhelm Weike, Mathilde Nolting/Franz Boas, Minden/New York, 13 October 1884]

Minden, Sunday, November 30, 1884.

Dear Herr Dr:
My sincere thanks for your letter.[9] It is really great to be back home again. But I still retain the greatest memories from the past year. We get endless pleasure when we get an essay to read aloud below here.[10] Our things have all arrived too, even the trading

---

6. Neighbours of the Boas family in Marienstraße in Minden.
7. Theodore Meyer (1844-1903), husband of Marie Krackowizer's older sister Helene (1856-1939) in New York (Boas, N. 2004:295).
8. Franz Boas had informed his family of his secret engagement to Marie Krackowizer on 28 May 1883 only at this time.
9. This letter did not survive.
10. What is probably meant is that the servants working in the basement of the Boas house were reading Franz Boas' series of articles in the *Berliner Tageblatt*.

chest and its contents.[11] The guns were very well packed. Every-thing is in the best condition. Singnar did not get the little concer-tina. It was still in the chest.[12]

Dear Herr Dr, I hope that you too will soon be coming over. If I know ahead of time that you are coming, I will pull hard so that you come over quickly. If Bill[13] comes back first and if you are writ-ing to him be so good as to greet him from me. Today Fräulein Hede [Hete] had a coffee gathering and I had to dress up as an Eskimo. I was standing in winter attire. I had laid out my sleeping bag in the living room, and then I had to crawl into it. But it is too warm for this clothing indoors here. I could not stand it for long. It is looking somewhat wintry outside here now too. Everything is white again. But it is not so cold. Give my regards to your lady bride. Many sincere thanks for your congratulations.[14] I hope that you will be back here by Christmas, and I wish you a good sea voyage.

Sincere greetings,
Your Wilhelm Weike.
[Wilhelm Weike/Franz Boas, Minden/New York, 30 November 1884]

Berlin, Monday, January 21, 1889.
Dear Herr Dr
After a long time I am writing to you again. So far things have been going well for us and Mathilde has adjusted very well to life in Berlin. I am still in the same job that I got when I first came here.[15] Whether a decision will be reached this year I still can't say, since the property is still under the management of the

---

11. The chest in which Franz Boas had taken trade articles with him for the Inuit.

12. See authors' discussion of the exchange of letters between James Mutch and Franz Boas at the end.

13. Wilhelm (Bill) Scherden.

14. Probably Boas' congratulations to Wilhelm Weike's engagement to Mathilde Nolting, the date of which is not known.

15. From January 1886 the Weikes were living in Berlin. In the Berlin directory Weike's occupation is listed as "doorman", probably in the apartment block he mentioned, over which the owners' heirs fought, and where he lived and worked at least until October 1889.

courts. The heirs were suing each other until last summer, but we've heard nothing as to what decision had been reached. I have a contract until October [1889].

Dear Herr Dr, it is a real pity that you are not in Berlin too, for since your dear parents have been here too,[16] for us it is just as when we were in Minden. I visit them almost every week and always hear how things are going with Herr Dr and when there are reports in the newspaper, I get them to read. I was there this evening and Frau Boas gave me a Prague newspaper to read, in which Herr Dr wrote about the fine December night when we were looking for Arnanitung.[17] It reads better than it was at the time. I still often think about the days we spent with the dear Eskimos. I have very fond memories. Many evenings I have sat and told my wife about it; she'll soon know how things were there, as well as I do myself.

Dear Herr Dr, how delighted we were to hear of your little daughter.[18] Fräulein Toni came and showed us her picture. Mathilde says she looks exactly like Herr Dr. The little one must be really cute. It must be great to have such a little being around. Happiness is just shining from your wife's eyes. I hope that you will come to visit very soon so that we can all admire your little daughter too. I've often said to Mathilde that if the little one were here she would be quite spoilt by her grandparents and aunts. Dear Herr Dr, I should like to thank you very much for the stamps you sent me, since stamp collecting is my evening pastime; I've already accumulated a thousand.

Many sincere regards from Mathilde for you and your wife. Best wishes, your

Wilhelm
Please forgive my bad writing, since this is one of my weak points.
[Wilhelm Weike/Franz Boas, Berlin/New York, January 21, 1889]

---

16. Boas Sr. and his wife moved from Minden to Berlin in 1887 (Cole 1999:109).
17. This refers to Boas' newspaper article "Trip to Anamitung" [Anarnitung] that was published on Sunday, 4 January 1885 in the *Berliner Tageblatt* (Volume 4, No. 5:6-7) and had probably been republished in Prague in a German-language newspaper (unidentified).
18. Helene Boas was born in New York in the fall of 1888 (Boas, N.F. 2006:292).

# PART 2

# WILHELM WEIKE
## Life in Germany
## and on Baffin Island
## (1859-1917)

*Wilhelm Weike's journal, which he kept in 1883-84, is a unique personal and literary document. Although it has been known about for years, for a long time it had been "slumbering" in the archives of the American Philosophical Society, in the bequest of his then employer, Franz Boas, of Minden, who became so famous. In its unfading freshness and directness, this journal and the few surviving letters convey how an ordinary working-class domestic servant from Westphalia in northwestern Germany experienced a one-year sojourn, initiated and shaped by scientific endeavour, in regions of the Arctic and among the Inuit, a people little known, or almost unknown, to Europeans of the time.*

## Youth in Häverstädt and servant in the Boas household in Minden (1859-1883)

Wilhelm Weike came from the eastern Westphalian town of Häverstädt, earlier also spelled Häverstedt. Sometimes, although rarely, the surname is also rendered as "Weicke," but from 1877 onwards it always appears in sources as "Weike." On January 25, 1884, he mentions his own surname, the only occasion that he does so, and renders it as "Weicke." He signed his later letters with "Weike."

This ordinary man kept a journal. Under the Prussian government, education was compulsory for everyone in Germany. Weike could therefore read and write. However, his spelling and punctuation were somewhat defective. He himself identifies this weakness in a later letter to Franz Boas: *"Please forgive my bad writing, for this is one of my weak points."* (Wilhelm Weike/Franz Boas, Berlin/New York, 21 January 1889).

One is nonetheless pleasantly surprised by his ability to express himself. Writing is not in Weike's blood, certainly, but despite that his language is clear, powerful, graphic, and sometimes full of irony. Still, the journal remains an assignment for him—an assignment that ends when he leaves the Arctic for the final entry occurs on September 1, 1884 on board the *Wolf.* The homeward voyage had begun and the journal ends.

Weike begins his journal less abruptly. He describes his last days on shore preceding the long sea voyage, and talks of friends and relatives whom he meets and from whom he takes his leave. At that point

Wilhelm Weike is working as servant and gardener in the Boas house-hold in Minden. He had trained as a gardener, for on November 6, 1877, at the age of almost eighteen, he had moved from Häverstädt to 4 Königstraße, Minden, home of August Ahlersmeyer, an artistic gardener who trained him and with whom he worked until September 30, 1879 (Residents' Registration Office, Municipal Archives, Minden). The profession of "artistic gardener" corresponds to today's "landscape artist."

Wilhelm Heinrich Christian Weike was born *"in wedlock,"* at 5 o'clock in the morning on November 28, 1859 in house No. 223, in today's Fliederstraße, in Häverstädt in eastern Westphalia, the village on the Wiehen as it is called locally. In the mid-nineteenth century this was a village of small farmers and craftsmen, located a few kilometres southwest of Minden/Westphalia, on the south slopes of the Wiehen Mountains. Wilhelm was the youngest of the three children of Louise Weike, née Bruns, and Christian Weike, whose occupation is not known. Little Wilhelm was baptized by pastor Ohley in the Evangelical-Lutheran St. Martini church in Minden on Monday, December 26, 1859, the second day of Christmas. His godparents were Heinrich Temme and Gottlieb Häger, both from Häverstädt (Entry no. 146, baptismal register 1859, Martini Land). Wilhelm Weike grew up in the house in which he was born. The house was part of a four-house development that then belonged to the municipality. In Häverstädt, until 1955 when street names were introduced, dwelling houses were given numbers in the sequence in which they were built (all information provided by Hubert Knicker/Bernd Gieseking, Häverstädt, 17 March 1997).

In 1856 there were 796 residents in Häverstädt; in 2006 there were over 4000. The community had become independent in 1811 and joined the City of Minden as part of the administrative reforms of 1973 (all data: Häverstädt 2007). In March 1997, from interviews with some older residents, Bernd Gieseking determined that neither the family nor the name Weike were known any longer, even in the house where Wilhelm Weike was born.

Wilhelm Weike attended the elementary school in Häverstädt, although it is not recorded when and for how long. The general compulsory education in Prussia was between the ages of six and fourteen; for Weike that would have been from Easter 1866 until Easter 1874. From

Grade 1 he was probably taught by teacher Busse, who was employed in the Häverstädt school from 1858 until 1898. At that time a school fee of one thaler and a heating fee of fifty pfennigs (about CAD$8.30 in 2011). had to be paid for each child (1861 data; Schulchronik Häverstädt 1878/79 to 1898). Franz Boas later expressed a verdict as to Wilhelm Weike's school education and capabilities: *I have just been teaching Wilhelm some more English. But he has a frightfully hard head, which it is difficult to get anything into. But that is not surprising, since he really has never learned anything* (June 25, 1883; Boas in Müller-Wille 1998:48).

Christian Weike, Wilhelm's father, was born in 1822, and died of consumption at 4 p.m. on Saturday, January 5, 1861, at the age of 36, as attested by the doctor, Dr Bronh. He left his wife Louise with three very young children; Wilhelm was just one year old. Christian Weike was buried on Wednesday, January 9, 1861. The *Colon* (tenant) Lange, who lived at House No. 33 (Entry No. 1, Register of deaths for the community of Häverstädt, 1861), was designated as guardian of the three fatherless children. (The names of Wilhelm's two older siblings could not be ascertained.) Shortly after that Wilhelm's grandfather Adolph Weike died on February 1, 1861, of old age, at the age of 73; he also lived in House no. 223 (Entry No. 4, Register of deaths for the community of Häverstädt 1861).

In his first journal entry, on June 10, 1883, immediately before he set off, Wilhelm Weike mentioned that he visited his father and older brother in Häverstädt, to say goodbye. It can therefore be assumed that Weike's mother had married again, and that here Weike was saying goodbye to his stepfather; his mother had already died. That is deduced from the files of the Minden Municipal Archives. On January 28, 1879, Wilhelm Weike, who was just nineteen years old, was transferred from the registry of his home-community of Häverstädt to the military rolls for the town of Minden as a conscript. His occupation is recorded as servant at the Ahlersmeyer gardener's business; it was also recorded that his parents were deceased (Minden Municipal Archives).

Whether Weike went to school until 1874 and where he was apprenticed or working between 1874 and 1877 cannot be determined. While he was travelling with Franz Boas on Baffin Island, Weike showed that he was well experienced with firearms—rifles and revolvers—whether in terms of cleaning, sighting-in or handling them, and with pouring bullets. Judging from his descriptions, he had considerable success at hunting there because of his unerring aim. The question is where and from whom had he learned that? One possibility is military service, but between 1877 and 1883 he was working. From the archival materials it is impossible to establish that Weike performed military service, which for regular recruits at that time lasted for three years; it is improbable, however.

In his journal, however, he mentions the military or uses descriptive references to it. In his letter of September 18, 1883, Weike mentions that they played *"Minden military music"* and that " Herr Dr," as Wilhelm always addressed Franz Boas and referred to him in his journal and letters, said that Weike must now be promoted from recruit to NCO (non-commissioned officer). Later, at the end of the expedition on August 14, 1884, both men, Boas and Weike, were marching around in their tented camp near Qivitung and, with the Inuit, were beating out the "changing of the guard" and the "last post" on tin drums, killing time while waiting for whaling ships. For their part, the Inuit believed that the two men were "ankuting," i.e., that it was some type of invocation of their gods.

From October 1, 1879, Wilhelm Weike, who was almost twenty years of age, was employed as gardener and house servant by Meyer Boas and his wife Sophie, née Meyer. They were owners of a textile business at the Market in Minden and were Franz Boas' parents. Weike was registered under their address. They had moved into their "Villa Boas," at 19 Marienstraße (sometimes also listed as No. 17), completed only in the late summer of that year. Weike's future wife, Mathilde Nolting, from Rinteln, was already working there. She had been employed as housemaid in the Boas household since October 17, 1876. Another woman, Sophie Barner, whom Weike mentioned in his letters, is listed as a housemaid with the Boas household (Minden Municipal Archives). Prior to Weike's departure for the Arctic in June 1883, another house-maid was engaged by the Boas family; her name was Linna (Boas spelled it Lina; her surname is unknown). In the fall of 1883 Weike sent joint letters to Linna and Mathilde from Baffin Island.

Franz Boas' parents lived in the "Villa Boas" until June 20, 1887; they sold it in February 1887. From Minden they moved to 2 Kurfürstenstraße in Berlin where their three daughters Antonie (Toni), Hedwig (Hete), and Aenna (Anna) had settled for employment and for family reasons. Meyer Boas had given up his Minden business, and in Berlin he founded an international business agency. Despite the protests of the people of Minden the "Villa Boas" was torn down in the summer of 1980 (Cole 1988: 130, 132, 134; Boas, N. 2004:4-5, 7).

But one cannot hide the fact that Franz Boas, in terms of both his life and work, is still unknown to wide sections of the Minden population. For a long time there was no attempt to make this world-famous scientist a part of the collective memory of the citizens of his hometown, and even today only a few individuals have made any such efforts (cf. Billing 1966; Rodekamp 1994; Langenkämper 2008; Mindener Museum ... 2007; Bender-Wittmann 2008). Since 1969 a small street in a then-new development has borne his name. The popular protest at the tearing-down of the house must rather be seen as an isolated manifestation. Even less well known is the fact that Boas took Wilhelm Weike with him as his companion on his first trip.

A story that Franz Boas wrote around 1900 about his sojourn with the Inuit on Baffin Island for his five adolescent children was recently edited and published by his grandson Norman F. Boas, physician and author (born 1922). Here Franz Boas wrote about Wilhelm Weike as follows:

> "It would not have been very pleasant to travel alone, so I needed a companion as well as someone to help in my work. You know Wilhelm who used to help grandpa in his office. At the time I was preparing for my trip, he was with your grandparents, tending their gardens. He wished very much to accompany me and I was very glad to take him along. He was able to help me in all my work, and it was very nice to have someone to whom I could talk about home." (Boas 2007:4).

Wilhelm Weike accompanied Franz Boas as his servant to Baffin Island in the eastern Canadian Arctic from June 20, 1883 until September 21, 1884; he returned to Minden from New York via Hamburg in the last week of September, arriving on October 9. Weike then continued to work at the "Villa Boas" for somewhat more than a year. In early January 1886 he moved to Berlin, having married Mathilde Nolting in the interim.

## Franz Boas—German polar research
## and expedition to Baffin Island (1882-1884)

Franz Boas' path to geography and ethnology and to the Inuit and whalers on Baffin Island has been discussed in detail elsewhere (Cole 1883, 1999; Cole and Müller-Wille 1984; Knötsch 1992; this chapter is mostly based on Müller-Wille 1998:6-11). Boas himself mentioned that already as a boy—around 1868-1869—he was very keen on the northern polar regions and their history of exploration and was reading books on the subject (among them most likely a book edited by Hermann Wagner [1867] that included a large fold-out map of Arctic North America; personal communication by Utz Maas, 2008). These were years when "polar fever" was gripping Germany and when expeditions were being sent to the Arctic Ocean and reported on extensively in the press. Boas began his studies at Heidelberg in the summer of 1877 and later studied at Kiel where he received his doctorate in 1881. In Kiel the geographer Theobald Fischer (1846-1910), with whom he had also studied at Bonn in 1877-78, influenced him through his lectures and seminars and led him to polar research by posing geographical and ethnological questions (Cole and Müller-Wille 1984:41).

The first German arctic voyages were carried out in 1868 and 1869-1870 in the Greenland Sea (Krause 1992). Greater, systematically designed research projects were planned that were to provide a more deeply penetrating understanding of the physical conditions and climatic interrelationships in the Arctic and Antarctic. In 1875, Karl Weyprecht (1838-1881), an influential German polar researcher living and working in Austria, was the first to propose the idea of an internationally and globally conceived research regime in European scientific circles (Alfred-Wegener-Institut 1993:53). The German Polar Commission, founded to attain this research goal, which was also nationalistically inspired under the energetic leadership of Georg von Neumayer (then head of the German Naval Observatory in Hamburg; 1826-1909), took a leading role in the planning and organization of this collaborative operation among the national expeditions within the framework of the Polar Year of 1882-83 (Alfred-Wegener-Institut 1993:53-56), later referred to as the First International Polar Year. Eleven nations participated in that very first year-of-science, with a total of fourteen research stations, twelve in the Arctic and two in the Antarctic, and three additional auxiliary stations (Barr 1985:4, 2008:7).

In addition to an expedition to South Georgia and a one-man-operation at Nain (Labrador), the German Polar Commission dispatched an expeditionary group of eleven men (seven scientists and four workers), on board the *Germania,* to the north end of Cumberland Sound, Baffin Island, in the summer of 1882. Between September 1882 and September 1883, the crew carried out station-based scheduled and regular environmental measurements of the most varied kind, using the most modern instruments, and took all recordings synchronously with all the other research stations (Neumayer and Börgen 1886; Neumayer 1890, 1891; see also Abbes 1992 [1884], Barr 1992; Barr and Tolley 1982).

The German personnel spent the year in a prefabricated, winterized house at Kingua, also known as Clearwater Fiord. The station hired one of the local Inuit, Ocheitu (Oqaitung, according to Boas), as "*local labour,*" or, to use the Germans' own expression "*our house-Eskimo*" (Ambronn 1883:352). Ocheitu lived for a year with his family in a tent or snow house barely 100 metres from the station, hunted and fished for the Germans, and in so doing learned a little German (Abbes 1890; Eliyak Keenainak/Ludger Müller-Wille, Salliq/St. Lambert (Canada), 17 September 1984). It was Ocheitu who, on December 21, 1883, very obligingly welcomed Franz Boas and Wilhelm Weike into his *iglu* at Anarnitung and looked after Weike, who had sustained very severe frostbite in both feet during their trek across the pack ice.

The Germans established relations, although only to a limited degree, with the Inuit and with the wintering Scottish and American whalers, whose crews were of various nationalities. After their return, in addition to their publications in natural sciences, some of the expedition members also published ethnographic papers on the Inuit (Abbes 1884, 1890; Ambronn 1883). They also brought back to Germany numerous ethnographic items that they had bought from the Inuit (see illustrations in Abbes 1884). These collections were private and could not be traced in museums.

At the time of the preparations for, and execution of, the Polar Year of 1882-83 Boas fulfilled his compulsory military service as a one-year volunteer in the 15th Infantry (Prince Friedrich of the Netherlands)

Regiment in Minden (October 1, 1881 until September 30, 1882). During that time he was allowed to continue to live at home. In parallel with his military service he found sufficient free time to plan and advance his scientific career. He decided on a year of field research with the Inuit of the *"British American Arctic"* (Cole 1988:129-131). Thus in telling his sister Hete about how he was spending his time in the military, he wrote: *"The only thing is that from time to time I can read something about my Eskimos, and take notes on them."* (Franz Boas/Hedwig Boas, Minden/ Paris, 14 May 1882; Boas in Müller-Wille 1998:33). Critical in his selection of the location in the Arctic were the winterized whaling stations in Cumberland Sound, especially on Kekerten Island (Boas writes Qeqerten), that had existed for decades; but so too was the fact that Christian missionaries had not yet established themselves in that region. Boas was counting on being able to investigate the *"natural unspoiled situation"* of the *"simple relationships between land and people,"* i.e., between the arctic environment and the Inuit. For Boas this turned out to be a fallacy, since the cultural and economic influence of the whalers on the Inuit society during the preceding few decades had increased and one could no longer speak of a culturally *"unspoiled situation."*

Members of the German Polar Commission and other arctic explorers, such as Moritz Lindeman (1823-1906) from Bremen, had promised Boas generous logistical assistance and had arranged contacts with Scottish whalers in Aberdeen and Dundee and with the British Admiralty in London. The latter body still played an important role in the Canadian Arctic although Great Britain had handed over its assumed sovereignty over the Arctic Archipelago to the Dominion of Canada in 1880. Boas also made contact with other scientists, and corresponded concerning the language of the Inuit (Inuktitut) with the Danish geographer and linguist Hinrich Johannes Rink (1819-1893), a former colonial official in Greenland, and with the philologist Heyman Steinthal (1823-1899) in Berlin. He visited both men in the spring of 1883. To what extent Boas had acquired a basic knowledge of the Inuit language prior to the expedition is not apparent from the sources.

In May 1883 he sent a list of questions, via the Crawford Noble Whaling Company, to James Mutch, the station manager on Baffin

Island, with a request that he translate them into Inuktitut (Franz Boas/ Crawford Noble, Minden/Aberdeen, May 1883). He probably received a reply only when he met Mutch at the end of August 1883 at his station on Kekerten. Boas made further intensive preparations for his arctic sojourn, by familiarizing himself with the literature available in German university libraries on the northern polar regions, on European and North American whaling and on the Inuit (Müller-Wille 1998:9).

In the winter of 1882-83 Franz Boas also spent some months in Berlin with a view to scientific preparation for his arctic expedition and in order to obtain the support of scientific institutions and of famous scientists such as Rudolf von Virchow (physical anthropologist; 1821-1902) and Adolf Bastian (ethnologist; 1826-1905). He also learned the latest topographic and cartographic survey techniques, as well as photography using a plate camera, which unfortunately failed him on Baffin Island since he overexposed or incorrectly developed the majority of the 48 glass plates that he took with him (Müller-Wille 1998:18). Only a few of his photos survived. Probably the best photo of the entire trip was taken by Wilhelm Weike; he photographed Franz Boas on August 6, 1883 on the deck of the *Germania* when she was cruising in a holding pattern off the pack ice in Cumberland Sound (see Weike's journal).

In terms of practical preparations for a wintering in the Arctic, Boas sought the advice of experienced "travellers of the Northern Sea," *Nordmeer-Reisende* (Cole and Müller-Wille 1984:42). He anticipated that during his sojourn he would have no contact with the outside world, would need to take care of himself independently, and would have to adapt to the local practices of the whalers and the culture of the Inuit. He could count on provisions and items of equipment left behind at the German polar station where he initially intended to winter. The Scottish whaling station on Kekerten Island in Cumberland Sound also offered itself as a base and as possible accommodation. Boas was wisely prepared for a second wintering in case no whaling ship could reach the Sound after the first winter. His equipment conformed to the most modern advances of the time: the finest survey instruments, camera, theodolite, rifles, revolvers, tent, boat, sledge, tools of every kind, an abundant supply of coal, clothing, adequate provisions, and trade items for the Inuit (Boas in Müller-Wille 1998:41-42).

It should be stressed here that Franz Boas financed his expedition entirely from private funds that his father made available. At that time Boas himself had no job and no income of any kind. After submitting two sample articles to the recently established *Berliner Tageblatt* in Berlin, he managed to negotiate with Rudolf Mosse (1843-1920), editor-in-chief, and Arthur Levysohn (1841-1908), its department head for foreign affairs, securing a contract for a series of sixteen articles, in part under the title "Northern Travel Sketches." For this series of articles, which were published partly before and partly after the expedition, between March 20, 1883 and April 27, 1885, he received 3000 marks (Cole and Müller-Wille 1984; see the list of newspaper articles in Müller-Wille 1984:117-120). That money was paid to him as a lump-sum advance prior to his trip, for which Boas Senior again stood surety. The total cost of the expedition is unknown; it included Weike's wages and expenses that were also paid for by Boas Senior. Today, the purchasing power of 3000 marks would amount to $35,700 in 2011 Canadian dollars (Matthäi 2007), a substantial sum for that time.

Boas received no direct monetary contributions from the public funds that the German imperial government had granted for polar research as a whole and for the Polar Year of 1882-1883 specifically (Cole and Müller-Wille 1984). Boas' expedition was thus not part of the enterprises officially carried out within that framework, and hence was never included in the relevant lists of German polar expeditions (Bundesarchiv, Acta des Auswärtigen Amts, Abteilung IIIb – Kunst und Forschung – Acta des Reichamtes des Inneren). In similar fashion, Boas' research on Baffin Island remained generally unheeded and unmentioned in general accounts of the history of the development of German polar research; on the other hand, some of his original drawings and maps that he produced on Baffin Island in 1883-84 were published without acknowledgement (Alfred-Wegener-Institut 1993:55, Fig. 87).

Boas managed nonetheless, through his contacts in Berlin scientific circles, to develop personal relationships with the German Polar Commission, and especially with Georg von Neumayer in Hamburg. Strong and positive recommendations from high-ranking figures in Berlin resulted in the Commission allowing Boas and Weike to travel free on board its expedition ship, the *Germania*. On Baffin Island, Boas received expeditionary items and provisions as well as survey instruments and rifles from the German polar station, the latter he returned to the Commission after the expedition (Boas in Müller-Wille 1998:41-42, 93). But all of that was linked to the requirement that Boas was to make data and information available to the Commission for the publications that were scheduled for later, and was to write contributions. That arrangement transpired only in part (Neumayer 1890, 1891; see Cole and Müller-Wille 1984; Müller-Wille 1998:6-11).

To ensure the free and undisturbed execution of his scientific work and for his own well-being, at the insistence of his family, especially his father, Franz Boas ultimately took Wilhelm Weike with him as his servant. Lieutenant von der Goltz (his Christian name is not known), who was scheduled to be his assistant upon the recommendation of the German Polar Commission but who had initially seemed dubious to Boas, decided shortly before the departure date not to join. Immediately, in May 1883, Boas informed Crawford Noble, the owner of a shipping company in Aberdeen and Dundee and of the whaling station on Kekerten, that he would now be coming to Baffin Island with only one companion. At the same time he asked Noble to let him and Weike live at the Scottish station during their sojourn (Franz Boas/Crawford Noble, Minden/Dundee, 20 May 1883). Boas abandoned his plan of living at the German polar station, since running it would have been too expensive and cumbersome for just two people. In addition, he would have been isolated from the Inuit, who lived in dispersed settlements and around the whaling stations farther south in Cumberland Sound.

Early in 1883 Boas wrote to his parents: *"Please now ask Wilhelm seriously, whether he would like to travel with me, and tell me his surname so that I can write to him myself."* (Franz Boas/parents, Berlin/Minden, 24 January 1883). The answer turned out to be positive. Later, even in reminiscences for his children, Boas wrote that Weike had himself wanted to accompany him. The fact that Boas did not know Wilhelm Weike's surname was not unusual in the context of the demarcation between the social classes that still prevailed; it probably also arose from the fact that he scarcely had anything to do with the "below-stairs" in his own home, especially because between 1877 and 1881 he spent his time studying in Heidelberg, Bonn, and Kiel, and also travelled extensively. Though, while living at home during his military service in 1881-82, he must certainly have had contact with Weike and other household staff members.

Shortly afterwards, Franz asked his parents that Wilhelm Weike should get himself examined by Dr Walzberg, the Boas family doctor, to see whether he was fit for the trip to the Arctic (Franz Boas/parents, Berlin/Minden, 8 February 1883). The doctor confirmed that Weike was in the best of health. After intensive preparations during the following few months, Franz Boas and Wilhelm Weike arrived in Hamburg from Minden, respectively on June 17 and 18, 1883, to embark aboard the *Germania*. She put to sea on June 20 under the command of Captain A.F.B. Mahlstede and with a crew of five, bound for Baffin Island. Mahlstede's mandate was to evacuate the personnel of the German polar station, whom he had taken there a year previously, and simultaneously to land Boas and Weike in Cumberland Sound.

For the young Boas this scientific expedition, his *Erstlingsreise* (first voyage), became an important phase in his life and academic career (Boas 1894:97). That was clearly the expectation his family expressed to their circle and community by this announcement in *The Jewish Chronicle* in London in July 1883.

*"A Jewish Polar explorer. — We learn with satisfaction that Dr Boss [sic], of Minden (Holland) [sic], intends to start at the end of the present month for the North Polar region, accompanied only by a servant, in order to make geographical, ethnographical, and meteorological researches in these regions. In furtherance of his plan he intends to make a lengthy stay among the Esquimaux, and he hopes to complete his labours within six months. Dr Boas, it is believed, will be the first Jewish traveller to the Polar regions." (The Jewish Chronicle 1883:12).*

His subsequent studies and research led Boas ultimately to Columbia University in New York where, for forty years, in both teaching and research as a Professor in the Department of Anthropology he established the fundamentals and outlines of "cultural anthropology" as the "science of man." After an eventful and full life Franz Boas died of a heart attack at the age of 84 on December 21, 1942 during a meal with colleagues and family members in the Faculty Room of Columbia University in New York (Boas, N. 2004:258-259; Lévi-Strauss 1984:9).

In the Arctic, Wilhelm Weike was indispensable for Franz Boas since he took care of almost all practical matters for him. For him the expedition became a "great adventure, a happy journey" as he called it, even when the expedition did not always run smoothly. His contribution meant that Boas could conduct his research that focused on the mutual understanding among individuals and peoples. Weike did so certainly unwittingly for his part; the same applied to the Inuit and whalers who imparted their knowledge to Boas. By way of publishing his journals and letter Weike's contributions are now fully documented and thus have received fair acknowledgment.

## Wilhelm Weike's writings—journal and letters (1883-1889)

Wilhelm Weike kept his journal regularly from June 10, 1883 until September 1, 1884, with only a few short breaks. Franz Boas wrote to his fiancée Marie Krackowizer (1861-1929) that he had begun his journal and letter-diaries and had simultaneously urged Weike to keep a journal as well (Franz Boas/Marie Krackowizer, Hamburg/Stuttgart, 11 June 1883). Weike took notebook and pen in hand and made his first entry promptly on the same day and continued the journal to the end of the sojourn in the Arctic. Only during the following periods—in all 14 days—did he not make any entries: from August 12 to 18, 1883, on board the *Germania*, during the long wait in the drift-ice and off the edge of the pack ice at the entrance to Cumberland Sound; from July 15 to 18, 1884, on the dog-sledge trip in the fiords north of Qivitung, when there was already water lying on the ice, and when driving the dogs was extremely difficult and strenuous; and from August 28 to 30, 1884, on the homeward voyage during the first days on board the *Wolf.* These periods were covered by the notes Franz Boas took and which were published earlier (see Boas in Müller-Wille 1998:63-66, 244-245, 258-259). Weike ended his journal on September 1, 1884 when he and Boas finally left the Arctic, southward bound. His service was over and with it too, apparently, the assignment of taking notes on daily events!

But from June 10, 1883 Weike had faithfully kept his journal. In it he made reference to Boas, whom he called " *Herr Dr,*" almost daily. Boas repeatedly commented that naturally he might at any time take a look and read what Weike had written. That certainly must have had an influence on how Weike wrote his journal. As Boas noted in a letter to his parents on July 2, 1883 from on board the *Germania*, he was particularly curious about what Weike was writing in his journal.

Weike wrote nothing emotional about Franz Boas, and nothing about his own mood, such as one may read in his few letters, always expressed in the most positive fashion. He was, we believe, *very much* aware that this journal would be read and evaluated. Weike's own feelings, loneliness, fears, even a love affair, were probably selectively filtered out. He was very capable of intense and emotional descriptions, assessments, and even negative evaluations, as one may glean at many places in his journal. On the other hand, he did not reflect on what was occurring and what he experienced; he did not compare or evaluate his experiences in the Arctic against his life in Germany, in the eastern Westphalian town of Minden on the Weser, which he mentions only a few times.

Wilhelm Weike mentioned quite frequently that he was about to sit down to write in his journal. He always took the trouble to record the events of the day chronologically: *"morning, noon and evening."* This often seemed to occur, at the whaling station, for example, in the morning after the very popular and indispensable coffee, or in the evening when it was quieter. He also described the inconveniences of writing with pen and ink in his sleeping bag in a snow-house. It is evident that he observed the strange environment and its inhabitants closely; he related events and the course of events accurately such as, for example, games, hunting methods, and customs in lively fashion. Also in his daily communication with the Inuit and whalers, he grasped the contexts in their basic outlines. He managed to learn important words in both foreign languages—English and Inuktitut—and mixed them in with his German, both in conversation and writing. It can be assumed that, for compiling the daily entries, he asked Boas for information and explanations when plans, daily routine, personal names or place names were involved. Weike records surprisingly many people and place names and thereby displays a deep understanding of "people" and "land."

Wilhelm Weike and the transcriber of his journal wrote in German Gothic script, also known as current (*Kurrentschrift*) or cursive script,

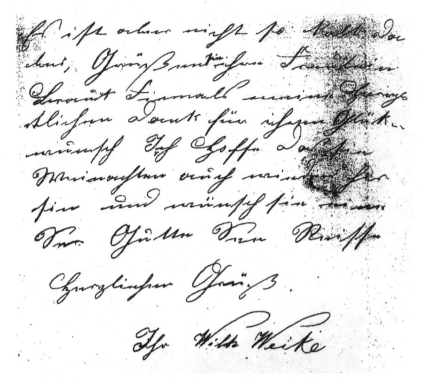

Wilhelm Weike's signature in letter to Franz Boas, Berlin / New York, 30 November 1884 (*American Philosophical Society*)

which in the nineteenth century was the script predominantly taught and generally used (Boas used the Roman script). In the case of the journal's copy, the copier used Roman transcription almost exclusively for foreign personal and place names, and for English and Inuktitut words, and generally also for dates (days of the week and months). He certainly corrected Wilhelm Weike's peculiarities of spelling, but left many words just as Weike wrote them. Thus, for example, Weike wrote *getz* for *jetzt* (now) and *kucken* for *gucken* (to see), following phonetically the pronunciation of his local Low German dialect, in the letters that are in his original handwriting. Unfortunately, it can no longer be determined to what degree the copier "improved" or changed Weike's writings and dialectal usage.

Weike did not worry too much about punctuation or capitalization. Commas, semicolons, and periods were only inserted to make sentence structure, the ends of sentences, and context clearer for the reader. The transcriber encountered some difficulties in deciphering Weike's handwriting, although actually in very few cases; those words he left blank, marked them with a question mark or simply wrote "unclear." Sometimes it appears that corrections were added later. It cannot be determined whether Weike was asked by the transcriber to decipher the illegible sections; that is probable, however, since the transcriber, Weike, and even Boas were all in Berlin when the copy was being made in the spring of 1886.

It is also not certain whether Boas instructed the transcriber to correct Weike's text, but it emerges from the text that that must have happened. Many names and words in English or Inuktitut, the latter based on Boas' transliterations, were written correctly in some places, although elsewhere they were rendered in Weike's own phonetic transcription. They could have been corrected by Boas. From both Boas' and Weike's journals, one can determine that at the start of their sojourn their phonetic transcription of Inuit personal names and place names was quite similar, reflecting their shared German language. Weike wrote as he heard the sounds converting them into German orthography reflecting his east Westphalian dialect. Gradually, Boas used exclusively the standardized orthography in his journals and later especially in his publications that had been developed for the language of the Inuit in Greenland in the mid-nineteenth century (Kleinschmidt 1851, 1871; Boas 1885a, 1894).

Weike's journal meant a great deal to Boas, for in early April 1886, when he was spending time in Berlin and knew that Weike and his journal were nearby, in a letter to his parents he remarked, *"I've had the whole of Wilhelm's journal copied, and I hope that it will substantially benefit me."* (Franz Boas/parents, Berlin/Minden, 5 April 1886). At that point Boas was planning to put together a popular description of his arctic expedition and experiences and to publish it with Brockhaus Publishing House in Leipzig. That plan did not materialize. It may be assumed that Franz Boas read Wilhelm Weike's journal after it had been copied. It cannot be established whether he used any of Weike's writing directly for his own publications. Only in his journals and letters did Boas refer to Weike's journal, but never as a source in his publications.

The version of Wilhelm Weike's journal conserved in the Franz Boas Professional Papers (American Philosophical Society) is the handwritten original of the copy, a collection of numbered loose pages, totalling 445, with sixteen lines on each and measuring 17 x 20 cm, and which at an earlier stage had been bound. The text runs to almost 40,000 words. The original journal must have remained in Wilhelm Weike's possession. Weike's estate could not be found in Berlin, whither he had moved in early 1886 and where he died in 1917. His wife Mathilde survived him at least by more than ten years; they had no children, and no evidence of other close relatives could be found.

The transcription of the journal and the letters for publication was mainly done from microfilm and occurred in several separate stages. For his edition of Franz Boas' Arctic journals and letters, Ludger Müller-Wille had copied several passages and worked them into the Boas text (Müller-Wille 1992 and 1994 in German, 1998 in English). In April 1997, while visiting Montréal, Bernd Gieseking prepared a handwritten copy of the journal for the periods June–October 1883 and February–September 1884. For a theatre play he used extensive passages from Boas' and Weike's journals in a collage, called *Im Eis* (In the Ice), accompanied by music and audiovisual effects (Gieseking 1998). Gieseking performed the play on November 21 and 22, 1998 in the Minden City Theatre as part of the 1200th anniversary of Minden. Müller-Wille produced a digital text from Gieseking's hand-written copy, compared it with the original, and transcribed the missing periods from microfilm between October and December 2006 and February and March 2007. The final editing of the document was completed by the end of November 2007. Weike's letters were transcribed and edited in July 2007. The English translation was carried out by William Barr and further editing and revising of the text was done by Linna Weber Müller-Wille and Ludger Müller-Wille between September 2008 and April 2011.

## People and Places in the Canadian Arctic (August 1883 to September 1884)

For Wilhelm Weike the expedition to Baffin Island was the first, and as far as can be determined, the only major journey of his life to distant places and among foreign people and cultures. His journal gives the reader a measure of his abilities to record remarkable things in an unaccustomed environment, and to adjust to local circumstances.

Nowadays, more than 125 years after Weike's and Boas' sojourn, Baffin Island (I. Qikiqtaaluk: the big island), the fifth largest island in the world and the largest in Canada at over 500,000 km², belongs to Nunavut (Our Land), a federal territory established in 1999. Before that Nunavut was part of the old Northwest Territories, which since then has existed as a separate territory still with the same name, embracing the Mackenzie Valley and the islands of the Western Arctic in northwestern Canada. Nunavut Territory includes 1.9 million square kilometres and, in early 2011, its population totalled 34,000 (2001: 26,746). These people live in 25 widely scattered, smaller and larger settlements with modern infrastructures. Inuit represented 84 percent of the population in 2006 (24,635 individuals), which is about 50 percent of all the Inuit who live in Canada (50,485) (all data according to Statistics Canada 2008-2011).

In southeastern Baffin Island, along the shores of Cumberland Sound and Davis Strait, the area in which Boas and Weike travelled, now there are two central settlements: Pangnirtung (also: Panniqtuuq) on Pangnirtung Fiord with 1,325 inhabitants and Qikiqtarjuaq, near Padli on the east coast of Baffin Island, with 473 inhabitants in 2006 (Bell 2004; Statistics Canada 2008). These settlements emerged mainly during the second half of the twentieth century. As compared to 1883-84 when Boas enumerated 250 inhabitants—Inuit and whalers (Boas 1885a:70)—at the start of the twenty-first century more than five times more people live in this region.

Nunavut Territory now has a democratically elected government, a modern administration and infrastructure, as well as attractions that draw thousands of tourists, including those from German-speaking countries, who want to get to know the land and people of the Arctic. Today, anyone who wishes may even follow Boas' and Weike's routes, escorted by Inuit guides. Kekerten Island, with the remains of the Inuit settlements and the whaling stations where Boas and Weike lived for more than eight months, is now uninhabited and has been declared a territorial historic park under strict rules of protection and preservation (Nunavut Handbook 2004).

Pangnirtung Fiord at low tide looking northeast, July 2007 (Photo: Bernd Gieseking)

## Peoples—Inuit, *Qallunaat* (whalers and Germans)

The economic, social and cultural structures and developments on Baffin Island during the second half of the nineteenth century are documented in some detail in the literature. This period saw the first intensive and persistent contact between the Inuit and the encroaching European and American whalers, as well as a few polar travellers and scientists, who, as Weike expressed it, *"were travelling to the North Pole"* (1 November 1883) in order to investigate the arctic environment and the lifestyle of the Inuit at first hand (Hall 1865; Abbes 1884, 1890; Ambronn 1883; Boas 1885a, 1888 [1974]; see also Stevenson 1997).

*Inuit*: Wilhelm Weike was familiar with the word *"Eskimo"* (pl. *"Eskimos"*) as the common designation for the Inuit in German; this word occurs over seventy times in his journal. He also frequently called the Inuit *"Eingeborene"* [natives] or *"Fremde"* [strangers]. Franz Boas generally termed them *"Eskimos"* although rarely he also used *"Inuit"* or *"Innuit"* (Boas 1888:420).

The word "Eskimo" is the designation applied by the Algonquian peoples, the aboriginal population of the northern forests, to the Inuit, who are their northern neighbours on the Québec-Labrador Peninsula in northeastern Canada. Linguists are not entirely unanimous as to the derivation of the word "Eskimo" in the Algonquian language family. One explanation suggests "raw meat eaters;" another "the strangers" or "the others," while a further derivation points to "snowshoe knitters" (see Mailhot 1978; Goddard 1984), a reference to the knitting or weaving of the webbing of snowshoes. As contacts between Algonquian, Inuit and finally Euro-Canadians became more intensive the term "Eskimo" acquired a condescending and extremely negative meaning, especially from the Inuit viewpoint. The word "Eskimo" emerged in English at the end of the sixteenth century, was adopted by every other European language, and finally achieved world-wide dissemination and application (Goddard 1984:5-7).

The most northerly aboriginal people of the arctic regions of Siberia, Alaska, Canada, and Greenland call themselves, with regional variations, Inuit. Since the early 1970s the term has gained acceptance, especially in Canada, and also at the international level. This process has been concurrently part of the efforts to champion human rights and recognize territorial claims by and political independence for the aboriginal peoples in the Arctic states and globally at the United Nations.

The word "*Inuit*" means "we, the people." The root is "*inu-*" = a person. The form "*inu-k*" means one person, "*inu-uk*" two people, and "*inu-it*" three or more people – hence "we, the people." In the Canadian Eastern Arctic the language of the Inuit is called "Inuk-titut", which translates as "what and how I speak." (Dorais 1996:7-8, 147-148).

During his expedition to Baffin Island, partly with Wilhelm Weike's assistance, Boas mapped Cumberland Sound and the west shore of Davis Strait, including the seasonal camps of the Inuit where they lived in caribou-skin *tupiks* (tents), sod huts, or snow-houses, depending on the season. Boas also conducted a census of the Inuit population. In this fashion he got to know the individual family units and regional population groupings, all of which identified themselves by names that were connected to their land use and settlement area (Boas 1885a, 1888). He placed particular weight on seasonally influenced migrations and hunting areas, as well as family relationships, and especially on name-giving.

As his starting point, Boas assumed that the Inuit population in 1840, when the whalers started hunting marine mammals in Cumberland Sound, totalled about 1000 people. That number was based on estimates. It had decreased to 350 by 1857-58 when a missionary from the *Herrnhuter Brüder-Unität* (Moravian Church) in Germany, Matthias Warmow, stayed with whalers in the Sound and conducted the first census (Warmow 1858; see also Harper 2009). In 1883-84, according to Boas, the number of Inuit in the same area—Cumberland Sound—totalled only 228 (Boas 1885a:70). This extraordinarily rapid decrease in the Inuit population can be ascribed to diseases introduced and spread by the whalers, such as syphilis, diphtheria, colds, pneumonia, and a high mortality rate among infants.

The census carried out by Boas put the population at 328 Inuit, spread among ten camps in Cumberland Sound (228) and along the Davis Strait coast (100); 82 of these people, the so-called "Station Inuit," lived on Kekerten Island. The total population consisted of 161 males (49.1 percent) and 167 females (50.9 percent); 50 boys and 48 girls were younger than fourteen years old (29.9 percent of total). During the year, eleven Inuit died; one man, four women, and six children, whose sex was only mentioned for some, representing 3.3 percent of the total population. In his journal, Weike mentioned the deaths of three women and six children during the same period. Boas recorded only two births and two miscarriages (all data from Boas 1885a:70, 1888:426).

*Qallunaat*: The Inuit call the strangers who came into their country from Europe from the late sixteenth century onwards *"qallunaat,"* which translates as "people (initially only men) with large eyebrows" (singular: *qallunaq; qallu* = eyebrow). During the first decades of the nineteenth century, ships of the British Navy began turning up with increasing frequency in the waters around Baffin Island, looking for a route through the Northwest Passage from Europe to China. Those expeditions encountered Inuit in various locations (cf. Dorais 1996:12ff.). Some Inuit even dared to travel with them voluntarily to Europe, to England and even to Germany; others were abducted against their will, several died in Europe, and few of those Inuit returned to their homeland (see Hall 1865; Ulrikab 2005).

*Whalers:* After 1820 the voyages of the European whaling fleets expanded into the arctic waters between Greenland and North America.

Qeqertudjuaq of Qeqerten [Kerkerten] Archipelago in drift ice, July 2007
(Photo: Bernd Gieseking)

High numbers of kills quickly reduced the populations of sought-after whale species; this applied especially to the bowhead whale. Moreover, losses of crews and sailing vessels in the difficult northern waters caused the industry to exploit other whaling grounds. That expansion led to the "discovery" and appropriation of Cumberland Sound as a productive whaling area by 1840, and finally, in 1857, to the building of the first wintering station by a Scottish company on Kekerten Island. Thereafter, several stations were established at other locations; as well, whaling ships increasingly wintered in the pack ice of Cumberland Sound. Thus there emerged a small, but permanent, *qallunaat* population. The Inuit whom the whalers employed as harpooners and boat' crews gradually settled near those stations or wintering places. In that fashion a close economic and social relationship developed, one characterized by mutual dependence and influence. When Boas and Weike reached Kekerten in late August 1883, intensive contact between Inuit and *qallunaat* had already existed for almost thirty years, i.e., for over a generation.

Twenty-four *qallunaat* wintered on Kekerten Island in Cumberland Sound in 1883-84. James Mutch managed the Scottish Station and

Kerkerten Harbour, site of former whaling station, and bowhead whale jaw as a memorial to the hunt by Inuit in 1998, July 2007 (Photo: Bernd Gieseking)

looked after the interests of the Crawford Noble Co. of Aberdeen, Scotland. The handyman at the American station was the Dane, Rasmussen (Christian name unknown), who was called Cooper (*Kuper* to Boas and Weike) and who, under the direction of Captain John Roach (see below), maintained the American Station for the Williams Co. of New London, Connecticut, U.S.A.

James Mutch, known as "Jimmy Mutchee" to the Inuit, had many years of experience as a whaler. He was born in Boddam, near Peterhead, Scotland, on December 15, 1847, the son of a carter, and he came to Baffin Island on board a whaling ship for the first time in 1865. Mutch returned soon after and lived on Kekerten and managed the station until 1900, interrupted several times by home-leaves. Thereafter, until 1922, he travelled regularly with Inuit to various locations on Baffin Island to hunt whales and other marine mammals, but generally returned to Scotland in the fall. He learned to speak Inuktitut fluently and, according to the Inuit, spoke "exactly like us." At Kekerten he had an Inuit wife, and they had a daughter called Annalukulu (Boas in Müller-Wille 1998:180, 191). Weike did not mention her, however. While

Mutch was in Scotland in 1885-86 he married Jessie (family name unknown) in Peterhead, and had a daughter. In 1922, at the age of 74, Mutch left the Canadian Arctic for good and lived in Peterhead. Later he moved with his wife to South Africa, where their only daughter lived, and died there in 1931 (all data on James Mutch according to Harper 2008).

Another whaler, the American ship *Lizzie P. Simmons* of the Williams Co., wintered off Naujatelling on the west side of the Sound under the command of Captain John Roach, a native of Montréal (Canada). He had been whaling in the Sound since 1876, partly for the American C. A. Williams Company of New London, Connecticut. In 1882-83 this ship had become frozen in the ice off the German polar station at Kingua and had wintered there. Little is known about her crew that totalled about twenty seamen and whalers, including the two German-American mates, Fred Grobschmidt and Wilhelm Scherden. The crew evidently consisted mainly of Americans, including some African-Americans and recently immigrated Europeans—hence a wide range of cultural backgrounds and languages. Weike mentioned an Italian and Boas also *"a countryman"* (German) and *"a Jew"* (Boas in Müller-Wille 1998:106). Roach, Grobschmidt, and Scherden often stayed at the American station and visited with Weike and Boas at Mutch's station. That year the whalers were active exclusively in Cumberland Sound. Thus, in addition to the 228 Inuit in the seven settlements in the Sound, in the winter of 1883-84 there were 22 *qallunaat*, plus Boas and Weike, i.e., they represented almost 10 percent of the total population. For some weeks, the number of whalers was further increased by the crew of the Scottish supply ship, *Catherine*, of the Noble Co., that stayed at Kekerten and in Cumberland Sound from September 6 until October 3, 1883. It could not be determined how many men were on board the ship, apart from the two returning Scots, one of them being Alexander Hall who was in Kekerten 1882-83 (Boas in Müller-Wille 1998:109).

The Scottish and American whalers were in strong competition with each other. Here, as on other arctic whaling grounds, the numbers of whales of different species had declined markedly in the previous years due to heavy exploitation. Whaling was waning and was no longer sufficiently lucrative (Boas 1885a:32-34; see also Ross 1985). There was no indication from Boas' or Weike's notes that they saw even a single whale either in the water or hauled ashore. In that year the whalers had their Inuit employees hunt just walrus and seals in order to obtain any oil at all. This rivalry led to tensions among the whalers as they courted the favour of the Inuit, since they were indispensable as crews for the whaleboats. Despite their spatial proximity, social relations among the whalers were rather cool, even when there were common, sociable evenings of music, games, and drinking, in which Boas and especially Weike actively participated.

By this point relations between Inuit and whalers embodied an inevitable symbiosis that had evolved over decades and established rules and sanctions. The whalers were the determining protagonists, since they were after the larger whales (e.g., baleen whales), which the Inuit themselves could hunt only under the most favourable conditions. Inuit men were employed for hunting the whales, but also walrus and seals in open whaleboats with six oarsmen and a harpooner in each. On shore they worked at the station flensing whales and doing other chores. Inuit women found employment as maids and sewing skin clothing. The Inuit population in the vicinity of the stations divided themselves according to their employer and, as Weike mentioned in his journal, were known simply as "Mutch Inuit" or "Roach Inuit."

This work relationship had developed into a well-practiced system that demanded loyalty and was renewed for each whaling season. For the Inuit the dependence and benefits involved imported provisions, equipment, and alcohol. Thus every Saturday, after a horn was blown as a signal, James Mutch, as the employer, would distribute rations to the women so that they could feed their husbands and families. The rations consisted of specific amounts of bread, coffee and molasses. The Inuit men also went hunting for the whalers and delivered fresh meat (caribou, seal, and walrus) and fish. For this hunting they had access to the station's boats, sledges, dogs, and equipment, which they could also use for their own needs.

At noon, every Friday there was an "assembly" for all the Station Inuit (probably just for the men), at which James Mutch gave out a shot of watered rum to "his Eskimos" as a reward. The puritanical Protestant Scots had also introduced Sunday strictly as a day of rest, on which the

Station Inuit did no work and were not allowed to go hunting, even if the weather was favourable and they urgently needed food. This "tradition" still survives among Anglican Inuit in Nunavut. Other religious communities behave differently, for example, the Catholics are more accommodating allowing the Inuit free rein to leave in the middle of a service to go hunting without reproach.

*Germans:* Apart from the German-American seamen who turned up sporadically among the whalers, between 1882 and 1884 the Inuit experienced an influx of thirteen Germans. The personnel of the German polar station, seven scientists and four workers, settled at Kingua from September 1882 until September 1883, to pursue research on behalf of the German Reich as member of the International Polar Commission. They conducted a rigorous simultaneous research program as part of the Polar Year. The Inuit had no knowledge of why, what, how, and for whom the research was being actively pursued. The Germans stayed almost exclusively at their station and had rather limited contact with the Inuit except for Ocheitu who was hired by the Germans to hunt and fish and lived next the station all year round (Abbes 1890, Ambronn 1883). During the Fourth International Polar Year 2007-2008 the interrelationship between external scientists and Inuit had changed. For the first time, Inuit and other aboriginal researchers became fully involved as partners in this international science programme in Nunavut and in the Arctic in general (Krupnik et al. 2005).

Oral traditions about the Germans' sojourn at Kingua continue to exist among the Inuit in Pangnirtung (Eliyak Keenainak/Ludger Müller-Wille, Salliq (Sadleq), N.W.T./St. Lambert, Québec (Canada), 17 September 1984). The station buildings were still standing until into the 1930s. A German-American whaler originally from Schwerin in Mecklenburg, Wilhelm Düwel (later William Duval; 1858-1931), used those buildings between 1885 and 1931. Duval had come to Cumberland Sound with Captain Roach in 1879. In 1883-84, while Boas and Weike were in the Sound, he had gone back to the U.S.A. for the year. He returned and married locally; his first Inuit wife died, and with his second wife he founded a family whose descendants still live in Pangnirtung and other locations in Nunavut. Duval was the only German from that period who stayed to live in the Arctic, spent his life there, and is buried there (all data on Duval based on Harper 2005).

Remains of the German polar station are still visible at Kingua as a reminder of that period.

Some Inuit in Pangnirtung still tell stories about Franz Boas and Wilhelm Weike, even though their names are not familiar. It is known where they travelled and that they collected place names and compiled a map. Yet it would take almost a hundred years before Franz Boas' major English-language publication about the Inuit, *The Central Eskimo* (1888), would be read by any of them, and its content assessed as to its significance for their own culture. The same happened in the case of the map that Boas compiled (1885a), on which he recorded almost exclusively Inuit place names, and on which descendants of those Inuit who had provided the place names to Boas, as they drew maps for him and explained their country, only recently set eyes for the first time. In August 1984 during a place name survey they commented on that map with the legitimate question, *"Why could this map with our place names be published in Germany over 100 years ago, yet until today it has not been available for us to see it?"* (Müller-Wille and Weber Müller-Wille 2006:217).

### Arctic environment

Weike's and Boas' writings also give us an insight into the natural conditions as they were in the eastern Canadian Arctic 125 years ago. These observations are of great significance, since they allow one to ascertain climatic and environmental changes in the arctic regions (see Wüthrich and Thannheiser 2002). For example, the *Germania* reached Kekerten Harbour on August 28, 1883, only after waiting for several weeks off the pack ice and in heavy drift ice to the south of the Kekerten Islands; in 2007, Cumberland Sound was already ice-free north of Kekerten by the end of June.

Weike was a very precise and careful observer. He took pleasure in nature and was interested in landforms, animals, plants, weather conditions, temperature, and the changeable light conditions of the arctic environment that was so alien to him. The area of Boas' and Weike's travels extended from 65° to 69° 30' N and from 61° to 65° W, an area of about 500 km N-S by 250 km E-W. At those latitudes they experienced the arctic night right on the Arctic Circle at Kekerten and Anarnitung, and the arctic day within the Circle on the Davis Strait coast. The alternation between arctic day and arctic night was a special experience for Weike, in particular the reappearance of the sun on the horizon in February 1884, which he recorded each day with minute accuracy. And Weike was also fascinated by the glittering and flickering of the northern lights, the calving glaciers, the steep, towering mountains, the treeless tundra, the great tidal range, and the constantly changing formations and crunching noises of the shore ice and pack ice.

Weike was a passionate hunter and often noted seeing or tracking animals, and then trying to kill them. He was preoccupied with the occurrence and behaviour of seals, bearded seals, walrus, as well as caribou, arctic hares, and foxes, which he hunted alone or with the Inuit whenever he found an opportunity. Although mentioned quite frequently in accounts by the Inuit, neither Boas nor Weike caught sight of a polar bear during their sojourn, apart from some tracks on the ice. Of the birds, it was the numerous gulls, ptarmigans, ducks, teals, crested grebes, terns, and even the very rare cranes that he pursued and brought home for the pot after a successful shot. The arctic raven was mentioned, but was rarely seen, although it was heard. In fall and summer Weike mentioned fish (salmon and trout) and edible mussels in the tidal zone that added to the menu. All these were the "country foods," *Landesprodukte*, which Weike appreciated greatly next to the foodstuffs such as canned meat, vegetables, and fruits, as well as coffee, tea, chocolate, bread, cheese, and Westphalian smoked–sausage spread that they had brought from Germany.

Apart from his own scientific interests, Boas had committed himself to obtaining collections of rock specimens, animals, insects and plants for museums in Germany, especially in Berlin. He instructed Weike to assist him in this collecting work by salting animals and pressing plants. Thus Weike also learned to recognize grasses, mosses, lichens, and berries, which he described with the names he was familiar with from eastern Westphalia. In the summer of 1884 he admired the explosive blossoming of the arctic vegetation, and, in a particularly great mood, he stuck flowers in his hat and brought Herr Dr a bouquet!

Between October 6, 1883 and April 29, 1884 Weike recorded weather and temperature data almost regularly, since Boas had set up a weather screen near the Scottish station in order to take readings at fixed times. These data are also listed in Boas' journals and, along with his astronomical data, he compiled and published an incomplete record (Boas 1885a:95-100) that probably was due to broken instruments.

During the period for which measurements were recorded, on October 6 the temperature was -1°C (the first frost had already been reported on board the *Germania* on July 26, 1883) and on April 29, 1884, the last date for which there are temperature data, -11°C. On average during October and November the temperature fluctuated between -10° C and -28°C. The lowest temperatures were recorded between December 7, 1883 and February 11, 1884—constantly between -30°C and -48°C; the latter, the lowest temperature, was recorded at Kekerten on January 25 and 26. During the tough, unfortunate journey on the ice to Anarnitung, when Weike froze his feet on December 21, 1883, the temperature remained below -35°C with the lowest reading of -49°C. The period after February 11, 1884 revealed temperature fluctuations between 0°C (March 9 and April 6) and -38°C (March 21).

## Daily life

*Languages: Inuktituk, English, Pidgin, and German*
It may be assumed that Wilhelm Weike grew up speaking the east Westphalian dialect and learned *Hochdeutsch* (High German) only in school. Those were the languages that Weike knew when he went to the Arctic. Franz Boas must have been familiar with the dialect spoken in the Minden area, but certainly spoke only High German. At high school next to other subjects he took French, along with Latin and Greek. English was not yet included in the curriculum (Franz Boas' high school leaving certificate, March 1877, Municipal Archives, Minden). The Boas family had wide-ranging family and business contacts in France, England, Canada, and the U.S.A., and hence a tutor was hired to teach him English as a youngster, but by 1883 he had not yet mastered it very well (Cole and Müller-Wille 1984:38). In preparation for his research in the Arctic and in light of the relevant literature on the Inuit, Boas also took pains to learn Danish, and, as far as it went, to acquire some Inuktitut as well, on the basis of teaching materials from Greenland and Labrador.

During the crossing on board *Germania* Boas gave Weike English lessons so that the latter could at least communicate a little with the English-speaking whalers and with the Inuit who had learned English from the whalers. Boas himself worked also on his English skills, since English, or the Pidgin English spoken on Baffin Island, was to become the real *lingua franca* for him. To conduct his research with the Inuit he made efforts to learn as much Inuktitut as was possible for him during his stay on Baffin Island. Weike expanded his command of English and Inuktitut orally, and progressed to the point that he could converse quite tolerably well with the Inuit and whalers. Boas took great pains to converse with the Inuit in Inuktitut, but often had difficulty in understanding them. Yet, with the Inuit he compiled a map on which about 800 Inuit place names are marked (Boas 1885a:90-95, Table 1), as well as numerous texts on "religious ideas and myths" (Boas 1888:583-643), and published a word list and glossary of the language of the Inuit of Cumberland Sound (Boas 1894). Yet he never felt very comfortable in the language of the Inuit, and often appeared to be frustrated by that (Cole and Müller-Wille 1984:54), even if he wrote optimistically and a bit boastingly in the *Berliner Tageblatt* on September 28, 1884, that he "*in time became fully familiar with the local language.*" (Boas 1884a).

Later on, in full recognition of his own linguistic limitations, he had to seek help from Moravian missionaries and in particular from Hinrich Rink in Copenhagen. In April 1885 he wrote Rink explaining his linguistic frustrations.

> "*You overestimate my knowledge of the Eskimo language, because my understanding of the songs is immensely deficient, some of them I almost do not understand at all; those which I master according to their content, I know due to the thorough narrations by the natives. ... Some unintelligible words might have originated from the erroneous recognition of the sounds on my part, which happens easily when knowledge of a language is incomplete. ... Indeed, I feel that I am in no way up to this task." (Franz Boas/Hinrich Rink, Minden/Copenhagen, 28 April 1885; see also A. F. Elsner/Franz Boas, Bremen/ Minden, 26 June 1885; both letters are in the Rink Papers, Archive of The Royal Library, Copenhagen).*

Again in the 1890s, when he finally published a vocabulary of the Inuit dialect of southern Baffin Island, Boas reiterated his linguistic shortcomings by acknowledging that the material he collected was "... *in many respects deficient and imperfect*" (Boas 1894:97). Boas' linguistic skills in Inuktitut and the level of insight into Inuit intellectual culture have been a matter of debate among scientists lately (e.g., see Saladin d'Anglure 2006:20; Harper 2008:57). Based on Boas' numerous contributions derived from Inuit knowledge, it is fair to say that he immersed himself sufficiently in Inuktitut to enable him, with the considerable help of Hinrich Rink and later James Mutch, to publish, in English translation, Inuit materials that are still recognized today (Cole and Müller-Wille 1984:53; Harper 2008:56; Krupnik and Müller-Wille 2010:378-380).

*Inuktitut:* The most widely spoken language on Baffin Island was Inuktitut, which at that time existed solely by way of oral transmission within the Inuit community. *Qallunaat* or outsiders might learn the language "by ear" from the Inuit on the spot. For Boas and Weike, James Mutch, who spoke Inuktitut fluently, was their most important linguistic intermediary, but so were also their companions, Singnar and other Inuit, who, according to Boas, also had a surprisingly good command of English and would translate for them. Daily association with the Inuit on boat and sledge trips, in tents and *iglus,* and at the station enabled Boas and Weike to learn as much Inuktitut as they did through direct interaction. This was certainly also assisted by the fact that between May 6 and August 25, 1884 they were alone with the Inuit and hence were obliged to learn and use Inuktitut increasingly. Both frequently allowed Inuit words or even sentences to enter their German writings (Boas inserted some eighty different Inuit words repeatedly and Weike close to thirty, not counting the numerous Inuit place names and personal names). To what degree the Inuit learned or simply adopted a few German words from them is unknown.

Despite all his efforts, Boas found it difficult to acquire a fluent command of Inuktitut so that he might converse effortlessly with the Inuit in their own language, and might acquire a feeling for their mode of thought and their behaviour. Boas found the language of the Inuit complicated and difficult, as he revealed repeatedly in his letters and journals (e.g., Boas 1894:97). He felt unsure as to how he should interpret the material he collected and, as mentioned above, had to enlist the assistance of Hinrich Rink and James Mutch. Weike, on the other hand, unaffectedly learned the words that seemed necessary to him, and strung them together as required to make himself understood and to be able to grasp situations and relationships.

*English*: English was the dominant language among the whalers, some of whom also spoke other European languages as their mother-tongue. It was the native tongue of James Mutch, John Roach, and several of their seamen. From the start of the contact period, English was the usual means of communication between whalers and Inuit; the latter very quickly acquired a command of English or of Pidgin English, since this seemed necessary and useful to them. The whalers also had the habit of giving English names to many of the Inuit, since they could not grasp or understand the complex naming system of the Inuit. Very rarely did the whalers acquire any knowledge of Inuktitut; there were exceptions such as James Mutch and William Duval (Wilhelm Düwel) mentioned above.

With Mutch and Captain John Roach, Boas spoke English exclusively, which at that time he spoke somewhat "stumblingly;" in that connection James Mutch's Scottish accent was certainly not always easily understandable for German ears. At the same time Mutch served as his "dictionary," as he delved deeper into English and Inuktitut. Initially Boas used English almost exclusively in talking to the Inuit, but soon shifted to using Inuktitut as well.

At the beginning Weike had difficulty in acquiring command of any foreign language. The linguistic situation represented an extraordinary challenge for him. At first, he limited himself to a few learned words, using gestures to make himself understood. His journal vividly reveals that he made progress, since more and more English words crop up there. (His text includes some fifty different English words, often used repeatedly, in contrast to Boas' thirty). Living with Mutch on a daily basis at the station, especially while his frostbitten feet were healing, also contributed to his expanding English vocabulary which, rudimentary as it was, he used without the least reserve.

*Pidgin:* Contact between several languages in the same area often leads to the emergence of a mixed language that fulfils the purpose of facilitating and maintaining comprehension between different linguistic communities living in close contact. In his entry for October 1, 1883, Boas gives an example of how such pidgin emerges from different languages when, in collaboration with Mutch and several Inuit, he compiled maps and collected Inuit place names using a mixture of English and Inuktituk (Boas in Müller-Wille 1998:107). Boas and Weike also participated in this pidgin and extended it to German by germanizing Inuit words – for example *"ankuten,"* which referred to the invocations of the shamans (I.: *angakkuq*).

*German:* Naturally Boas and Weike spoke German together. They used the formal *"Sie"* form of address to each other, Boas saying *"Sie, Wilhelm!"* and Weike: *"Sie, Herr Doktor!"* Both were pleasantly surprised at finding in Fred Grobschmidt, Wilhelm Scherden, and the Dane, Rasmussen, people who spoke German. Among the Inuit there was Ocheitu, who had acquired a limited German vocabulary during his year-long sojourn next to of the German polar station, and was very proud of it (Abbes 1884).

### Work, service, and duty

Wilhelm Weike had been the gardener and domestic servant in the Boas family household. His work and servant duties were certainly transferred to his new appointment during the arctic expedition. During this period Franz Boas was his boss and always referred to him as his servant. However, the tasks expected of him in the Arctic had little in common with his work in Minden. Weike became a jack-of-all-trades who was at the bidding of his employer, *Herr Dr*, round the clock. He was in charge of provisions and functioned as cook and baker, laundryman and cleaner, joiner and carpenter, bullet-pourer and gun-cleaner, smith, tailor, oarsman, dog-team driver, hunter and even nurse and scientific assistant—a considerable range of tasks for one person.

Weike's efforts benefited not only *Herr Doktor* but also James Mutch, who frequently called on him to keep the dwelling house, workshop, and storage sheds at the whaling station in order, to prepare meals and to make tea. One may assume that this represented a *quid pro quo* for Boas and Weike staying at the station. Weike's tasks included keeping their furnishings and equipment in good condition and repairing them; he also kept regularly track of their supplies. While preparing for the long dog-sledge trips and while packing up their goods for shipping, Weike developed into a true master of manufacturing and sealing-up wooden cases. Although Boas alluded to Weike's lethargy and laziness a few times (e.g., on July 27, 1884), his reproach does not seem justified, since, despite the impairment caused by his frostbitten feet, Weike performed and mastered all his duties effortlessly. By contrast Weike refrained from criticizing *Herr Dr.*in his journal; he knew better because Boas might review his writings.

*Travels, living conditions and mobility*

Wilhelm Weike had set out on what was practically a world-trip that started with the 70-day crossing of the North Sea and the North Atlantic on board the *Germania*, which took him through the arctic ice to Kekerten. During his sojourn on Baffin Island, along with Boas, Weike first travelled the shores of Cumberland Sound, then crossed the high pass to Davis Strait on the east coast of Baffin Island, and finally explored the numerous islands and fiords of that coastal region.

From August 28, 1883 until May 5, 1884 the Scottish whaling station on Kekerten Island (65° 43' N; 65° 48' W) was Boas' and Weike's main base. From there, in September and October Weike accompanied Boas, along with three Inuit, on three boat trips into the eastern fiords of Cumberland Sound. From December 11, 1883 until January 7, 1884 Boas and Weike, accompanied only by Singnar, undertook their first trip on foot on the sea ice. For Weike that trip ended tragically because, due to poor clothing and very low temperatures, he suffered severe frostbite on both feet. Between January and April 1884 he remained at the station to treat his frozen feet and to let them heal. By April he had sufficiently recovered that he was able to undertake sledge journeys. From May 6 until July 19, he and Boas, along with several Inuit, were constantly on the move by dog-sledge on the sea ice and overland along the shores of Davis Strait. On July 4 they reached their most northerly point (69° 35' N; 67° 30' W), the island of Siorartijung, east of Aulitiving. They spent the remaining time until their departure on August 25 with several Inuit families in a tented camp at Qivitung (67° 55' N; 65° W).

Before the winter started Franz Boas was at pains to acquire his own dog team, in order to be able, once ice had formed, to conduct his geographical explorations and survey work independently. That was more difficult than he had anticipated. In the fall of 1883 a devastating epidemic raged in Cumberland Sound among the 100 or so sledge dogs of the Inuit and whalers. By February 1884 there were only sixteen dogs left at Kekerten. Yet by March 8, 1884 Boas had succeeded in buying fifteen dogs from other Inuit settlements. This he achieved only by applying some pressure, threatening to give out no more ammunition to the Inuit—something that he had previously been doing very generously (Boas in Müller-Wille 1998:172). Those fifteen dogs formed the team that Boas used around Cumberland Sound and was later driven mainly by Weike to and along Davis Strait. The journal confirms that dogs had especially taken Weike's fancy. He came to love and hate the dogs. Securing food for the dogs—seal and fish—turned out to be an arduous task. Yet the dogs were indispensable for their travels. Boas mentioned that with a fully loaded sledge they could sometimes achieve a maximum distance of up to 90 kilometres in fifteen hours on the sea ice (Boas 1884b).

It is difficult to calculate how many kilometres Boas and Weike covered on foot, by boat, and by dog-sledge on Baffin Island. Weike's share alone amounted to roughly more than 1000 kilometres. Those journeys, on which he spent the nights in tents and snow-houses, took him into the most captivating regions of the Canadian Arctic and must have left images that stuck in Weike's memory for the rest of his life.

*Pleasures and leisure-time*
Despite all his chores, Wilhelm Weike found leisure time to occupy himself with things that brought him diversion and relaxation. He much preferred to be out in the open air. He loved to go on long hikes, to hunt and fish. On Kekerten, both at the station and in the tents of the Inuit, he commonly took part in sociable games or even in *ankuten* events. The Inuit and whalers, as well as Boas and Weike, often played music or sang; both men played the quite common concertina, which was very popular with the Inuit. Weike played chess and cards with Boas and Rasmussen and observed the Inuit at their card games. He learned games of strength and endurance from the Inuit, while freely getting together with them in uncomplicated fashion in their tents and snow-houses.

He also found pleasant and humorous reading material; in particular he liked the "comedies" among the books that Boas had brought with him (see November 6, 1883). Boas gave him Cervantes' *Don Quixote* for his birthday. There is no evidence as to whether he read it. He probably preferred lighter literature. In addition, the regular writing of his journal seemed to provide him with a welcome outlet.

Weike loved to smoke his pipe. Like Boas, he drank his daily and mandatory fresh coffee that represented both a pleasure and a ritual. In addition he liked to drink a glass of cognac, schnapps, wine, or some other drink, either in company or alone. For him all of these activities often represented *"a real pleasure;"* he felt as if he were *"enjoying a night out,"* and when he was savouring the sheer pleasure of hunting with the Inuit he remarked, *"We've stolen dear God's sweet time."* (26 June 1884).

## Health and illness

Weike and Boas were two young, strong, healthy men when they set off on their arctic expedition. With such constitutions they could withstand the physical and mental stresses they might have anticipated. Nonetheless on the outward voyage Boas had to contend with severe seasickness. After some intense travels by dog team he experienced attacks of faintness and dizziness as a result of exhaustion, as well as some colds. On their first short sledge trip both men sustained some minor frostbite on their faces. They also frequently had to contend with snow-blindness. They did not mention whether they used the effective snow goggles developed by the Inuit and made from wood, bone or leather, with a narrow slit for looking through. In June 1884 Weike suffered an attack of hives on the sun-drenched sea ice, and treated it with the panacea of vinegar. Both men had to cope repeatedly with toothache and dental ulcers, for which they gave no explanation, but from which they always quickly recovered.

The greatest impairment in terms of Weike's state of health was the third-degree frostbite inflicted on his feet in late December 1883. Boas and Weike were running a serious risk when they set off on that first winter trip dangerously unprepared. They had forgotten very important items of equipment, such as their kerosene stove. In addition, the caribou-skin winter clothing that had been ordered from the Inuit women for Weike had not been completed in time. But he absolutely wanted to go with Boas on that first winter outing. James Mutch helped by lending him his own clothes, including a pair of cloth pants, which, however, were too big for him and thereby did not keep him adequately warm.

A catastrophe could be anticipated, and was only averted by Signar's perseverance and finally the accommodating welcome they received from the Inuit of Anarnitung who, in their own fashion, and in response to the circumstances, immediately recognized and properly treated Weike's severe frostbite. Yet it still took almost three months before his feet and toes were fully recovered. That they had completely and successfully healed was proved by Weike's energetic, physical performance on the subsequent, very strenuous sledge trip. After his recuperation he never again mentioned the frostbite nor any after-effects.

### Insights into Inuit culture

At a few places in his journal Wilhelm Weike described various aspects of Inuit culture that he perceived as extraordinary. These are not detailed ethnographic descriptions but rather plain references to the heterogeneous nature of hunting methods, customs as to clothing and meals, games and ceremonies such as the *"Fall Festival"* on November 11, 1883 at which the Sedna legend, the Inuit's origin myth, was dramatized by disguised players. In addition, he became involved with their language and with learning the numerous personal names and place names. He also purchased articles of the Inuit material culture, such as a complete suit of skin clothing and tools and ordered ivory carvings for himself. He took all these with him back to Germany and they probably became part of his home in Berlin. Boas also collected and bought articles for himself and especially for the Royal Museum of Ethnology in Berlin (today Ethnological Museum, National Museums in Berlin) where he sent items of Inuit material culture and some original maps drawn by Inuit that are still part of the general collection (Königliches Museum für Völkerkunde, Sammlung Boas, 1885-1887, Inventory IV A 6692-6726, 6727-6734, 6819–6854, Berlin).

Weike was a religious fellow, moulded by the evangelical Lutheran church. It says much for him that he took a great interest, with an open mind, in the spiritual concerns of the Inuit, expressed especially in the invocations of the *angakkuq*, the shaman. He mentioned these invocations eight times in his journal. The acts of the shamans, which were mainly aimed at healing sick people, took place in tents and snow-houses and even at the Scottish station. They made a lasting impression on Weike and Boas, so that for their own use they rendered the concept of *angak-kuq* as the verb *"ankuten"* [to *ankut*] in German. Unlike Boas, Weike did not remain at an observing distance, but participated directly in the events and was accepted by the Inuit by joining their circle. He revealed himself to be strongly moved by these invocations. His observations were precise and even embraced the current material changes that were integrated by the shamans. For example, he mentioned that a shaman used a European cooking pot when the traditional drum, a circular wooden frame, over which a tanned sealskin is stretched, was not available.

Weike's generally positive attitude towards the Inuit is in contrast to some condescending remarks that he wrote about them, especially the women, at the beginning of his sojourn. At that point he commented on their appearance, cleanliness, and smell—all of which were alien to him, yet he wrote that the Inuit *"are very friendly, that one has to con-cede."* (Letter, 28 August 1883). And yet Weike ultimately adapted to the local conditions, repeatedly let an Inuk cut his hair in the *"Eskimo fash-ion,"* visited their tents, played games with them, and took part in com-munal meals of seal meat. All this meant that he felt uninhibitedly at home among the Inuit.

## Alcohol—the questionable drink of the Qallunaat

Prior to contact with Europeans, the *qallunaat,* the Inuit, like other aboriginal populations in North America, were unfamiliar with alco-holic drinks. The "explorers" and the whalers took alcohol with them in large quantities for their own use, and often shared it generously with the Inuit. Hence, alcohol became a regular element in the early economic and social relations between them and the Inuit. The Inuit could not handle alcohol like the *qallunaat,* who for centuries had integrated it as a normal component of their diet, culture and customs, but who now frequently employed it as a "means of persuasion" with regard to the Inuit in order to achieve certain goals. Boas and Weike, who were well supplied with alcohol in their stocks of provisions, also became an ele-ment in this unequal and inglorious situation. Nowadays in Nunavut the sale and consumption of alcoholic drinks is strictly regulated by the government. The two modern settlements that are located in Weike's and Boas' travel area, are "dry," i.e., "prohibited communities" where import, sale, and consumption of all alcohol is absolutely prohibited by law (Nunavut Liquor Act 2006).

In his journal and letters Wilhelm Weike mentioned alcohol and its use in more than twenty places, most frequently in September and October 1883 when the crews on board the whaling ships and *Germania* were liberally celebrating their meeting and then a "wet" leave-taking. During the fall boat trips that Boas and Weike made along with three Inuit, schnapps was always present; it was administered in German fashion, at any time of day, in order to help invigorate the limbs and the spirits in cold weather. The whalers, whether Scottish or American, always took a supply of spirits (rum or whisky) with them; serving it to the Inuit became a regular component of relations with them. James Mutch, who was a strict teetotaller (Boas in Müller-Wille 1998:103), nonetheless unscrupulously distributed a "ceremonial" shot of rum as a reward to "*his Eskimos*" once a week. Weike described this as follows: "*A bucket full of rum and a bucket full of water was the schnapps that the Eskimos received.*" (21 January 1884).

The German polar station at Kingua was more than abundantly provided with alcoholic drinks. That led, among other things, to considerable problems among the eleven-man staff. When the station was being closed down in September 1883 the leader, Wilhelm Giese, had to give orders that all remaining bottles be smashed, to prevent further drinking among the restless personnel. This was unsuccessful, however (Boas in Müller-Wille 1998:88). Apart from beer, which was the first to be exhausted, there were wine, champagne, liqueur and hard liquor, of which the commissary issued a daily ration during the wintering. By the end there was still a surplus, of which Boas alone accepted forty bottles of rum! (Boas in Müller-Wille 1998:93). The Germans' consumption of alcohol did not remain a secret from the local Inuit, since one of them, Ocheitu, worked for them for a year, had some experience with Germans who drank, and certainly also received alcohol from them.

Boas and Weike also had an adequate supply of wine, punch, schnapps (*Korn;* grain liquor), rum, and cognac. They mainly drank

254 ♦ Inuit and Whalers on Baffin Island through German Eyes

this alcohol themselves, but also shared it freely with the Inuit or gave it to them as a reward. In December 1883 they had rum or schnapps with them on their trek across the sea ice. Singnar carried the bottle against his chest to prevent it from freezing. Once they had drunk it all, Weike prepared a potent and far-from-innocuous drink from warmed-up pure alcohol, enriched with sugar. On New Year's Eve 1883, when supplies from Kekerten reached the camp at Anarnitung, these included sufficient amounts of cognac and Swedish punch, which they shared with Ocheitu. Weike repeatedly noted that from time to time he would treat himself to a mulled cognac or rum for pleasure or to deaden the pain caused by his frostbite.

## Return to Minden—readjusting and marriage (October 1884 to December 1885)

Wilhelm Weike ended his journal without fanfare or any transition on September 1, 1884 when, along with Franz Boas, he was aboard the whaling ship *Wolf* in Exeter Bay, Baffin Island, and she was homeward bound to St. John's, Newfoundland. They arrived there on September 7, and arranged passage on board the steamer *Ardandhu*, which sailed from St. John's on September 10, called at Halifax (Nova Scotia) and reached New York on September 21.

On September 23 Boas set off as quickly as possible by train for Bolton Landing, to the summer home of the family of his fiancée, Marie Krackowizer, on Lake George in northern New York State. He left Weike behind in New York, and arranged for him to make the trans-Atlantic crossing from New York to Hamburg on board the next steamer, thereby returning to Minden. Ostensibly, Weike was now very homesick. Boas made sure that his servant reached home quickly since he intended to remain in the United States and concentrate on his research, and, not least, wished to be with his fiancée and her family. Boas Senior was not keen on that decision, since he expected his son to return to Germany as soon as possible to advance his academic career (Correspondence between Franz Boas/parents, New York/Minden, October – December 1884).

Wilhelm Weike travelled from Hoboken, New Jersey to Hamburg on board either the *Albingia* or the *Allemania* of the Hamburg-America (HAPAG) line between September 25 and 27, arriving on October 8 or early on October 9, 1884; the relevant schedules were not on record in the archives. Depending on the location and size of the cabin, a crossing cost between 80 and 120 marks per person (HAPAG 2007). From Hamburg, Weike took the train to Minden; on changing at Hanover he unexpectedly encountered an old friend. He wrote to Boas: *"L. Kloy, when I was leaving last year, was the last of my friends that I saw at the station in Hannover, now he was the first one I saw."* (Wilhelm Weike/ Franz Boas, Minden/New York, 13 October 1884). But probably more important was the fact that Mathilde Nolting had travelled from Minden to Hamburg to greet Wilhelm Weike (Toni Boas/Franz Boas, Minden/New York, October 1884). They became engaged soon after his return.

The Prussian administration has provided today's researcher and reader with a charming oddity. The official at the Minden Residents' Registration Office duly recorded Wilhelm Weike's name and particulars on October 10, 1884. In the column, entitled *"Location from which the incomer has moved,"* "Nordpol" (North Pole) is clearly indicated as the location from which Weike had returned (Minden Municipal Archives; City of Minden, F 2149, serial no. 41/1884, under letter W). Adding to this story, Monika M. Schulte, Minden City Archivist, wrote to the authors on December 14, 2007: *"The entry for Wilhelm Weike is located in the lower half of the book; the previous entry (somebody else had moved from the Grand Duchy of Oldenburg) has unfortunately spilled over into the line for Wilhelm Weike, so that the entry in the immigration box relating to Wilhelm Weike's last place residence reads "Grand Duchy North Pole."* The North Pole, more than 2500 kilometres—as the crow flies— north from southern Baffin Island, was not 'discovered' until more than twenty years later. Had Weike been unwittingly to the North Pole and thus the 'first conqueror' of the sought-after imaginary location? But how could Weike, who had been introduced to geographical and cartographic methods by Boas, have explained to a Prussian official of that time where he had really been? Or was it that for the official himself, the names of places such as *Baffin-Land, Kekerten* or *Kivitung* seemed

Mathilde Weike, née Nolting, and Wilhelm Weike, Berlin, 1886 (Photo: Studio Theodor Wenzel, Berlin East; *American Philosophical Society*)

to be from a totally alien world? Or had Weike with his sense of the comical and humorous given that answer purely out of mischief?

Soon after his return from the Arctic, Boas asked his father what he had paid Weike as wages for the entire year of the expedition (Franz Boas/parents, Alma Farm, Lake George, NY/Minden, 25 September 1884). His answer has not survived. No information can be found as to the amount. How the payment was calculated is unfortunately also not clear. The question poses itself as to what Wilhelm Weike's work was worth to the Boas family. Franz Boas' father covered all the costs, including Weike's wages during his sojourn in the Canadian Arctic and for the sea passage from North America (Müller-Wille 1998:10). Was it adequate remuneration for a year during which Weike subsequently risked his life and would not know when or if he would return? Had ice conditions been different their journey could easily have stretched to at least two years. Was Weike living with "free board and lodgings" plus salary and travel expenses? After a year without expenses, was he for a time well-off for his situation, as a result of these savings and of his steadily accumulating wages? Money is not mentioned at all in Weike's journal. Answers to these questions would certainly also provide more information as to why the Weike-Nolting couple moved from Minden to Berlin, apart from the fact that the ties of employment continued with the Boas family, whose daughters had already moved to Berlin before Weike's return.

After his return, until the official notice of his departure from Minden on December 30, 1885, Wilhelm Weike again lived at 19 Marienstraße. In the fall of 1884 Boas enquired of his parents as to Weike's health; the latter had just turned 25 on November 28 and seemed healthy (Franz Boas/parents, Washington, D.C./Minden 30 November 1884). It would appear that Weike had very quickly settled down in Minden again; his few letters to Boas testify to that.

Wilhelm Weike had known Mathilde Nolting since 1879; she had been employed as maid to the Boas family since October 1876, and later also worked in the "Villa Boas." She was born in Rinteln on June 2, 1858, where she presumably also grew up. She must have had a position in Hausberge on the eastern bank of the Weser a short distance south of Minden, for on November 22, 1875 she moved from Hausberge to

43 Bäckerstraße in Minden where she served as maid to the Schmidt family. From October 17, 1876 she was registered at 66/67 Markt, then the business premises and residence of Meyer Boas, and from the summer of 1879 at the newly completed "Villa Boas." Mathilde Nolting and Wilhelm Weike got engaged in the fall of 1884, were married on December 30, 1885 in a civil ceremony in Minden and moved immediately to Berlin (Minden Municipal Archives).

Franz Boas returned to Germany only in March 1885, and stayed mainly in Berlin. From there he corresponded with his parents with regard to Weike, who had expressed a wish to move to Berlin to find work there (Franz Boas/parents, Berlin/Minden, 23 July 1885). In November 1885, Boas even posted a newspaper advertisement to find him a position as domestic servant. But Boas had first ascertained from his parents whether Weike could also serve with gloves (Franz Boas/parents, Berlin/Minden, 23 November 1885). Shortly thereafter Boas informed his fiancée that Weike had found a job and could marry and move to Berlin (Franz Boas/Marie Krackowizer, Berlin/New York, 27 November 1885).

## Move to and life in Berlin (1886-1917)

After the wedding, Wilhelm Weike is officially registered as leaving Minden as a married man, along with his wife Frau Mathilde, née Nolting. The marriage remained childless. Weike's first address in Berlin and probably the young couple's first home was recorded at 16 Prinzessinenstraße in Kreuzberg for the year 1886-87. His occupation was listed as doorman. He was still registered at that address with the same occupation in 1889. Between 1890 and 1896 there was no entry for him in the Berlin directory. During those years the Weikes probably lived and worked as servant and maid in Franz Boas' parents' house at 9 and office at 13A Großbeerenstraße, where Boas Senior also conducted his international business agency. As of 1897 until Wilhelm's death in 1917 the couple lived in the third floor of the second house at the back court of 62a Kottbuser Ufer (changed to Cottbuser Ufer in 1919), now 44 Fraenkelufer, in Kreuzberg near the synagogue, and very close to the Urbanhafen on the Landwehrkanal. Weike's occupations during that period were recorded variously as house-servant, business servant, and business assistant; he must probably have changed his job quite frequently. It is not known where or by whom Wilhelm Weike was first employed in Berlin (all data: Berliner Adreß-Buch 1873-1895; Berliner Adressbuch 1896-1943).

The close connection with the Boas family continued, as he himself mentioned in his letters to Boas. In part, like his wife, he served various members of the Boas family. In the fall of 1885, Boas asked his parents that Wilhelm Weike send him his *"Eskimo clothes"* for an exhibition, probably at the Royal Museum of Ethnology in Berlin (Franz Boas/parents, Berlin/Minden, 11 September 1885). Later, after Weike and his wife had moved to Berlin, Boas visited them and hired Mathilde Weike to do his laundry (Franz Boas/parents, Berlin/Minden, 5 February 1886). Over the next few years contact between Boas and Weike became more sporadic. Between October 1884 and January 1889 Wilhelm Weike sent *"Herr Dr"* a few letters from Minden and Berlin to New York (see above texts of letters following the journal). The Weike couple always got together when Boas and his family visited his parents and sisters in Berlin.

In his children's story about the year in the Arctic Franz Boas mentioned, *"You know Wilhelm, who helped* [your] *grandfather in the office."* (Boas 2007:4). Between 1890 and 1913 Boas, along with his wife and children, visited Germany almost every second year, so that their children, who were born between 1888 and 1902, probably met Weike frequently at their grandparents' or aunts' homes (Cole 1999:150; Boas, N. 2004:292). In 1901 Weike received a portrait photo of Boas with a dedication. The Weikes congratulated Marie and Franz Boas on their silver wedding on March 10, 1912, and in the summer of 1913 they got together in Berlin for the last time.

Wilhelm Weike died in Berlin-Kreuzberg on Monday, June 11, 1917. The death and funeral registry reads: *"Wilhelm Weike, house-servant, age 57 years, 6 months, 13 days, died on 11 June 1917, resident 62a Kottbusser Ufer, interment on 14 June 1917, in the Jacobi Churchyard II; cause of death: cardiac arrest."* (Death register No. 793, Registry Office Berlin Va, Friedrichshain-Kreuzberg).

Weike was buried in the Jakobi II Cemetery in grave C II 826, indicating section and grave number. That section lies on the left side of the cemetery. This cemetery still functions at present; the arrangement of the sections by letter still continues, but the record of burials now runs only up to 500. Weike's grave plot was not retained by his wife or the family, and over the course of time it was reoccupied at least three to four times (personal communication by Stephanie Reibnitz, June 2007). Weike's wife, Mathilde, is not listed in the burial records of Sankt Simeon parish, to which the Jakobi Cemetery belongs, at any time before 1932 inclusive (Evangelisches Landeskirchliches Archiv/Bernd Gieseking, Berlin/Dortmund, 11 June 2007). After Weike's death his widow continued to be a tenant at that address until 1929 after which no trace can be found of her whereabouts or her death (Berliner Adressbuch 1896-1943). In Berlin the destruction of the archives in World War II as well as the partial evacuation and less-than-successful return of many documents is a constant problem in finding individuals' vital data.

Despite the war between Germany and the U.S.A., which began with the American declaration of war on April 6, 1917, the news of Wilhelm Weike's death reached Franz Boas very quickly via his colleague William C. Thalbitzer (1873-1858) in neutral Denmark. The reaction of Franz Boas and his family was sadness and shock (Toni Boas/Franz Boas, Berlin/New York, June 1917). At his summer place in Bolton Landing in upstate New York on July 21, 1917 Boas wrote his eldest son Ernst Philip Boas (1891-1955), who was serving in the American army as a doctor: *"I can hardly tell you how depressed my mood is. The news of Wilhelm's death has moved me painfully. It is very painful when one's whole youth begins to die off on all sides. One becomes so aware of aging."*

In July 1917, Franz Boas had just turned 59. A few days later he informed James Mutch in Scotland about Wilhelm Weike's early death: *"I want to let you know that Wilhelm, my faithful companion during our stay in Cumberland Sound and on Davis Strait, died early this month of hardening of the arteries. I saw him last four years ago [1913] when I was in Europe. He leaves a widow who, I think, is fairly well provided for. They have no children. Both Wilhelm and his wife have always been closely associated with our family, and my sisters have seen him quite often."* (Franz Boas/James Mutch, Bolton Landing, New York/Peterhead, Scotland, 26 July 1917).

Almost a year later, on May 12, 1918 James Mutch replied *"... William has gone to where we have to take our turn by & by."* He added that he had visited Inuit recently at *"Muckleman's place"* at Cape Mercy/Uibarn and that *"Eenewyak"* was still alive and that *"Kanacker and a few more whom you met are all old looking, but old and young know about you."*

## Messages to and from Baffin Island (1884-1886)

After his arrival in New York in September 1884 Franz Boas maintained an active correspondence with the captains of the whaling ships that he had encountered off Qivitung and to whom he had entrusted copies of his research data and ethnographic items for transport to Germany. Captain Burnett of the *Wolf* wrote that the belongings that Boas had asked him to take had arrived safely in Dundee and would be forwarded to Minden (Burnett/Franz Boas, Dundee/New York, 20 October 1884). He also sent *"Greetings to Willie"* (Wilhelm Weike). Earlier, in New York on March 14, 1885 Franz Boas had embarked on board the passenger steamer *Donau* of the North German Lloyd Line (*Nordeutscher Lloyd*), bound for Bremerhaven. He arrived back home in Minden on March 26, 1885, after an absence of 21 months.

During the following year he lived in Berlin to write his post-doctoral thesis (*Habilitationsschrift*) in Geography at the Friedrich-Wilhelms University (since 1949 called Humboldt University); it was published late in 1885 (Boas 1885a). On May 27, 1886 he gave his *Habilitation* lecture and on June 5 his inaugural lecture, and thereafter was appointed unpaid lecturer (*Privatdozent*) in Geography in the Faculty of Philosophy. He never filled that position, but left Germany again on July 8, 1886, reaching New York on July 27, and remained permanently in the United States thereafter (cf. Cole 1999:105ff.; Verne 2004). He married Marie Krackowizer in New York on March 10, 1887 (Boas, N. 2004: 81).

James Mutch, who was on home-leave in Scotland in 1885-86 reported in detail to Boas on life at the American and Scottish whaling stations at Kekerten, and mentioned that *"Attinak and Oman"* (the woman Atteina and the man Oman) still spoke often about *"William"* (Wilhelm); also *"Nockakchew"* (Nachojaschi), who had been on boat trips with them and had often come to the station and sung for Boas, had not forgotten the two of them (James Mutch/Franz Boas/Peterhead/Minden, 18 November 1885). In a later letter in December 1885 he mentioned that

*"At=hwak"* (unidentified) was still at Kekerten and that Boas should relay this to Wilhelm Weike. Mutch also took pains to clear up an apparent misunderstanding. *"Signah"* (Ssigna/Singnar) had never said that Boas had treated him unfairly not always giving him three meals per day while he was hunting seals. Captain Roach had been spreading that unfounded rumour among the Inuit and had been trying to stir up animosity among them towards Boas.

This demonstrates that misunderstandings and a certain rivalry had existed between Franz Boas and Captain Roach. The Inuit found themselves caught in the middle. Roach was apparently also irritated that Boas had arranged for Mutch to distribute his gift of thirty pounds of tobacco to express his gratitude to all *"his Eskimos."* Boas had had the tobacco, to the value of £20, sent to Mutch in Scotland via the Noble shipping company in the spring of 1886. There is no evidence of any exchange of letters between Franz Boas and Captain Roach; his correspondence with Mutch was to continue extensively until the 1920s. Boas also got Mutch to collaborate in publications about the Inuit (Boas 1901, 1907) and Mutch (1906) wrote a contribution to the commemorative volume for Franz Boas that was published in 1906 to mark the twenty-fifth anniversary of his doctorate (Laufer and Andrews 1906; see also Harper 2008).

In the letter quoted above, Mutch also informed Boas that the German-Americans, Fred Grobschmidt and Wilhelm Scherden, as well as the Dane Rasmussen had left Kekerten—the latter due to ill health—and had travelled south via St. John's, and that *"Signah,"* Boas' Inuit companion, had worked for Captain Roach in 1884-85 and had brought to Kekerten the locked boxes that Boas had cached on Kingnait Pass. They were sent to Minden via Dundee. Another crate, containing equipment and other items belonging to the German Polar Commission, which Boas had borrowed, were also shipped to Germany.

Early in 1886 Boas informed Mutch about Weike's marriage to Mathilde Nolting. He also intimated that he intended travelling back to Baffin Island, accompanied by Weike, in the fall of 1886, to continue his research among the Inuit. In his next letter to Boas James Mutch expressed his interest in Weike's life in Berlin and wrote *"I hope William is happy with his new wife. You had better tell him not to mention about*

*Tookavay or she, Mrs. W.* [Weike], *might be jealous. Should he go with you again possibly, even though he has said that he is not to go. Probably we might all not meet again where we met first. However happy new year to them and may they have as many sons + daughters as they both wish."* (James Mutch/Franz Boas, Peterhead/Berlin, 14 January 1886). It cannot be proven, but it seems likely that Weike never mentioned Tookavay to his wife—a love story untold.

In 1886, James Mutch got married in Aberdeen before he returned alone to Kekerten (Harper 2008). He was expecting Boas and Weike back on Baffin Island in the fall, and later asked Boas whether Weike wanted to send greetings to *"Tookavay, Oman or Athinak"* (Tokaving, Oman, Atteina) (James Mutch/Franz Boas, Peterhead/Berlin, 8 May 1886). The relationship with Tookavay never crops up in Wilhelm Weike's journal, although Atteina, Oman's wife does; nor did he mention Oman by name. In 1908 James Mutch wrote to Franz Boas once again and recalled Wilhelm Weike: *"William, not King William* [an allusion to Kaiser Wilhelm II], *your man you had with you in Cumberland Gulf. He will be making Lager beer in his own country and quite well I hope."* (James Mutch/Franz Boas, Peterhead/New York, 1 February 1908).

In the spring of 1886, Franz Boas, writing from Berlin, had enquired of Robert Bell (1841-1917), geologist and arctic researcher with the Geological Survey of Canada in Ottawa, whether he could travel with him to Baffin Island on board a Canadian government ship. On May 26, Bell sent Boas a telegram to the effect that his request had been approved and that the ship would sail from Halifax on June 24 and could take him to Baffin Island. Franz Boas did not pursue his plan further. Instead, he had decided to move to New York to develop his career there, and to marry his fiancée as soon as possible. Thus, Wilhelm Weike's prospect for another trip to the Arctic came to naught.

## Wilhelm Weike through Franz Boas' eyes

Franz Boas mentioned Wilhelm Weike at least 145 times in the journals and letters that he wrote on Baffin Island. Some of these mentions are very informative as to Boas' attitude towards and relations with Weike, and hence have been inserted in italics and in square brackets into

Weike's journal (Boas' quotations taken from Müller-Wille 1998). In Boas' post-doctoral dissertation *Baffin-Land* (1885a) and also in the series of articles in the *Berliner Tageblatt* (see listing in Müller-Wille 1984) Weike crops up only a few times. Boas refers to him generally as his accompanying *"servant"* (1885a:1,8), but never alludes to his contribution and merits. On the other hand he describes in detail Weike's frostbite, which he had looked upon almost as an impediment to his own work. He writes *"During our trek through the rough ice poor Wilhelm had frozen his feet and thereafter had to stay for weeks in the snow-house of my host* [Ocheitu at Anarnitung], *until I could move him to the Scottish whaling station at Qeqerten; he was not able to leave it again for the remainder of the winter. On the 24*[th] [December 1883] *I went back to Qeqerten to fetch provisions for Wilhelm and gifts for the Eskimos who had received us so hospitably."* (Boas 1885a:10).

For Franz Boas the arctic expedition to Baffin Island and to the Inuit was a key experience leading to an exceptional career as a scientist. Nowadays, one attributes to him the re-casting of the then so-called "savage natives," as far as western-oriented society was concerned, into "civilized people," since he had identified *"Herzensbildung,"* noble-heartedness, among the Inuit (Boas in Müller-Wille 1994:161, 1998:159; see also Cole 1983:50). He, Franz Boas, the modern scientist, enters the *iglus* of the Inuit—figuratively speaking—and becomes the first to see them at the same level as his own culture, that of European civilization, and this naturally entirely from his own viewpoint (cf. Tilg and Pöhl 2007) – *"while I lived among them as one of them,"* as Boas himself expressed it (Boas 1885b:5).

But the relationship between servant and master, between Wilhelm Weike and Franz Boas, their mutual recognition, did not include any such acknowledgment. The social hierarchy of contemporary German society remained intact. After all, in Germany the two men would never have spent the night in the same room; here in the Arctic they spent days and nights in close physical proximity in tents and *iglus,* or on the same sledge. But at the Scottish station each had a separate bed recess. And yet for Weike Boas always remained *"Herr Doktor"* and he, in return, addressed him always with *"Wilhelm, Sie,"* i.e., there was a clear and distinct social hierarchy that was not overcome or reduced by common experiences.

Weike did not match Boas' educational level; with disarming honesty Boas revealed that difference in a letter journal he kept for his sister Toni. *"If one sends a person into the barren solitude, such as I experienced— for Wilhelm is hardly company—he will feel the need to communicate, the need to see people around him with whom he can live, and how much I long for work."* (12 July 1884).

It appears that Boas did not let Weike be on par with him; he saw everything in terms of science and of the academic career toward which he was striving. The collection and discovery of new plants, mapping, and all fame and every deed of this expedition were solely the achievement of *"Herr Doktor."* Weike's observations expressed in his journal are neither cited nor recognized. For an entire year that they spent together on the ice and the tundra under the most difficult conditions, on a journey that might at least have cost Weike a foot—and here due to his hurry and impatience Boas bears considerable blame—his appreciation and valuation of Weike are wanting. This is understandable, perhaps, given contemporary attitudes, but disappointing nonetheless, in light of Boas' perceptions presented in his perhaps greatest works *"The Mind of Primitive Man"* (Boas 1911) and *"Kultur und Rasse"* (Culture and Race; Boas 1914). Who conquered Mount Everest? Edmund Hillary or Tenzing Norgay?

After the expedition, relations between Boas and Weike remained intact as a continuation of the respectful but distant link between master and servant. One has to assume that for the rest of their lives Mathilde and Wilhelm Weike remained part of the Boas families, who displayed a strong sense of responsibility for them. The reaction of Franz Boas and other family members at Wilhelm Weike's death, which was a moment of belated reflection, is thus understandable.

## The Inuit and the Arctic–the Boasian enigma

One has to realize that Franz Boas was not a very happy man in the Arctic—and not at all happy right after that. It was icily cold in the Arctic; it was arduous; for various reasons he had not completed all the tasks that he had intended. He was an unfortunate young scientist who was afraid that he could not realize the ambitious goals that he had set himself in Germany, and was afraid that the exertions of the trip had been in vain.

Having started on this trip as a geographer, but already with ethnological lines of questioning, he himself was almost totally dissatisfied with its progress. While in the Arctic he had had to adapt constantly his travel goals to the circumstances. Moreover, he was very much in love, had secretly become engaged immediately before his departure, and felt painfully alone, even though his fiancée was in New York on the North American continent. With a mania for communicating—his publications, like his letter-diaries and correspondence, are impressive in terms of volume—he felt himself cut off, without a conversational partner with whom he had similar interests and with whom he might have exchanged ideas. Culturally he felt downright isolated on this expedition.

He felt that he often missed the mark in his research and assessments. His cartographic survey work was more than noteworthy. When the Canadian government published new maps of Baffin Island in the 1920s and 1930s, Boas' map of 1883-84 was taken as the baseline. His book *The Central Eskimo* (1888), the ethnological treatise based on his sojourn, became a classic of cultural anthropology, and has remained so to the present day. Other publications that appeared later (Boas 1901, 1907) are standard works on the ethnohistory of the Inuit.

Despite this success, Boas had apparently inwardly finished with the Arctic as a field for his own direct research. From today's vantage point, he abandoned his short-lived plan to return to Baffin Island surprisingly quickly. Why did that second trip not materialize? The authors suspect the cause was a strong inner rejection of coldness, hardships and loneliness, and the prospect of a long wintering with an uncertain return certainly made him hesitate. Also he felt his considerable shortcomings with respect to the Inuit whose language and culture, despite all the efforts, seemed to elude him and became his enigma. Furthermore, at that time more conveniently and comfortably accessible research areas among the aboriginal peoples on the Northwest Coast of Canada became more interesting, and were to occupy him for the rest of his life (cf. Cole 1999; Boas, N. 2004).

A very negative aspect of late nineteenth century ethnology, in which Franz Boas was also involved, should be mentioned here: on the one hand, the compulsion for grave robbing, i.e., the acquisition of human skeletons, bones, and skulls without the permission or approval of the descendants concerned, and on the other, the degrading practice of exhibiting individuals and groups of so-called "primitive peoples" in European and North American museums and zoos, as well as the portrayal of those people as "museum objects" for "purely scientific purposes"—not exactly a page to be proud of in the history of the "science of mankind" (cf. Harper 2000; see also Pöhl and Tilg 2009; Schmuhl 2009). In the Arctic Boas was totally unsuccessful and defeated at grave robbing, since the Inuit met that idea with a clear *"verboten"* and a distinct rejection (Boas in Müller-Wille 1998:116; Pöhl 2008; see also Müller-Wille 2008).

The experiences and writings of Franz Boas and Wilhelm Weike should also be seen in the light of the recently published journal of Abraham Ulrikab, who, along with seven other Inuit—men, women and children—reached Germany from Labrador in 1880 under reprehensible circumstances. In plain and simple words, he recorded the sojourn of those eight Inuit and their exhibit in "popular shows" that were frequented by many Germans and covered extensively in the German press. The story ended tragically, since all the Inuit died of smallpox in Berlin and other places within five months, due to the careless omission of any vaccination. The Inuit were buried in unmarked graves in Berlin. Abraham Ulrikab's journal, written in Inuktitut and intended for his relatives and for the missionaries of the *Herrnhuter Brüder-Unität* (Moravian Church) in Labrador, is a devastating testimony on how he saw the world of Germans, where his fellow-travellers and ultimately he himself, died (Ulrikab 2005).

## And who was Wilhelm Weike?

Nowadays one would probably say that Weike was a "fantastic guy and a good buddy"—an ordinary, unassuming person who had grown up under arduous circumstances. His father died early and his mother before he was twenty. He trained with a landscape gardener and then joined the Boas household as a servant at what was certainly one of the best addresses in Minden. Meyer Boas was a wealthy businessman, the town's most successful textile merchant at that time. His only son Franz obtained his school-leaving certificate, studied, and gained his doctorate. These two young men were of almost the same age and lived in the same house, but it would appear that there was scarcely any contact, if any, between them.

As was revealed in the Arctic, Weike was a clever young man—*ein gewitzter Mensch*, as they say in his homeland, eastern Westphalia—smart with little formal education. Or at least not in the traditional sense. He quickly learned what was essential for such a journey. What on earth moved him to commit himself to accompanying Boas for one year. Love of adventure? An attempt at breaking out of his world? Was it the money that Boas Senior offered him? Daren't he say "No"? Did he have any concept of what lay in store for him? Weike was the sole person who accompanied Boas after Lieutenant von der Goltz, Boas' intended assistant, had dropped out for unknown reasons. Above all, among Weike's special abilities were his communicative skills and gregariousness. He succeeded in making himself understood to the Inuit and whalers, the local population of that strange world, although initially with practically no command of English or Inuktitut. For him there were no constraints. Weike would set foot in the *tupiks* and *iglus* of the Inuit, eat with them, and take part in their lives, and would live with and visit whalers at their stations. Weike made himself understood at their own level; he learned and was receptive to new things, was a passionate hunter, became an expert arctic cook, assisted Boas in endless chores, kept a regular journal, grasped the life, spirituality, culture and thoughts of the Inuit and forged friendships. But these he did not cultivate further later on. Why not? The Inuit culture was entirely oral at that time. And James Mutch, their host, the head of the Scottish whaling station, was himself another *"Mister"* as far as Weike was concerned, i.e., from another social stratum; by contrast the Inuit were a society without hierarchies or barriers.

At the same time Weike was a wonderfully humorous character; he described many things with great irony and with an eye for the comical and the grotesque. During the winter, when he was hanging laundry out, he comments jokingly, it froze to *"stiff blokes"* in no time. With regard to hygiene, Weike remarked, *"Even if I have to steal the water, I'll do the laundry come what may."* (Letter, 28 August 1883). He was also musically gifted; he sang with the Inuit, the seamen and whalers, or made music with *Herrn Doktor.* And—again to use an east Westphalian expression—*"er spuckt nicht ins Glas"* literally *"he wouldn't spit in the glass,"* i.e., wouldn't refuse a drink. He enjoyed a drink, and liked to celebrate. During the nights before the European ships left the Sound in the fall of 1883, their departure was celebrated in boisterous fashion.

He also learned to drive sledge dogs, and here another character trait comes into play. Weike drove his team with a very firm hand and even killed a pup by throwing a rock at it. But this was the wrong century and the wrong place for an animal rights protester or a vegetarian. Also when he was *"preserving animals,"* by which he meant immersing mollusks and animals in alcohol, this clearly gave him pleasure.

In a few places in his journal Weike provides an insight into his own spirituality and a glimpse at his open and keen interest in shamanistic activities by the Inuit. Weike, as a Lutheran, was religious. At the start of 1884 he wrote a dedication for the New Year, *"The New Year has begun; God has given it to us."* Back in Minden, the regular life set in again; he became engaged and married Mathilde Nolting. He remained a houseservant. Did he have no opportunity for anything else? Was he happy as he was? Were his prospects or abilities limited? Did the Arctic expedition offer a personal escape or greater liberty? Weike had an intimate relationship with Tookavay, an Inuit woman at Kekerten. One can deduce this much from the letters that Mutch later wrote to Boas. One has to read between the lines. During weeks when Boas was travelling Weike, with his injured feet, was tied to the station and was often alone there, or perhaps not entirely alone.

After this year of extreme challenges Wilhelm Weike fell back into formation, to use a military expression as he himself sometimes did, and initially again became a servant in the Boas family—in the narrow confines of a business household, after a year of wide-ranging freedom and responsibility and the most unusual experiences. Why then the move to Berlin? There he became a doorman and later a house-servant again. A jack-of-all-trades, which was what he did best—serving people.

## Finale

In the end many questions remain unanswered. How did Weike spend his childhood and youth? Why, after his excursion into the world of the Arctic, did Weike subsequently stay at home, or was collecting stamps satisfying to him as a substitute for travels in the wider world? Were his experiences too extreme for him? Why did he not stay longer in Minden? Why did he change jobs? Did Boas try to help him to find work in America, and if so, why did Weike not emigrate? When did the relationship between Wilhelm Weike and Mathilde Nolting begin? The marriage remained childless; were there contacts with other family members? Where are the original of his journal and his Inuit skin clothing? Where are the carvings that he purchased or received as gifts? Was he "famous" in Minden or later in Berlin after he returned from the Arctic?

Most of these questions will never be answered. What Wilhelm Weike has left behind are the fascinating writings of a young man who, through pure chance, set off on a trip to a strange people and to regions then totally unknown to Germans and Europeans in general. His journal is the rare literary legacy of an ordinary man of his time. Weike accompanied Boas and looked after him on the trip, supported him in all his work, lived with the Inuit, and met whalers, scientists and seamen. His impressions, always filtered knowing that Franz Boas would also be reading what he wrote, are fresh, lively, and often with a hint of irony.

His journal and letters offer an impressive glimpse into the world and perceptions of Wilhelm Weike, whose collaboration with Boas cannot be judged highly enough. He went to Berlin, remained a servant, and his wife Mathilde did Franz Boas' laundry when he visited Berlin. As an ordinary man Weike contributed unequivocally to the first scientific journey by Boas, who began and ended his academic world career in New York. Evidence of the intimate presence of Wilhelm Weike survived solely through his journal and his letters in the Boas Papers housed in the American Philosophical Society in Philadelphia. By making them public in both German and English Wilhelm Weike has been accorded—next to Franz Boas—a place in history.

# Acknowledgements

During the preparation of the original German version and the English translation of Wilhelm Weike's journal and letters the authors/editors received generous support and help from a number of individuals and institutions in carrying out the investigations and in producing this book. We would like to thank them all very sincerely. Special thanks are due to the Board of Directors of the Minden Historical Society and to its executive director, Monika M. Schulte, who accepted the original version of this book in the Society's publication series, and who funded its design and printing from the Society's own resources. For publishing the English version we are grateful to Robin Philpot of Baraka Books in Montréal (Québec) in Canada who, in an uncomplicated and flexible fashion, accepted the book manuscript upon the kind suggestion by William Barr who did the translation into English.

## Individuals

William Barr (geographer, arctic historian and translator, Arctic Institute of North America, University of Calgary, Calgary, Alberta, Canada)

Ursula Bender-Wittmann and Petra Brinkmann (Curators, Minden Museum of History, Regional Studies, and Folklore, Minden, Germany)

Bert Buchholz (archivist, Evangelical National Church Archives, Berlin, Germany)

Hermann Gieseking and Ilse Gieseking (local assistance, Kutenhausen/ Minden)

Charles B. Greifenstein (Manuscript Librarian, American Philosophical Society, Manuscript Library, Philadelphia, Pennsylvania, U.S.A.)

Kenn Harper (entrepreneur, arctic historian and writer, Iqaluit, Nunavut, Canada)

Hubert Knicker (historian, Häverstädt/Minden, Germany)

Josée Lalancette (graphic artist, Folio infographie, Montréal, Québec, Canada)

Jürgen Langenkämper (journalist, daily newspaper *Mindener Tageblatt*, Minden, Germany)

Martina Lorenz (graphic artist, Etage Eins/publicity, design, web design, Minden Germany)

Utz Maas (linguist, Department of Linguistics, University of Osnabrück, Osnabrück, Germany)

Linna Weber Müller-Wille and Ragnar Müller-Wille (editorial, linguistic and technical assistance and graphic design, Myriad Pursuits, Saint-Lambert, Québec, Canada)

Manfred Nolting and Ursula Nolting (editorial and linguistic assistance, Appelhülsen, Germany)

Robin Philpot (publisher, Baraka Books, Montréal, Québec, Canada)

Stephanie Reibnitz (owner, Schmidt Grabmale, Berlin, Germany)

Monika M. Schulte, Vinzenz Lübben and colleagues (archivists, Minden Municipal Archives—Archives of the City of Minden and of the Minden-Lübbecke District, Minden, Germany)

William A. Weber (botanist, Herbarium, COLO, Botany Section, University of Colorado Museum of Natural History, Boulder, Colorado, U.S.A.)

## Institutions

Bundesamt für Seeschifffahrt und Hydrographie, Bibliothek und Archiv, Bundesministerium für Verkehr, Bau and Stadtentwicklung, Hamburg (formerly Deutsche Seewarte)

Bundesarchiv, Berlin-Lichterfelde

Deutsches Schifffahrtsmuseum, Bremerhaven

Evangelisches Zentralarchiv in Berlin, Kirchenbuchamt, Berlin

Friedhofsgemeinde St. Jacobi, Berlin

Geheimes Staatsarchiv Preußischer Kulturbesitz, Berlin-Dahlem

Haus der Kirche, Minden

Kommunalarchiv Minden, Archiv der Stadt Minden und des Kreises Minden-Lübbecke, Minden

Mindener Geschichtsverein, Minden

# Bibliography

Abbes, H[einrich] 1884. Die Eskimos des Cumberland-Sundes. Eine ethnographische Skizze. *Globus* 46:198-201, 213-218.

— 1890. Die Eskimos des Cumberlandgolfes. In: Neumayer, Georg von, ed. *Die internationale Polarforschung 1882-1883. Die Deutschen Expeditionen und ihre Ergebnisse.* Band II: *Beschreibende Naturwissenschaften in einzelnen Abhandlungen* Hamburg: Deutsche Polar-Kommission, 1-60.

— 1992 [1884]. The German Expedition of the First International Polar Year to Cumberland Sound, Baffin Island, 1882-1883. Translated by William Barr. *Polar Geography and Geography* 4:272-304.

Alfred-Wegener-Institut für Polar- und Meeresforschung (ed.) 1993. *125 Jahre deutsche Polarforschung.* Bremerhaven: Alfred-Wegener-Institut für Polar- und Meeresforschung.

[Ambronn, Leopold] L. A. 1883. Bemerkungen über den Cumberland-Sund und seine Bewohner. *Deutsche Geographische Blätter* 6:347-357.

American Philosophical Society 2007. Franz Boas Collections, 1862-1942, B:B61. Franz Boas Professional Papers, B:B61p; Franz Boas Family Papers, B:B61p, B:B61.5; Franz Boas Print Collection, B:B61, No. 1-34. Philadelphia, Pennsylvania, U.S.A.: American Philosophical Society. http://www.amphilsoc.org/library/mole/b/boas.htm (consulted March-December 2007)

*Archives Israélites 1883.* 2 August 1883. Paris: Bureau des Archives Israélites de France.

Barr, William 1985. *The expeditions of the First International Polar Year.* (2$^{nd}$ Edition 2008). Calgary AB: Arctic Institute of North America.

— 1992. Background to the German Expedition to Clearwater Fiord, Baffin Island, as part of the First International Polar Year 1882-1883. *Polar Geography and Geology* 16(4):265-271.

— and Chuck Tolley 1982. The German Expedition at Clearwater Fiord 1882-1883. *The Beaver* 313(2):36-44.

Bell, Jim 2004. Nunavut's population nears 30,000. *Nunatsiaq News,* 18 June 2004. Iqaluit, Nunavut.

Bender-Wittmann, Ursula 2008. Franz Boas (1858-1942): Begründer der Kulturanthropologie, Humanist und Demokrat. *Schriftenreihe der Münzfreunde Minden und Umgebung* 25:17-92.

*Berliner Adreß-Buch* 1875/1895. Published with the cooperation of H. Schwabe (and of W. and S. Loewenthal from 1881). Berlin 1873/1895. http://adressbuch.zlb.de/ (consulted 18-19 April 2007).

— *1896/1943 unter Benutzung amtlicher Quellen.* Berlin: Scherl 1896/1943. http://adressbuch.zlb.de/ (consulted 18-19 April 2007).

Boas, Franz 1884a. Kurzer Bericht über meine Reisen in Baffinland. *Berliner Tageblatt*, 13<sup>th</sup> year, No. 455, Sunday, 28 September 1884.

— 1884b. Der Hundeschlitten. Nordische Reiseskizzen für das Berliner Tageblatt. *Berliner Tageblatt*, 13<sup>th</sup> year, No. 551, Sunday, 23 November 1884.

— 1885a. *Baffin-Land. Geographische Ergebnisse einer in den Jahren 1883 und 1884 ausgeführten Forschungsreise.* Supplement to *Petermanns Mitteilungen*, No. 80:1-100. Gotha: Justus Perthes. (Reprint: Saarbrücken: Bibliophiler Fines Mundi Verlag 2006; http://www.fines-mundi.de).

— 1885b. Aus dem hohen Norden. Die letzten Wochen im Lande des ewigen Eises. *Berliner Tageblatt,* 14<sup>th</sup> year, No. 170, Good Friday, 3April 1885, p. 4-5.

— 1888. *The Central Eskimo.* Sixth Annual Report of the Bureau of Ethnology 1884-85:399-675. Washington, D.C.: Bureau of Ethnology. (Reprint: With an introduction by Henry B. Collins. Lincoln: University of Nebraska Press / Bison Book with Smithsonian Institution 1964; facsimile reprint: Coles Canadian Collection. Toronto: Coles Publishing Co. Ltd.1974, two plates).

— 1894. Das Eskimo-Dialekt des Cumberland-Sundes. *Mittheilungen der Anthropologischen Gesellschaft in Wien* 24 (New Series 14):97-114.

— 1901. The Eskimo of Baffin Land and Hudson Bay: from notes collected by George Comer, James S. Mutch and E.J. Peck. *Bulletin of the American Museum of Natural History* 15(1):1-370. New York: American Museum of Natural History.

— 1907. Second report on the Eskimo of Baffin Land and Hudson Bay: from notes collected by George Comer, James S. Mutch, and E.J. Peck. *Bulletin of the American Museum of Natural History* 15(2):371-570. New York: American Museum of Natural History.

— 1911. *The Mind of Primitive Man.* New York: Macmillan Company.

— 1914. *Kultur und Rasse.* Leipzig: Veit and Co. (German translation of *The Mind of Primitive Man,* 1911).

— 2007. *Eskimo story (Written for my children). My arctic expedition 1883-1884.* Edited by Norman Francis Boas. Mystic Connecticut: Seaport Autographs Press (http://www.seaportautographs.com).

Boas, Norman Francis 2004. *Franz Boas 1858-1942. An illustrated biography.* Mystic, Connecticut: Seaport Autographs Press (http://www.seaportautographs.com).

Brilling, B[ernhard] 1966. Die Vorfahren des Professors Franz Boas. *Mindener Heimatblätter* (Special supplement to *Mindener Tageblatt*) 3-4/1966:[1-2].

Cole, Douglas 1983. "The value of a person lies in his *Herzensbildung.*" Franz Boas' Baffin Island letter-diary, 1883-1884. In: George W. Stocking, Jr., ed. *Observers observed. Essays on ethnographic fieldwork. History of anthropology*, Vol. 1. Madison: University of Wisconsin Press:13-52.

— 1988. Kindheit und Jugend von Franz Boas. Minden in der zweiten Hälfte des 19. Jahrhunderts. *Mitteilungen des Mindener Geschichtsverein, Mindener Heimatblätter* 60:111-134. Minden: Mindener Geschichtsverein.

— 1994. Franz Boas. Ein Wissenschaftler und Patriot zwischen zwei Ländern. In: Volker Rodekamp, ed. *Franz Boas 1858-1942. Ein amerikanischer Anthropologe aus Minden. Texte und Materialien aus dem Mindener Museum* 11:9-23. Bielefeld: Verlag für Regionalgeschichte.

— 1999. *Franz Boas. The early years 1858-1906*. Vancouver/Toronto: Douglas and McIntyre; Seattle and London: University of Washington Press.

— and Ludger Müller-Wille 1984. Franz Boas' expedition to Baffin Island 1883-1884. *Études/Inuit/Studies* 8(1):37-63.

Dorais, Louis-Jacques 1996. *La parole inuit. Langue, culture et société dans l'Arctique nord-américain*. Paris: Edition Peeters.

Gieseking, Bernd 1998. *Im Eis. Aus den Tagebüchern von Franz Boas und Wilhelm Weike*. A dramatic reading of text pieces by Bernd Gieseking. Music by Reinhard Karger. Historical City of Minden 798-1998 – the City's 1200th anniversary. Stadttheater Minden, performances on 21 and 22 November 1998. Unpublished manuscript.

Gieseking, Bernd 2010. Die Farbe des Wassers. Ein Theaterstück über eine Arktisreise. Theatre Performance, World Premiere, City Theatre, City of Minden, October 24, 2010. Köln: Hartmann & Stauffacher Verlag.

Goddard, Ives 1984. Synonymy. In: Introduction by David Damas. *Handbook of North American Indians*, Vol. 5: *Arctic*. Washington, D.C.: Smithsonian Institution:5-7.

*Häverstädt 2007*. http://freenet-homepage.de/dorfgemeinschaft/geschichte.htm and http//www.haeverstaedt.de (consulted May and December 2007)

Hall, Charles Francis 1865. *Arctic researches and life among the Esquimaux: being the narrative of an expedition in search of Sir John Franklin, in the years 1860, 1861 and 1862*. New York: Harper.

HAPAG [Hamburg-Amerikanische-Packetfahrt-Actien-Gesellschaft] 2007. http://www.schiffe-maxim.de/HAPAG.htm (consulted 13 December 2007).

Harper, Kenn 2000. *Give me my father's body: the life of Minik, the New York Eskimo.* South Royalton, VT: Steerforth Press and New York: Washinton Square Press. (Original edition: Frobisher Bay, N.W.T. [Iqaluit, Nunavut]: Blacklead Books, 1986).

— 2005. Feb. 13, 1858 – The birth of Sivutiksaq [William Duval]. *Taissumani, Nunatsiaq News,* February 11, 2005. Iqaluit, Nunavut.

— 2008. The collaboration of James Mutch and Franz Boas, 1883-1922. *Études/ Inuit/Studies* 32(2):53-71.

— 2009. The Moravians in Cumberland Sound, Part 1-3. *Tassumani, Nunatsiaq News,* 18 and 25 September, 2 October 2009. Iqaluit, Nunavut.

Kleinschmidt, Samuel 1851. *Grammatik der grönländischen Sprache mit teilweisem Einschluss des Labradordialektes.* Berlin: Walter de Gruyter & Co. (Reprint: Hildesheim: Georg Olms Verlagsbuchhandlung 1968).

— 1871. *Den grønlandske Ordbog.* [Greenlandic Dictionary.] København: Louis Kleins Bogtrykkeri.

Knötsch, Carol Cathleen 1992. *Franz Boas bei den kanadischen Inuit im Jahre 1883-1884. Mundus, Reihe Ethnologie* 60. Bonn: Holos Verlag (M.A. thesis, Bonn 1988).

Krause, Reinhard A. 1992. *Die Gründungsphase deutscher Polarforschung, 1865-1875. Berichte zur Polarforschung* 114. Bremerhaven: Alfred-Wegener-Institut für Polar- und Meeresforschung.

Krupnik, Igor, Michael Bravo, Yvon Csonka, Grete Hovelsrud-Broda, Ludger Müller-Wille, Birger Poppel, Peter Schweitzer and Sverker Sörlin 2005. Social sciences and humanities in the International Polar Year 2007-2008: an integrating mission. *Arctic* 58(1):89-95.

Krupnik, Igor and Ludger Müller-Wille 2010. Franz Boas and Inuktitut Terminology for Ice and Snow: From the Emergence of the Field to the "Great Eskimo Vocabulary Hoax." In: Igor Krupnik, Claudio Aporta, Shari Gearheard, Gita J. Laidler and Lene Kielsen Holm, eds. SIKU: Our Ice. Documenting Inuit Sea-Ice Knowledge and Use. Heidelberg: Springer:377-400.

Langenkämper, Jürgen 2008. Franz Boas - Ein Vorbild für Forscher. *Schriftenreihe der Münzfreunde Minden und Umgebung* 25:93-135.

Laufer, Berthold and H.A. Andrews (eds.) 1906. *Boas Anniversary Volume. Anthropological papers written in honor of Franz Boas. Presented to him on the twenty-fifth anniversary of his doctorate, ninth of August, nineteen hundred and six.* New York: G.E. Stechert & Co. [Published 1907.]

Lévi-Strauss, Claude 1984. Claude Lévi-Strauss' testimony on Franz Boas. *Études/ Inuit/Studies* 8(1):7-9.

Mailhot, José 1978. L'étymologie du mot "esquimau" – revue et corrigée. *Études/ Inuit/Studies* 2(2):59-69.

Matthäi, Fredrik 2007. http://home.arcor.de/fredrik.matthaei/HVV/kaufkraft. htm (consulted 24 December 2007).

Mindener Museum für Geschichte, Landes- und Volkskunde 2007. *Das Franz Boas Projekt Minden 2008.* http://www.franz-boas.de. (consulted August 2007 to May 2008; November 2010)

Minden-Lübbecker Kreisblatt 1883. Local-Berichte. *Minden-Lübbecker Kreisblatt,* Tuesday, 26 June 1883. Minden.

Müller-Wille, Ludger 1983. Franz Boas (1858-1942). In: Arctic Profiles. *Arctic* 36(2):212-213.

— 1992. Franz Boas: Auszüge aus seinem Baffin-Tagebuch, 1883-1884 (19. September bis 15. Oktober 1883. In: Dürr, Michael and Erich Kasten, Egon Renner, eds., *Franz Boas: Ethnologe, Anthropologe, Sprachwissenschaftler. Ein Wegbereiter der modernen Wissenschaft von Menschen. Ausstellungskataloge, Neue Folge* 4:39-56. Wiesbaden: Reichert.

— 1994. Franz Boas und seine Forschungen bei den Inuit. Der Beginn einer arktischen Ethnologie. In: Volker Rodekamp, ed. *Franz Boas 1858-1942. Ein amerikanischer Anthropologe aus Minden. Texte und Materialien aus dem Mindener Museum* 11:25-38. Bielefeld: Verlag für Regionalgeschichte.

— (ed..) 1984. Document: Two papers by Franz Boas. Introduction. *Études/Inuit/ Studies* 81(1):117-120.

— (ed.) 1994. *Franz Boas. Bei den Inuit in Baffinland 1883-1884. Tagebücher und Briefe. (Ethnologische Beiträge zur Circumpolarforschung* 1, Erich Kasten, ed.) Berlin: Schletzer Verlag.

— (ed.) 1998. *Franz Boas among the Inuit of Baffin Island 1883-1884. Journals and letters.* Translated by William Barr. Toronto: University of Toronto Press.

— (ed.) 2008. Franz Boas and the Inuit. *Études/Inuit/Studies* 32(2):5- 84.

— and Linna Weber Müller-Wille 2006. Inuit geographical knowledge one hundred years apart. In: Pamela Stern and Lisa Stevenson, eds. *Critical Inuit studies. An anthology of contemporary arctic ethnography.* Lincoln, Nebraska: University of Nebraska Press:217-229.

Mutch, James 1906. Whaling in Ponds Bay. In: Laufer and Andrews 1906:485-500.

Neumayer, Georg von (ed.) 1891. *Die internationale Polarforschung 1882-1883. Die Deutschen Expeditionen und ihre Ergebnisse. Band I: Geschichtlicher Teil.* Hamburg: Deutsche Polar-Commission.

— and C[arl]. Börgen (eds.) 1886. *Die internationale Polarforschung 1882-83. Die Beobachtungsergebnisse der deutschen Stationen. Band 1-2.* Berlin: Asher.

Nunavut Handbook 2004. *The Nunavut Handbook: travelling in Canada's Arctic.* Iqaluit: Ayaya Publishing & Communications.

Nunavat Liquor Act 2006. http://www.lex-nu.ca/index.html (consulted 19 March 2011)

Pöhl, Friedrich 2008. Assessing Franz Boas' ethics in his arctic and later anthropological field work. *Études/Inuit/Studies* 32(2):35-52.

Pöhl, Friedrich and Bernhard Tilg (eds.) 2009. *Franz Boas - Kultur, Sprache, Rasse. Wege einer antirassistischen Anthropologie.* Ethnologie - Forschung und Wissenschaft, Volume 19. Wien: LIT Verlag.

Rodekamp, Volker (ed.) 1994. *Franz Boas (1858-1942). Ein amerikanischer Anthropologe aus Minden. Texte und Materialien aus dem Mindener Museum* 11. Bielefeld: Verlag für Regionalgeschichte.

Ross, W. Gilles 1985. Arctic Whalers, Icy Seas: Narratives of the Davis Strait Whale Fisheries. Toronto: Irwin.

Royal Library (Det Kongelige Bibliotek), Manuscript Division. The Hinrich Rink Papers. The New Royal Collection, No. 2488. Copenhagen, Denmark.

Saladin d'Anglure, Bernard 2006. The influence of Marcel Mauss on the anthropology of the Inuit. *Études/Inuit/Studies* 30(2):19-31.

Schmuhl, Hans-Walter (ed.) 2009. *Kulturrelativismus und Antirassismus. Der Anthropologe Franz Boas (1858-1942).* Bielefeld: *transcript* Verlag.

Schneider, Lucien 1985. *Ulirnaisigutiit. An Inuktitut-English dictionary of Northern Quebec, Labrador and Eastern Arctic dialects (with an English-Inuktitut index).* Québec: Les Presses de l'Université Laval.

Statistics Canada 2008-2011. *Census 2006.* http://www12.statcan.ca/english/census06 (consulted 15 January 2008); *Nunavut's Population Clock.* http://www.statcan.gc.ca/ig-gi/pop-nu-eng.htm (consulted March 19, 2011).

Stevenson, Marc G. 1997. *Inuit, whalers and cultural persistence: structure in Cumberland Sound and Central Inuit social organization.* Toronto: Oxford University Press.

*The Jewish Chronicle* 1883. A Jewish explorer. June 1883. July 6, 1883:12. London. http://www.thejc.com/home.aspx (consulted 17 January 2008).

Tilg, Bernhard Josef and Friedrich Pöhl 2007. "Donnerwetter, wir sprechen Deutsch!" Erinnerung an Franz Boas (1858-1942). *Anthropos* 102:547-559.

Ulrikab, Abraham 2005. *The diary of Abraham Ulrikab: text and context.* Translated from German by Hartmut Lutz and students at the Universität Greifswald. Ottawa: University of Ottawa Press.

Verne, Markus 2004. Promotion, Expedition, Habilitation, Emigration. Franz Boas und der schwierige Prozeß, ein wissenschaftliches Leben zu planen. *Paideuma* 50:79-99.

von der Eltz, Christian and Regina Schick 2007. *Erfrierungen – Frostbeulen.* http://www.meinegesundheit.de/300.0.html (consulted 3 June 2007).

von Nida, C. A. 1893. Neues Liederbuch für Artilleristen. Altendorf/Rheinland. http://www.volksliederarchiv.de/text2707.html (consulted 16 December 2009).

Wagner, Hermann (ed.) 1867. *Die Franklin-Expeditionen und ihr Ausgang. Entdeckung der nordwestlichen Durchfahrt durch Mac Clure sowie Auffindung der Ueberreste von Sir John Franklin's Expedition durch Kapitän Sir M'Clintock, R.N. L.* Leipzig: Verlag von Otto Spamer.

Warmow, Matthias 1858. *Extracts from Br. Matthias Warmow's journal of his residence in Cumberland Inlet, during the winter of 1857-1858. (Periodical Accounts relating to the Missions of the Church of the United Brethren, established among the Heathen,* Vol. 23). London: The Brethren's Society for the Furtherance of the Gospel among the Heathen.

Wüthrich, Christoph and Dietbert Thannheiser 2002. *Die Polargebiete.* Braunschweig: Westermann Schulbuchverlag GmbH.

# Index*

(Personal and ships' names in italics)

# MORE NONFICTION FROM BARAKA BOOKS

JOSEPH-ELZÉAR BERNIER
*Champion of Canadian Arctic Sovereignty*
Marjolaine Saint-Pierre (translated by William Barr)

A PEOPLE'S HISTORY OF QUEBEC
Jacques Lacoursière & Robin Philpot

AN INDEPENDENT QUEBEC
*The past, the present and the future*
Jacques Parizeau, former Premier of Quebec (1994-96)

TRUDEAU'S DARKEST HOUR
*War Measures in Time of Peace, October 1970*
Edited by Guy Bouthillier & Édouard Cloutier

THE RIOT THAT NEVER WAS
*The military shooting of three Montrealers in 1832
and the official cover-up*
James Jackson

THE FIRST JEWS OF NORTH AMERICA (Spring 2012)
*The Extraordinary Hart Family (1760-1860)*
Denis Vaugeois & Käthe Roth

THE QUESTION OF SEPARATISM
*Quebec and the Struggle over Sovereignty*
Jane Jacobs

SOLDIERS FOR SALE (1776-83)
*German "Mercenaries" with the British in Canada
during the American Revolution*
Jean-Pierre Wilhelmy

**Marquis Book Printing Inc.**

Québec, Canada
2011